I0801597

ADVANCE PRAISE FOR

Bridges, not Blockades:

Transcending University Politics

"Much has been made of higher education in the political realm, but less attention has been paid to politics within higher education. At the same time, external social forces are affecting interpersonal relationships on campuses, making them counterproductive or, in some cases, even toxic. This timely collection provides desperately needed relationship strategies that faculty, staff, and administrators can use to navigate conflict so that we may band together in service of our students and our industry. The essays here provide historical and theoretical frameworks for understanding how we arrived at our current state, as well as concrete recommendations for creating agile institutions and higher education practitioners capable of effective and ethical response to contemporary challenges."

Lindsey Bernhagen,
Director, Center for Inclusive Teaching and Learning
Editor, To Improve the Academy

"*Bridges, not Blockades* provides readers with much needed relief from the cynicism framing public perceptions of higher education. The success stories in this collection remind us that higher education is not a monolith and offers a roadmap for collaborations that work."

Lori Mumpower, Ph.D.
Director, Center for Teaching and Learning Excellence – DB Campus
Embry-Riddle Aeronautical University

"*Bridges, not Blockades: Transcending University Politics* is an idea whose time has come. The scope of topics covered and the expertise involved in writing this book provide a good foundation for understanding strategies for successfully navigating today's political climate in higher education. Understanding the importance of politics in higher education is the first step towards a successful career."

Lynda Ransdell, Ph.D., FACSM, CSCS
Dean and Professor
College of Health and Human Services
Northern Arizona University

"*Bridges, not Blockades: Transcending University Politics* is a must-read series of insightful and thought-provoking essays written specifically for anyone employed in or preparing for a higher education career. Navigating the unwritten rules of university and college politics is needlessly perplexing and can even be maddening. *Bridges, not Blockades: Transcending University Politics* is a refreshing series of insightful and thought-provoking essays that unravels the politically charged world of the academe and offers refreshing solutions to age old issues."

Mark A Heinrich, Ph.D.
President, Shelton State Community College (2008–2012)
Chancellor, Alabama Community College System, Retired

"The contributors to *Bridges, not Blockades: Transcending University Politics* carefully and courageously name and describe multiple political issues facing the faculty, administrators, and students who work and learn in college and university communities across our nation. In doing so, they diminish the greater power each issue gains by our silent endurance and reduce the isolation experienced when navigating complex political dynamics on our own campuses. And, they do not stop there. Each chapter humbly presents solutions that build upon the confidence and belonging we need to transform our institutions and higher education more generally into the transparent, supportive, and curiosity-inducing environments they are meant to be."

Sally Heilstedt
Dean of Instruction – Engagement and Learning
Lake Washington Institute of Technology

Bridges, not Blockades

Critical Studies in Teacher Leadership series

Eleanor J. Blair, *Editor*

Teacher leadership as a term is used broadly to describe the many roles and responsibilities of good teachers working in 21st-century schools. Teacher leaders, acting in both formal and informal roles, are instrumental in doing at least three things: facilitating and sustaining teacher voice; building leadership capacity in schools and communities; and addressing teaching and learning issues and concerns with best practices evidence and research. Research on the intersection of teacher leadership, school culture, and school improvement is extremely limited, particularly as it pertains to school reform efforts that occur in diverse geographical and social contexts. Important factors that affect the work of teacher leaders include, but are not limited to, issues such as race; urban and rural education; socio-economics; ethnicity; politics; and ideological differences. Critical efforts to link teacher leadership with increased power and agency in teachers' work are limited. Teacher leadership that is both transformative and critical serves the purpose of redefining teachers' work to include new roles and responsibilities, such as advocacy leadership and a commitment to the principles of social justice as key components of teachers' work. As such, a better understanding of teacher leadership and the way that it functions in schools and communities has the potential to nurture new conceptualizations of the teaching profession, but also on the work of teachers advocating for both academic and social reform in public spaces for teaching and learning.

Books in the Series

A Cross-Cultural Consideration of Teacher Leaders' Narratives of Power, Agency and School Culture: England, Jamaica and the United States
by Eleanor J. Blair, Carmel Roofe, and Susan Timmons (2020)

Bridges, not Blockades: Transcending University Politics
by Gayle Maddox and Martha Diede (2020)

Stewarding the Profession: Stories of Early Career Teacher Leadership
by Carrie Rogers (2020)

Interested authors and collection editors are invited to contact:

Eleanor J. Blair
ejblair@email.wcu.edu

Bridges, not Blockades

Transcending University Politics

Edited by Martha Diede
and Gayle Maddox

Myers Education Press

GORHAM, MAINE

Myers Education Press

Published by Myers Education Press, LLC
P.O. Box 424 Gorham, ME 04038

Myers Education Press is an academic publisher specializing in books, e-books, and digital content in the field of education. All of our books are subjected to a rigorous peer review process and produced in compliance with the standards of the Council on Library and Information Resources.

Library of Congress Cataloging-in-Publication Data available from Library of Congress.

13-digit ISBN 978-1-9755-0119-8 (paperback)
13-digit ISBN 978-1-9755-0118-1 (hard cover)
13-digit ISBN 978-1-9755-0120-4 (library networkable e-edition)
13-digit ISBN 978-1-9755-0121-1 (consumer e-edition)

Printed in the United States of America.

All first editions printed on acid-free paper that meets the American National Standards Institute Z39-48 standard.

Books published by Myers Education Press may be purchased at special quantity discount rates for groups, workshops, training organizations, and classroom usage. Please call our customer service department at 1-800-232-0223 for details.

Cover and text design by Sophie Appel

Visit us on the web at **www.myersedpress.com** to browse our complete list of titles.

CONTENTS

DEDICATIONS

This book is dedicated to my dad, Dr. J. Cordell Maddox,
who spent forty years as a leader in higher education.
His kind and generous spirit modeled servant leadership for me
as I embarked on my own career in higher education.
His ability to see the "big picture" on campus
has helped me navigate the politics of the university.
His compassion to forgive and move forward taught me
that people are always more important than politics.
—Gayle Maddox

My mother worked most of her career in banking, and she often worked
with clients who behaved in less-than-optimal ways.
A praying woman, she prayed that she would be
the person who—both personally and professionally—would stand in the gap.
She then attended to a wide variety of gaps between people—cultural,
linguistic, behavioral, familial, class, and many others.
This book is dedicated to her. She taught me to look for the gaps
and to build the bridges that would eliminate those gaps.
—Martha Diede

ACKNOWLEDGMENTS

BRINGING THIS BOOK FROM an idea in a coffee shop to a group of finished essays took a team effort. There were many friends and colleagues who built bridges across disciplines and across the country to help us develop the themes and titles for this edition. In fact, we share the book title with one of our contributors as it so accurately describes what we want to do. Coming to share a title—unusual in an edited collection—represents precisely the kind of bridge-building that we seek to encourage.

We also could not have put this work together without the tremendous work of our Series Editor, Dr. Eleanor Blair, along with the staff of Myers Education Press. Their belief in this book provided invaluable support throughout the process.

Finally, we would like to thank our universities for providing us with workplaces we love, our tremendous colleagues for supporting us as mentors and friends, and, most importantly, our families for encouraging us to thrive.

FOREWORD

Carol Burton
Vice Provost for Academic Affairs
Western Carolina University

After more than thirty years as an administrator in higher education, I perceive the increasing uptick of the impact of politics on this industry. Politics pervades almost every aspect of higher education, particularly state-funded universities and colleges; governance, enrollment, funding, faculty, staff, curriculum, students, facilities, mission/vision, and strategic planning, to name a few areas, are all affected by politics. While much has been written about the impact of politics on higher education, relatively little in this arena has been suggested from the faculty perspective, those at the heart of the educational enterprise. This collection of essays affords us the benefit of understanding the roles, implications, and challenges of politics in higher education, from internal and external perspectives, and suggests some ways to identify common ground to solve problems and advance our institutions.

We are inundated daily with examples of colleges and universities that are heavily influenced (in positive or negative ways) by politics. This century heralded a new normal of bold decisions guided by politically charged governing boards, state legislators, lobby and advocacy groups, and accrediting bodies. Mass media regularly takes turns critiquing the costs, effectiveness, and value of higher education. External and internal politics impact our world, with each playing an increasing role in defining the evolving role of colleges and universities—our primary purpose, our achievement of our purpose, and the nexus of faculty, students, staff, administration, parents, alumni, governing boards, and community partners, politicians, accrediting bodies, donors, journalists, and the list goes on. Universities can be microcosms of society at large and, as such, the way we serve our constituents (students), manage and utilize resources, address conflicts, and fulfill our primary mission often adopts the practices employed outside of our "walls."

Mergers; closings; budget cuts; civil and criminal court cases; racial, sexual orientation, and religious tensions; resource mismanagement; and conflicts of interest are becoming as commonplace in institutions of higher education as they are in the world outside the academy. Add healthy doses of athletics misdemeanors, fraternity misdeeds, donor undue influence, and admission scandals, and it becomes apparent that teaching and learning aren't the only activities taking center stage on college campuses. To be fair, many of the 4,500-plus institutions aren't necessarily grappling with many or even any, of these issues, and yet it appears that the lines between higher learning and the broader society are becoming increasingly blurred; the walls that used to insulate or separate postsecondary institutions are more permeable than ever. To be sure, this is not necessarily a negative development. Many institutions with a regional engagement focus are purposeful in their efforts to connect with their communities and provide opportunities for student learning beyond the boundaries of a physical campus. These institutions also provide an avenue for all members of a campus community to engage in the academic enterprise together; staff play a critical role in student success and sometimes offer unique perspectives on higher education.

Recently, our search for a new chancellor was suspended abruptly because of system-level politics. Extreme patience, committed staff, board members, faculty, students and alumni, community members, and administrators ensured that the search process regained its footing and culminated in a successful candidate. Student activism correctly called our administration to task over inaction and miscommunication on topics such as sexual orientation, gender inequality, and racial identity. Again, progress occurred because staff, students, faculty, and administrators worked together to understand the concerns, were committed to a sense of purpose, and dispensed with the fear of potential political fallout. I have observed faculty become demoralized by internal politics and administrators disheartened by faculty wars promulgated under the guise of shared governance. I have experienced institutional gridlock because of internal politics at senior levels played at the expense of the greater good. I have led institutional priorities fraught with emotion and tension because of perceived threats to resources and positions. And I have observed the benefits to institutions when staff have been key and valued partners in the academy. Politics does not have to be pejorative; it can result in positive or negative outcomes. *Bridges not Blockades:*

Transcending University Politics offers avenues for faculty, staff, and administrators to collaborate on shared goals, issues, and opportunities while harnessing the power of politics for increased institutional effectiveness.

A former academic administrator colleague used to challenge faculty with the statement "Don't confuse governance with administration." It's a delicate balance, but healthy academic institutions understand and respect the differences between the roles of faculty, staff, and administrators; carefully crafted roles are delineated, supported, and valued in an environment of trust. *Bridges not Blockades: Transcending University Politics* attempts to first understand the nature of internal politics from the faculty perspective, and second to present opportunities for overcoming the barriers that are fostered by university politics and undermine the commonalities that make us more effective institutions; we truly are greater than the sum of our parts.

CHAPTER ONE

Why We Need to Build Bridges in University Politics

Gayle Maddox

During one single week in the spring of 2016, three events took place that encouraged me to write this book. The first was a newspaper article about a state legislative body that was involving itself in the workings of a diversity office at a state university. Several local politicians were objecting to university funds going to support certain diversity programs on campus. Even campus memos about the use of inclusive terms reflecting diversity were being questioned by state legislators. Ultimately, the Tennessee General Assembly cut off funding to the diversity office for at least a year. UT Knoxville Chancellor Jimmy Cheek told the campus community about the cut in an email. "It saddens me to share with you that a new state law requires us to defund the Office of Diversity and Inclusion from July 1, 2016, to June 30, 2017," Cheek said. "This means no funds can go to operate the office." (M. Boehnke, personal communication, May 20, 2016).

A second event that week involved a conversation with a colleague who is a campus administrator across the country. He related that his institution's academic offices had a great deal in common with some of the student services offices on campus, so the groups had been talking about meeting once a month over lunch to discuss common concerns. The meetings had not taken place, however, because the administrators of each office could not agree on a "neutral" territory to hold the lunches. Neither party would go to the other's offices for fear of yielding power. Those meetings were ultimately canceled—not for lack of interest but because the two division leaders couldn't agree on who would get to "host" the meetings. In other words, the problem couldn't be solved because they couldn't agree on whose conference room to use.

The third event involved a local man whose wife worked at the state university in his town. He was standing at a local restaurant and started talking with another man visiting from out of state. Something was said about the university, and the visitor said that all the people "at that school are just overeducated liberals." Because the local man was married to a college employee, he wasn't really surprised at that sentiment coming from an outsider, but he was surprised by the brazenness to say this to a complete stranger in a university town.

It seems we have a political problem on campus.

Usually, when I tell people I am working on a book on university politics, they look perplexed. Given the state of both local and national politics these days, most people are looking for ways to "tune out" the political noise, not dive headfirst into political culture. To me, however, this culture of politics we are living in makes it that much more important that we have conversations about the politics of higher education. Those of us in higher education must reflect on our own campus cultures and seek to make colleges and universities safe places for innovation, critical thought, and creativity.

Before delving into the world of university politics, I want to be upfront—I think working on a university campus is one of the best jobs a person can have. My father worked in higher education for forty years, and I followed in his footsteps, first as a staff member and later as a full-time tenured faculty member. When I was growing up, we lived on a college campus. Many of my earliest memories involve college events such as concerts, athletic events, and student functions. As an adult, I have spent the better part of the last twenty-five years working in higher education at both private institutions and state universities. I have seen the politics of the college when church denominations get involved, and I have worked at public universities that are at the whim of state party politics. My coeditor has also worked at a private, research university. Politics, we can attest, are everywhere.

On top of that, I loved my own college experience. My college years helped shape who I am as an adult. I remember taking a college history class focused on the events of the 20th century and walking out of that final exam thinking the class changed the way I viewed the world. I remember reading books in a Southern literature class that helped me understand my own Southern experience. I remember looking in a microscope and learning to appreciate a world I could never see. For me, a college campus can be a magical place—a place of ideas, friendship, opportunity, and learning.

For a traditional student, the years between 18 and 22 are transitional years. In fact, I would say that for many students, those years can be magical. Many students enter college as one person and emerge four or five years later with a more complicated understanding of the world, new skills, and new prospects for the future. If a student embraces the college experience, he or she will graduate a different person from the kid who sat in freshman orientation.

Part of this change is the exposure to new people, different ideas, and a concentrated time period where it is safe to explore complicated thinking. Part of this change is related to classroom activities, and some of this learning happens outside the classroom. And, part of this transformation for the traditional-aged student is the massive change in brain activity happening during the late teen years/early adult years. As Jenson (2015) writes, the teenage and young adult brain is more powerful and more vulnerable than any other time in life. In her book *The Teenage Brain*, Jensen (2015) states, "The teenage brain is a wondrous organ, capable of titanic stimulation and stunning feats of learning" (p. 6). Brain development during this time is ripe for neural plasticity, which is another way of saying learning. So, the potential for student learning is massive. The opportunity for the university to guide student development is an exciting, awesome responsibility.

With all that said, I profoundly believe that higher education has real issues that need to be addressed. Despite the wonders of college, serious concerns bubble at the surface, and outside forces present real threats to higher education. Here are some of the issues that are fairly universal on college campuses:

- Budget money—who has it and who wants it?
- Rising costs of college/student debt
- Space issues
- Tenure and promotion

- The role of instructors and adjunct faculty
- Collegiality and the role that plays in promotion
- Societal threats to higher education
- Bullying in academe
- Poor leaders and poor leadership
- View of higher education as a business model
- Students who arrive unprepared academically
- Diversity concerns
- Students arriving on campus with complex mental/physical health issues
- Pressures to change the way we teach and learn
- The impact of assessment on teaching and learning

A myriad of terrific books address the issues facing higher education. A quick survey of current literature in higher education highlights some of these concerns. In many ways, higher education is in a tough spot—universities need to stay competitive with other institutions, yet the uniqueness of a campus is what often draws students to a place. For sure, universities are being compelled to move toward a business model, with all the marketing, austerity measures, assessment, and budgeting concerns that come with it.

Many colleges and universities believe they must embrace a business model in order to meet the needs of today's student market. Fabricant and Brier (2016) argue that the decreasing investments from the state into public higher education have created the need to move toward a business model. As state funding has declined in recent years, universities have been forced to raise tuition, cut budgets, seek outside support and fundraising, and look toward research and grant funding to maintain academic programs. Several universities have liquidated art collections and historical pieces in order to raise money for the operating budget (Kinsella, 2018).

McGee (2015) makes a compelling point that universities are a changing marketplace and must adjust to the times to survive in a modern economy. He points out that economic, cultural, and demographic changes are occurring on university campuses and suggests using data on these changes when making administrative decisions on campus. In this sense, assessment will be a crucial piece of the workplace. In other words, colleges and universities must think strategically about the economic market if they hope to survive in the 21st century.

In contrast, Smyth (2017) makes the case that the university is under assault by neoliberalism and the view of universities as another area of a global market culture. Smyth (2017) states, "Universities are one of the few crucial remaining places for the construction, preservation, and contestation of knowledge and ideas, and all of us stand to lose if this process is corrupted and corroded" (p. 19). There is danger in viewing education like other commodities. Not all parts of learning or experience in college can be quantified, marketed, or assessed. The process of learning does not always fit with business tenets or the economic models such as neoliberalism.

The financial health of a university is paramount to its survival, but the need to manage money can lead to other concerns on campus. A concern commonly expressed in the literature is the tension between the faculty "legs of the three-legged stool"—research, teaching, and service. While teaching is usually cited as a strength for a university, Callier, Singiser, and Vanderford (2015) suggest that research is the main priority for many college administrators because it can bring in both money and prestige. While some tenured faculty conduct prestigious research, instructors and adjuncts are asked to teach large classes of students. Although the mission of the university is teaching, that mission is often superseded by a push for research since grant dollars flow into departmental budgets.

There have been concerted efforts to refresh the tenure system and equalize the three legs of the stool, but those efforts have not fully taken hold (Boyer, 1990). Tenure and promotion are often tied to research in a higher proportion than either teaching or service. University leaders periodically discuss the creation of new paths to full professor status, suggesting the route to promotion could include paths through research as well as excellent teaching. Both could earn the rank of full professor. These ideas are not new to academe, but they cause a great deal of debate on campus and can politicize members of the faculty and the administration (Burgan, 2006). For example, many universities discuss a more diversified workload of teaching, service, and research that could lead to promotion and/or tenure for faculty, but changing the emphasis on publication will take strong leadership. Despite conversations to the contrary, at many research universities the dollars generated by grant funding and publications always seems to supersede both teaching and service when it comes to earning tenure or promotion. Faculty who hope to advance their careers through strong teaching and service still feel the pressure to make sure they also have the "right number" of publications, and many of these faculty just fall back into the established tenure system in order to survive.

These types of debates and the issues surrounding tenure and promotion can lead to issues beyond just anxiety. In *Faculty Incivility*, Twale and De Luca (2008) discuss a bullying culture that exists in higher education. Incivility can happen in many forms. It may be outright aggression such as retaliation or harassment, or it may be hidden through indifference, manipulation, or exclusion. Such bullying makes collegiality among faculty and staff difficult. Gappa, Austin, and Trice (2007) suggest that improving civility enhances the intellectual strength of the campus, yet pressures on faculty are making a sense of collegiality harder and harder to achieve. Faculty are teaching, attending committee meetings, and working on research projects in an environment where resources may be scarce and competition is fierce. This type of individualized work can lead to the "silo" effect in higher education—where all I see is my work in my discipline. When that happens, it's easy to lose sight of the big picture of the university, and other faculty can be viewed as competitors rather than colleagues. If we aren't careful, that type of environment can devolve into a culture of bullying.

Perhaps the biggest problem with this bullying culture is how it can impact students. When I was working on my PhD in 1994, I was told by my dissertation adviser that there were certain faculty who disliked each other so much they would not serve together on committees. I needed to choose one of the faculty but not the other. I was perplexed by this as a young graduate student, but when I mentioned this to an older friend in higher education he told me that in the 1960s he had the same problem on his doctoral committee. I also remember a situation in my undergraduate experience where two professionals had offices next to each other but would only communicate through e-mail. Even as a college kid, I thought that was strange. It certainly did not model adult behavior in the workplace. These colleagues surrounded themselves with blockades.

Within the university system, there has also been debate on what content should be taught in classes and how to improve teaching strategies to help students learn that content. In *Whatever Happened to the Faculty*, Burgan (2006) discusses the debate over the best approach to reform classroom practices. These issues can also create some political discord on campus.

On one side are the pedagogical reformers who want to change how classes are conducted. This includes more student-centered learning, more discussion, and less lecture. On the other side are the curriculum reformers who suggest that universities need a return to the liberal arts education or "great ideas" that are at the root of American higher education. Each of these camps is trying to find the best way to increase student learning, but these debates can be contentious. While these are important discussions to have on campus, classroom faculty can get caught in the middle. To meet the needs of both the faculty and the students, these discussions need to find common ground.

Student needs are changing as well. Many students are facing tremendous debt to attend college (Fabricant & Brier, 2016). Because of growing debt, students frequently see the experience as career preparation. Learning for the sake of learning is not always a top priority. Instead, students are trying to work, take classes, maintain relationships, and prepare for the job market. These student needs are creating new challenges for faculty and staff on campus.

Some students are arriving at college unprepared for the challenges of academe. College, for them, was the next step in life, not something they actually wanted to do. For many families, college is an expectation. For example, Pew researchers in 2012 found that 90% of parents with a child under the age of 18 expected their child to attend college. Yet, Mortimer and Sathre (2007) state that many students attend college without the intention to graduate in four years—they go to college in order to get away from home, socially mature, or for other cultural reasons.

Today's students are different in many ways from the faculty who are teaching them. Each year our university sends out a "who are the freshmen" factsheet. My freshmen students this year were born in the year 2000. The first U.S. president most of them remember is Barack Obama. The Vietnam War, the Cold War, Ronald Reagan, or even Bill Clinton seem like historical people and events from long ago. Students today, the "Generation Z" kids, like to communicate through apps like Snapchat. A large percentage of my students don't read, even when it is required in a class. Many students don't even take the time to read email anymore. Pedagogy is changing, and not all faculty are happy with the changes.

One of the things that frustrates faculty is the lack of "deep learning" taking place in academic classes. Rather than embrace critical thinking, some students are surface learners—they are strategic learners who have figured out that grades are all they want. Moreover, they have chosen what grades they will pursue and in what classes. In many ways, students have been conditioned in school to be surface or strategic learners (Bain, 2004). Most faculty want their students to develop a deep curiosity about the course content, strive to think critically about real-world issues, and discover a passion for a subject that can impact the world around them. Instead, Bain (2004) argues that students often employ models of learning they have developed over a decade in school—the model to do enough work to get the grade that will get them to the next step in life. This is not true of all college students, but many faculty struggle with motivating students to really *think*.

Most schools want to encourage critical thought, so students remain inquisitive after the college years. Many college programs also seek to help students develop leadership skills, appreciate diversity, and, ultimately, become better citizens. While students and parents may appreciate this effort by the university, students also hope the end goal will be career placement and advancement. McGee (2015) suggests that instead of college being a transformational experience for some students, it has become a transactional one.

It is important to note the frustration in having different learning goals for faculty and students. Studies show that over time faculty develop a teaching fatigue that starts with disenchantment and moves to malaise and then to stasis (Gould & Hazelgrove, 2018). Faculty who start careers with a passion and energy for teaching can fall into a sense of weariness and futility, even complacency, when they perceive there is a lack of learning. In a classroom, ideas should be unfettered. For faculty, an academic discussion should be a place of ideas, collaboration, discussion, and change. Some students buy into that while others secretly, and sometimes not so secretly, count the minutes until the end of class.

In the article "Why Are Associate Professors So Unhappy?" Wilson

(2012) writes that mid-level career academics across the country are struggling with "exhaustion, doubt, and even depression." After achieving tenure, many faculty see the disparity between their expectations and the reality of the job. Faculty also report a lack of appreciation from the university and a lack of comradery with colleagues. Add to this the idea that many tenured faculty feel "stuck" at their university, as it is difficult to move in the faculty world unless you choose to move into administration.

Other issues may revolve around the decrease in the number of full-time, tenure-track faculty hired at a university. Departments are being downsized, which adds to the workload of tenured faculty. Out of 1.5 million faculty, only 53% are employed full time and only one-third of all instructional employees at four-year colleges are tenured or on the tenure track (U.S. Department of Education, 2018). Because the number of tenure-track faculty has declined, adjuncts now represent 75% of the national instructional workforce (House Committee on Education and the Workforce, 2014). Adjuncts teach classes only; their contracts do not require any of the advising or administrative work necessary for departments to function. That burden falls on the full-time, tenure-track, or tenured faculty. As positions are eliminated or repurposed, that burden increases.

In addition to issues of job expectation, many faculty feel frustration over salary disparities. You can't really talk about the politics on campus without talking about money. This conversation necessarily includes budgeting, salaries, scholarships, grants, and travel funds. For some faculty and staff, the disparity is related to gender. Women in the same fields as men may make less money on some campuses. For others, salary disparities are related to disciplines. Fields like education and liberal arts do not command the same salaries as hard sciences or healthcare fields. Even within academic units, certain fields are paid more than others.

And, then there is the issue over space. Issues over space on campus can become bitter arguments (Olson, 2014). Control over offices, classrooms, parking areas, and student buildings can create nasty divisions on a campus. Space is the core of our existence. Faculty are confined to offices and labs and may teach in the same classrooms year after year. As Olson (2014) states, space is a commodity that people will fight over in an economy of scarcity. The politics of space can seem silly on the surface, but this issue is ubiquitous on campus. Departments try to control office space, classrooms, student spaces, and labs as faculty and staff struggle to find space to work. Even within academic programs, disciplinary politics often come into play with space. Certain disciplines receive new modern spaces while other programs are forced to work in older buildings—all based on the "value" of the disciplines.

And, those are just some of the political issues *on campus*.

Additionally, more and more colleges and universities are facing pressure from outside entities, such as state politicians, church groups, donors, and corporate leaders. Depending on the worldview of these outside groups, the college environment may be asked, coerced, or even forced to reexamine academic freedom. Across the country, corporate leaders are engaging universities by making donations with some strings attached. These situations expose the challenge facing universities as they seek to balance a need for more revenue while making sure a donor's demands don't hinder academic freedom (Ball, 2016). A real threat appears when donations seek to influence what is taught on campus. In 2018, gifts to colleges and universities topped $41 billion, and 15.1% of that money came from corporations. Most gifts are earmarked for specific programs (Seltzer, 2018).

College and university leaders are facing more and more issues over diversity concerns on campus, and hostility surrounding these issues is on the rise. For example, in recent years, the North Carolina university system has been facing political pressure concerning Confederate monuments on the campus of the University of North Carolina at Chapel Hill. Some groups in the state want the statue removed because it represents antiquated ideas that no longer have a place on an academic campus. Other groups see the statue as a part of the state's history and insist that it belongs on campus. The chancellor of the university ordered the statue of "Silent Sam" removed due to growing threats to safety surrounding both sides of the issue. Facing criticism from a politically appointed conservative board, the chancellor was forced out by the Board of Governors (Dalesio, 2019).

In addition, politicians, media personalities, and the general public regularly attack higher education for its so-called liberalism. In a 2017 interview, Matthew Quick, the acclaimed novelist, recounted the story of what his grandfather told him before he entered college. Quick (2017) said, "[M]y grandfather pulled me aside and told me, 'You need a college degree.' He didn't have one, and he said, 'Do whatever you have to do to get your piece of paper, but I want you to know that they're going to lie to you.' He meant the professors. He said, 'I don't want you to believe anything that they tell you. Just get your piece of paper.'" In my own teaching, I often encounter students who are concerned about ideas that might "change" them. Most students will embrace critical thought, but it takes time for them to develop their own opinions and ideas separate from the way they were raised. Our current political culture of identity politics makes this even more challenging.

Faculty are frequently under attack in the current culture wars. In a 2018 report on NPR, Kamenetz reported that in the previous 18 months, at least 250 university professors had been targeted by off-campus right-wing online campaigns because of their research, their teaching, or their social media posts. Faculty have also been targeted by left-wing political groups, and some of that harassment emerges from within the academic community itself. In the NPR article, Hans-Joerg Tiede of the American Association of University Professors says no matter what side you're on politically, it's clear that academic freedom is under assault.

Extreme politicians and members of the mass media portray faculty as attempting to radicalize students, but most faculty just want students to realize that issues are complicated. Simple answers may sound good in politics, but they will not work for real 21st-century challenges like climate change, poverty, health care, or a globalized economy.

In his essay "From Die Hard Conservative to Liberal Humanist: Education and the 'Corruption' of Students," DiPaolo (2013) recounts his own movement from conservative ideology to a more liberal worldview as he advanced through his education. As a faculty member now, he stresses his desire to have his students *learn* to think for themselves, so they can discover their own political views, spiritual insights, and core values. The real threats to higher education come from those who do not want students to think on their own.

Universities have also become lightning rods for politicians, if that cause helps them with constituents. For example, in 2019, the president of the United States issued an executive order to protect freedom of speech on university campuses. President Trump has repeatedly complained about alleged suppression of free speech on campuses, especially speech by conservative students. However, freedom of speech is already protected by the First Amendment, and universities have a strong commitment to an open exchange of ideas. Julie Schmid, executive director of the American Association of University Professors, said the executive order appeared to accomplish little procedurally, "but is troubling in that it serves a broader goal of attempting to discredit higher education" (Kreighbaum, 2019, p. 2). It seems the politics of higher education has reached the highest levels of government, yet the real concerns on campus such as limited resources, rising student debt, and pressure from outside entities are not part of the conversation.

This enumeration of concerns names only some parts of the sentiment we face in higher education, and it creates our conundrum: How can we help students understand the complexity of issues without being attacked for changing their worldview? How can we rally together both with colleagues on our own campus and across the country to change that sentiment? How can parents expect students to learn without expecting them to change in some way? How can we regain the trust of the broader society so they do not fall prey to rumors and political attacks on "liberal" faculty? How can we do our jobs in higher education and stay out of the fray of politics just beyond the campus gates?

These are real questions that universities face in the 21st century. But before we tackle the politics outside the campus gates, I would contend that we must get our own academic house in order, so we are better prepared for the challenges waiting for us. We need to make sure we are working together to make our campuses better, not giving in to the temptations to get involved in petty fights.

To do that, we need to be honest about the politics *on* campus. And, we need to realize that the political problems across campuses and across the country are actually very similar. A few years ago, I was asked to conduct a workshop on university politics at a national organization in higher education. The workshop had attendees from a variety of campuses across the country. To prepare for the workshop, I created case studies of different faculty situations.

All of the examples were stories that originated at my home campus. However, when we started going over the case studies, the workshop attendees started saying things like, "That guy works at my institution," or "That same thing is happening in my department," or "Our administration is saying those same things." It was enlightening to see that the problems at *my* institution are just archetypes, and those same problems exist at *most* schools. I don't know if there is comfort in that or not, but it says something that we are all struggling with similar issues in our workplace.

What is needed now more than ever is good leadership on campus. We need leaders who are creative, courageous, and conciliatory. We also need leaders who can step back from a problem and see the big picture. Many campuses have strong leadership already, and those leaders can be mentors to young professionals. Leadership training can also be valuable both on campus and across disciplinary associations. Leadership exists in the classroom, in our departmental areas, on campus, and across all of academe. The work of higher education is invaluable, but meeting the challenges facing colleges and universities in the 21st century will require people working together. We need leadership at all levels, and that leadership should be about bringing people together.

This book cannot cover all the political issues in higher education. But, if the problems are similar across campuses all over the country, perhaps the solutions might be similar as well. At least talking about the issues and bringing them to light will move the conversation along. Perhaps it is as simple as working to communicate better and compromise more. Perhaps it is as simple as following some basic rules of kindness: empathy for others, seeing the big picture, keeping things in context, and forgiving mistakes.

With that in mind, this book will highlight some of the political issues on college campuses, but, more importantly, this book will offer some solutions to those issues. The following chapters represent a variety of political concerns on campuses across the country.

There is a story in Roman history that in AD 64 the emperor Nero chose to play music while the citizens of Rome watched helplessly as their city burned for six days. After it was over, 70% of the city had been destroyed. While the historical fact of Nero's actions can be debated, the story has taken on a more current meaning reflecting poor leadership and a lack of action in the face of crises. The old adage of "fiddling while Rome burned" applies to higher education in the 21st century. If we are not careful, we will spend our time arguing among ourselves on campus while real problems attack the campus gates. This book is an attempt to keep the conversation going on how to build bridges, not barriers, in higher education.

References

Bain, K. (2004). *What the best college teachers do.* Cambridge, MA: Harvard University Press.

Ball, J. (2016, April 3). When strings are attached to university donations. *Asheville Citizen Times*, pp. A1, A4.

Boehnke, M. (2016, May 20). University of Tennessee disbands Office of Diversity. *The Tennessean.* Retrieved from http://tnne.ws/1NCwH2H

Boyer, E. (1990). *Scholarship reconsidered: Priorities of the professoriate.* Princeton, NJ: Carnegie Foundation for the Advancement of Teaching.

Burgan, M. (2006). *Whatever happened to the faculty?* Baltimore, MD: St. John's Press.

Callier, V., Singiser, R., & Vandeford, N. (2015). The parlous state of academia: When politics, prestige and proxies overtake higher education's teaching mission. *Australian Universities Review, 57*(1), 13–16.

Dalesio, E. (2019, January 16). University head yanks Confederate marker, is forced out. *Asheville Citizen Times*, pp. A1, A5.

DiPaolo, M. (2013). From die-hard conservative to liberal humanist: Education and "corruption" of students. In E. Watson (Ed.), *Generation X professors speak* (pp. 67–93) Lanham, MD: Scarecrow Press.

Fabricant, M., & Brier, S. (2016). *Austerity blues: Fighting for the soul of public higher education.* Baltimore, MD: Johns Hopkins University Press.

Gappa, J., Austin, A., & Trice, A. (2007). *Rethinking faculty work.* San Francisco, CA: Jossey-Bass.

Gould, J., & Hazelgrove, T. (2018). *Igniting the teaching soul.* Paper presented at the National Learning Communities Conference, Bay City, MI.

House Committee on Education and the Workforce, Democratic Staff. (2014). *The just in time professor.* US House of Representatives. https://edlabor.house.gov/imo/media/doc/1.24.14-AdjunctEforumReport.pdf

Jensen, F. (2015). *The teenage brain.* New York, NY: Harper.

Kamenetz, A. (2018, April 4). Professors are targets in online culture wars; some fight back. *All Things Considered.* Retrieved from https://www.npr.org/sections/ed/2018/04/04/590928008/professor-harassmenthttps://www.npr.org **This is an afternoon news program on NPR. I'm not sure how to add that to the citation.**

Kinsella, E. (2018, January 5). Outrage mounts as LaSalle University forges ahead with plans to sell works from museum's collection. *Artnet News.* Retrieved from https://news.artnet.com/art-world/la-salle-university-decision-to-deaccession-artworks-sparks-outrage-1193042

Kreighbaum. A. (2019, March 22). White House executive order prods colleges on free speech, program-level data and risk sharing. *Inside Higher Ed.* Retrieved from https://www.insidehighered.com/news/2019/03/22/white-house-executive-order-prods-colleges-free-speech-program-level-data-and-risk

McGee, J. (2015). *Breakpoint: The changing marketplace for higher education.* Baltimore, MD: Johns Hopkins University Press.

Mortimer, K., & Sathre, C. (2007). *The art and politics of academic governance: Relations among boards, presidents, and faculty.* Westport, CT: Praeger.

Olson, G. (2014). The politics of academic space. *Chronicle of Higher Education, 60*(17), 21–23.

Pew Research Center. (2012, May 17). *College graduation: Weighing the cost and the payoff.* Retrieved from https://www.pewresearch.org/2012/05/17/college-graduation-weighing-the-cost-and-the-payoff/

Quick, M. (2017, July 18). Interview by Frank Stasio (Digital recording). *The State of Things.* Retrieved from https://www.wunc.org/post/silver-linings-playbook-author-debuts-new-novel-featuring-brazen-veteran

Seltzer, R. (2018, February 8). Giving to colleges rises by 6.3%. *Inside Higher Ed.* Retrieved from https://www.insidehighered.com/news/2018/02/06/personal-giving-pushes-donations-colleges-and-universities-new-level-2017

Smyth, J. (2017). *The toxic university: Zombie leadership, academic rock stars, and neoliberal ideology.* London, UK: Palgrave Macmillan.

Twale, D., & De Luca, B. (2008). *Faculty incivility: The rise of the academic bully culture and what to do about it.* San Francisco, CA: Jossey-Bass.

U.S. Department of Education, National Center for Education Statistics. (2018). *The Condition of Education 2018* (NCES 2018-144), Characteristics of Postsecondary Faculty. https://nces.ed.gov/programs/coe/indicator_csc.asp

Wilson, R. (2012, June 3). Why are associate professors so unhappy? *Chronicle of Higher Education.* Retrieved from https://www.chronicle.com/article/Why-Are-Associate-Professors/132071

CHAPTER TWO

Organizational Physiology and Transcending Ambiguity

Betty A. Block

This book is about university politics, the aspects of university life that happen at and around the university, and the manner in which these aspects are managed and governed through policy. All of the issues that the various authors present in this book are part of a larger system. My contribution to this book is to outline the larger picture for you. I will identify the aspects of the age of super-complexity, the ambiguous nature of higher education, and provide overarching but practical solutions for transcending ambiguity.

In higher education, no decision can ever stand alone. For illustration, I begin this chapter with a scenario. It is a story as told to me by a vice president when I was a new department head. It illustrates the fragile balance that exists at the university and the manner in which departments, communication across departments, and decision-making at every level connect. I call the scenario the *diploma dilemma.*

> ***The diploma dilemma:*** *The dilemma begins when a well-meaning clerk in the Purchasing Department found larger, more beautiful diploma covers for the same price as the smaller ones the university had been using. The information about the diploma covers was shared with the clerk's supervisor who ran the idea of purchasing them to the provost. The provost approved the purchase of the larger diploma covers with little thought. The registrar soon found out that the size of the actual diploma was too small for the larger diploma cover and was forced to purchase larger, more ex-*

pensive paper to print them on. This caused the Marketing Department to redesign the artwork on the larger diplomas, which resulted in an increase in printing costs. When the physical plant workers retrieved the diploma covers to cart them to the auditorium for graduation, they found that the boxes that held the diploma covers were too heavy for the small cart they had used to carry diploma covers in the past. They were forced to go back to their supervisor to ask for a larger cart. The university did not own a larger cart and had to rent one. After the diplomas arrived at the auditorium and were unboxed, they found that the table that was set to hold the diplomas was too small to hold them. The table had to be replaced with a larger one. Arranging the larger table on the stage next to the president resulted in the removal of some of the leather arm chairs on the stage. This meant that several faculty members who needed to be on stage to hood doctoral students had no place to sit. The chairs had to be replaced with smaller chairs so that everyone who needed to be on the stage would fit. The decision was made to use chairs from surplus rather than purchasing new ones. After the graduation ceremony, an alumnus wrote a letter to the president complaining that the chairs on the stage were "tacky and embarrassing" for the institution's size and prestige. A happy outcome was that a large number of students contacted the dean of students to thank her for the beautiful diploma covers.

The point of the story is this: Without signaling processes in place (or proper communication through the chain of command), a seemingly simple decision can easily disrupt balance and affect many people. Universities are intricately connected—just like a living organism—which is the point of this chapter. We will examine in this chapter more important issues that are relevant to the life of the university than diploma covers. However, the diploma dilemma was important for those people who were involved with solving the problem, because each person in the chain of command had a job to do. In the end, those were affected by changing the size of the diplomas were these: Purchasing Department, the physical plant, the registrar's office, the provost's office, the Marketing Department, the print shop, Alumni Affairs, the president's office, dean of students office, Contracts Department, and the business office. The people who were affected by this change were primarily staff members who work behind the scenes to help keep the university running. Faculty and students had no idea that there was a problem at all. The staff members who were solving the problems associated with the diploma dilemma are the people who are generally involved with implementing procedures. They see to the day-to-day operations at the university; nevertheless, they are rarely consulted when decisions that affect them are made.

THE UNIVERSITY AS A LIVING SYSTEM

For something to be *alive* it must have a heritage, the ability to reproduce, respond, and grow into something stronger and more adaptable to the environment in which it is situated. Functionally, it must have signaling and self-sustaining processes that enable it to maintain homeostasis (the ability to maintain balance within the system). To live, the organism must interact with other organisms and the environment where each compete for limited resources. In this chapter, the university is compared to a living organism with a unique organizational physiology.

The university is thought to be situated like an organism or a biological entity in the world that exists within a fragile ecosphere. To thrive, the university must maintain the ability to signal and put into place self-sustaining processes that can protect and indeed transcend the potential disruptions that invaders can cause. Our diploma cover issue would not have been an issue at all had the appropriate people been signaled. Instead, the purchasing supervisor jumped several levels and went directly to the provost for a decision. Similarly, the provost added to the issue by failing to push the decision to those responsible for diploma covers.

In a perfect environment, the university could anticipate and alleviate problems before they happen. Small problems can become incredibly large problems very easily without the appropriate leadership and chain of command. Large problems can be devastating to the life of the university if not handled properly. The university exists in a complex world environment rife with unpredictability caused by ambiguous situations; therefore, the university must be adaptive, nimble, and responsive like an organism in an unstable environment.

Organizational Physiology

The phrase *organizational physiology* has to do with the unique set of mechanisms and functions that keep the university operational and effective.

Mechanisms are the units of the university such as academic and student affairs, institutional research, the business and finance unit, the physical plant, and so forth that provide structure to the functional systems. The functional systems include the roles and responsibilities of employees, the beliefs and values that guide purposeful decision making, the policies and procedures that govern behaviors, and a unique social system that evolves from the interaction of each. Every university has is its own individual organizational physiology that is situated within a global and networked world; however, we will refer to all universities in this chapter as a single entity: the university.

The term *homeostasis* will be used often in this chapter as disruptions to balance are critical to the life of the university. Homeostasis can be defined as the tendency for an organizational system to maintain stability even within conditions of imbalance. Identifying and understanding the forces that affect the organizational physiology of the university is critical to maintaining homeostasis. For instance, outside forces can pull the university out of balance if not counteracted. Conversely, opportunities can be missed if not seized upon in a timely manner. In other words, the organizational physiology of the university can be penetrated by things that are antithetical to the university's mission. Once introduced into the system these things can create disorder and imbalance with homeostasis. To thrive, mechanisms (units that provide structure) at the university must maintain a keen sense of place and an awareness of the functions (roles, values, beliefs, responsibilities) that sustain them; otherwise, the system will be unable to respond and adapt when penetrated.

Governmental Influence

To illustrate the connection between governmental politics and university homeostasis, let us consider a governor who must present a budget in an economy that is wavering. Citizens know that budget cuts are inevitable. The university knows that funds have been diverted steadily for years; the governor's system is at risk of being compromised. The governor will be forced to navigate complex political and social tides antithetical to the functions of the university regardless of her positive views on higher education. Therefore, in order to maintain homeostasis, the university must proactively identify new funding sources and diminish reliance on the state by working with corporations, alumni, and friends to maintain stability in a wavering economy. The university's organizational physiology must be sound—the governor's beliefs and values must not waver, and the roles and responsibilities of her personnel must see her through times of imbalance. Being futuristic in her thinking (signaling) and anticipating solutions to problems (self-sustaining processes) are the best ways for the university to transcend the politics that plague elected officials.

Dissecting the Problems in Higher Education

At this point, an identification of the aspects of the age that define the invading forces that are penetrating the postmodern university is in order. The age is the era after postmodern times that Barnett (2000) called super-complex. This is followed by a discussion of ambiguity in higher education. The super-complex time is a time when the global and digital world magnifies and extends the aspects of the age at a more pervasive and faster rate, causing ambiguous situations that confuse and misdirect the university into environments that are unsuited to its mission. The next part of the discussion will contain strategies to deal with the aspects of the age that we face in universities. Understanding the importance of using policy development to our advantage, sustaining a healthy culture, and leadership training is key to constraining invading influences that disrupt the homeostasis of the university.

Super-Complexity

Super-complexity is a term coined by Barnett (2000) to explain the postmodern condition of the world. Decades before the turn of the century, higher education administrators began to notice a prodigious penetration of higher education by the wider society; undeniably, the ambiguity between the life of a scholar and the demands of a networked world have become disruptive. This is an era when the frameworks of meaning that define who we are and what we do in the academy are being systematically dismantled. Traditional frameworks of meaning at universities used to look like these: The composition of the student body was composed of high-achieving, competitive students with ambitious goals. Professors were held in high esteem and were rarely questioned. The primary role of the professor was to search for and teach the truth. Academic administrators came from the ranks of the faculty. Students were responsible for their own schedules, degree planning, and study habits. Professors had academic freedom to follow a research question to conclusion. Students were responsible for their own success. Professors could design their own courses, grading criteria, and teaching strategies without interference.

Conflicting Frameworks of Meaning

Today, the traditional frameworks of meaning seem absurd. The organizational physiology of the postmodern university is dramatically different than the modern university. Accreditors hold universities to the standards that disciplinary experts and society at large have set. Our student bodies have changed considerably. Universities are now as diverse as the nation. Research is questioned for relevancy and applicability. Many academic administrators are drawn from the ranks of business and politics because universities are now expected to run like businesses. Universities are mandated to provide advisement, career counseling, tutoring, developmental courses, counseling, and health services to students. And, professors are held to student learning outcomes and strict reporting standards. Administrators are expected to compete for students and market programs, as well as answer to state legislators and boards of regents. These are only a few examples of frameworks that are continuing to evolve. The manner in which universities recognize and address these frameworks of meaning will determine levels of funding, graduation rates, faculty success, workforce placement, and enrollment. In other words, the entire organizational physiology of the university has evolved into something that looks more like an ecosphere that supports all aspects of the student rather than a single purpose entity designed to search for and disseminate truth.

Student Success

Understanding the changing nature of frameworks of meaning in the moment is important to addressing the issues that come along with them. There are calls for equal access and opportunity that have changed admission requirements, and consequently for good or ill, the composition of our student bodies. The idea that everyone should have access to a university education, while laudable, has changed the organizational physiology of the university. It is one of those situations whereby the university is being assessed as both the problem and solution to the issues related to an uneducated workforce. This is happening even as legislators are decrying vocational education in high schools as discriminatory toward low socioeconomic populations and minorities that track them into low-level jobs. Further, universities are expected to create spaces that support students who may not be ready or interested to engage in university-level work. Universities are required by law to offer course material in multiple formats for students with disabilities. That means that we must create different opportunities for success and participation for students sitting in the same course. Additionally, students who cannot afford to attend university are burdened with debt that follows them for decades, while some legislators and the wider society call for free higher education for everyone.

Workforce Demands

An overarching distraction to student success is the idea that a university degree is a ticket into the workforce or a ticket out of poverty with little regard for student ability or interest in participating in higher learning. There are calls for university programs to meet the demands of a postmodern workforce much like a vocational or technical education would meet. As a result, universities are being asked to make curricular changes that, in general, have diminished liberal education in favor of career-driven professional programs.

Competition

Delivery of content has also changed with the evolving nature of students, the advent of online education platforms, competition from for-profit universities, and digital technologies. These delivery changes have resulted in the development of multiple formats and delivery systems that scholars must learn to navigate. On top of this change is the introduction of the heavy hand of globalism into higher education. Globalization has caused universities to become more like businesses and knowledge has become a commodity to be bought and sold. Therefore, scholars are called on to market their research and programs with little to no marketing training. They also must compete with nimble private online institutions who have technology and marketing experts who plan programs via indicators that point toward profits. They provide flashy learning management systems, package knowledge, and sell it publicly. The for-profit institutions protect knowledge and treat it as a commodity. These for-profit institutions can come up with a concept one day and begin implementing it the next. Scholars in public institutions must navigate through complex bureaucracies and state boards to push through innovative concepts. They are also most likely working with outdated equipment and technical support that is unequal to for-profit institutions. Additionally, scholars are expected to share the scholarship of teaching innovations that they develop and put it out into the world for review and inspection; for-profits do not.

Digital Technology

The effects of technology crept up on many of us in higher education over the past few decades. The ability to transcend space and time through technology pulls all of us, students and professors, into different dimensions of ourselves when we should be focusing on learning, adding to the body of knowledge, teaching, and serving others through learning and research. Before we recognized it, the impact that technology was having on our day-to-day existence became invasive. We noticed a bombardment of communication from all fronts: A great increase of e-mail messages from administrators, students who expect instant responses to queries of questionable importance at all hours, and requests from outside educational service providers to test or buy their products all distract us from our stated roles and responsibilities as scholars.

Penetration by Society

Legislators and the wider society have unfettered access to university administrators. The academic decisions of university administrators rest in part on the opinions of outside voices. Often, what we do as a university becomes part of the public discourse. Careers can begin and end with legislators and people of influence who have the ability to pressure administrators to do their bidding. Their influence trickles down to faculty and staff instantaneously. It is not uncommon that faculty and staff are expected to implement dubious research and program agendas brought forward by legislators and benefactors. The resulting effects can be nebulous and unsettling. Additionally, because of technology, these reports and policies are expected to be produced at a quicker rate and evaluated and reviewed by multiple constituencies with multiple reviews and revisions prior to dissemination. These seemingly benign requests from administrators take away valuable time from research, teaching, and service and can cause great disruptions to organizational physiology. On a personal level, instant access disrupts the life of scholars. Often administrators expect faculty and staff to be available after hours, often texting or e-mailing long after office hours are over for the day. These invasions into personal time take away time that could be spent on reflection and recuperation.

Digital Natives

Technology has changed the nature of our students as well. The manner in which we interact and teach students has been forever changed as digital natives sit in university classrooms. They are digital warriors who are savvy and sophisticated navigating the World Wide Web and social media. They grew up with technology and do not know a world without it. These students are distracted by vast amounts of readily accessible information and can easily confuse fact with fiction. They document their experiences on social media in the moment and communicate to the wider society while they are engaged in social and academic activities. They are capable of navigating the rules of student honesty by using technological tools that help them plagiarize, share information, and record content with ease. The ability that they have at their disposal to instantly access knowledge and information (true or not) and to disseminate it competes with the true quest for knowledge that we want students to practice at the university.

AMBIGUITY

The characteristics of super-complexity are exemplars of the ambiguity that exists in the organizational physiology of the university. They illustrate the ways that known functions and structures at the university conflict with the present realities of the age. The university seems to be losing its soul; professors feel marginalized and dismissed as being out of touch with the real world, even as professors are addressing the aspects of the age with their research, service, and teaching. The wider society view professors as liberal elitists who are out of touch with reality, even as professors are attempting to define reality for the 21st century. Ambiguity is enhanced because the wider society has penetrated the walls of the university and is trying to redefine the roles of the scholar and the mission of the university. Scholarship and research have been placed below service and workforce demands. Administrators feel pressure to appease big donors and legislators. These are just a few of the situations that cause ambiguity at the university.

The 21st century is already proving to be rife with ambiguous situations that stretch our abilities and imaginations far beyond those of the past. Ambiguity has been fueled by the introduction of multiple sets of conflicting information that make policy formation nebulous because they vie and contend with the information educators traditionally accepted as true. Nebulous policy development results in ambiguity in leadership and ambiguous changes in the roles and responsibilities of university personnel.

The characteristics of super-complexity that have infiltrated higher education were not intentionally created as a grand scheme to disrupt homeostasis, but rather an aspect of the age; even so, these characteristics can be ambiguous and disruptive to the lives of scholars. For instance, ambiguity is caused when reasonable arguments for the greater good, ideals that we can all buy into, replace the basic principles that we espouse in higher education. Their insertion into inappropriate settings or without being fully vetted by scholars can cause great disruption to the organizational physiology of the university. This disruption can pull us away from being fully present, disrupt the academic life of the scholar, and interfere with who we are and what we do at the university. The interesting thing about existing in an environment of ambiguity is that mundane things seem alluring. Negatives can be interpreted as positives that confuse legislators and administrators into transforming university policy into what the wider society expects.

Most often while faculty are searching for truth and adding to the body of knowledge in their respective disciplines, the organizational physiology is quietly being compromised. In many cases, homeostasis is disrupted before faculty and some administrators understand the full impact of the problem. Identifying the sources of the disruptions, the specific aspects of the university's organizational physiology that are being upset, and novel ways to operate outside the traditions and customs in academe are the first steps to take while coping with ambiguity. In so doing, leaders can be poised to create policies and procedures that pull the organization back into balance.

Transcending Ambiguity

This discussion sounds rather bleak for higher education; nevertheless, we can transcend ambiguity if we identify, understand, and, as odd it might seem, work with the wider society to reposition the university in this new century. It is possible to regain homeostasis in the university organizational physiology. Attending to political and social realities, being keenly aware when political and social windows open, and most importantly getting out of the walls of the university and engaging, informing, and leading educational reform issues is vital to success. In so doing, university personnel can work together to anticipate, plan for, and create legislation ideas that move the university in the right direction.

Consider this scenario: Forces outside the university with the full support of parents and legislators are calling for lower admission standards and customer-based operational models where students are treated like customers and knowledge as a commodity to be bought and sold. These efforts are reinforced by accrediting bodies and state regulators as a matter of course. As a result, university programming, the manner in which professors teach, their scholarship and research funding, and the types of services professors are expected to engage in are affected. Further, in an effort to accommodate freer access, tenure-track positions are slowly being replaced by professional-track faculty who focus on teaching and workforce readiness, not necessarily research and service. Understanding the big picture will help us recognize the aspects of the age that affect our organizational physiology.

Recognizing Signs of Supercomplexity

There are strong signals in this scenario that point us to the aspects of the age that have thrown our organizational physiology off balance and changed the direction of higher education over the past few decades: the calls for equal access, opportunity, and participation; the marketization of higher education programs to attract students and resultant competition with university peers; digitalization of curricula to attract a global audience of students to competitive online formats; and meeting the oversight efforts of the wider society are clearly present. These frameworks (access, opportunity, participation, marketization, competition, oversight, digitization, and globalization) will continue to create ambiguity at the university by growing, expanding, and disrupting. It is the savvy university that identifies the frameworks of meaning that vie and contend with the health of the organizational physiology and deploys self-sustaining processes to address them. Universities can and will be able to maintain homeostasis if prepared.

To begin, the university must search out the forces that have penetrated its organizational physiology, acknowledge the penetration, and create defensive policies and procedures against their disruptive influence. It is not too late to redirect the university away from ambiguity. Indeed, scholars have the benefit of routinely engaging in unfettered thought and objective analysis. Scholars at the university are capable of protecting the university with the contention that they have the discipline to understand the forces that disrupt the physiology more than the forces understand themselves. Professors fact-check, verify, analyze, and produce objective data before making major decisions with the end goal in mind. In other words, the university is the perfect place to employ sound research methodologies to shape policies and procedures. In other words, professors must save the life of the university with their intellect, reasoning, and research skills.

Strategies for Transcendence

There are specific strategies that university professors, staff, and administrators can use to transcend ambiguity and keep the organizational physiology of the university intact. Some of the major issues that face the university and contribute to ambiguity can be addressed through policy development, culture, and leadership training. Policy development is the process whereby beliefs and values are operationalized. Culture is the environment within which all aspects of the university exist. Leadership training is the essential component necessary to sustaining life, maintaining the core beliefs and values of the university, and sustaining homeostasis in times of ambiguity.

Policy Development

The university must create policies and procedures that hold students, staff, and faculty accountable to the beliefs, values, and mission of the institution above all else. It is easy to drift into areas that do not fit with university values when individuals of influence are unclear of values that form the foundation of the university culture. This drift can result in mission ambiguity—a state whereby the university is steered off the course of the stated mission. Similarly, every individual is a vital part of the organizational physiology and must recognize his or her function and purpose with regard to the values and mission of the university. Role ambiguity can happen if one does not uphold his or her function and purpose within the stated policies of the organization as described. The university community members must understand their roles within the mission, just as biological entities have specific roles to play in an ecosphere. Therefore, all community members must have a voice in the development of policy. Shared governance is a way that affords an opportunity for all voices to be included. A mission can be derailed very easily if a powerful administrator makes arbitrary decisions without considering the input of the entire university. This leads to another strategy for transcending ambiguity: culture.

Culture

In biological terms a culture is a condition suitable for growth. A little cell grows and develops to its full potential in the right culture. Think of a biologist and a research team made up of lab assistants, graduate assistants, and students. Together they create, monitor, and attend to providing for a healthy culture for the little cell. They study the latest literature on the conditions that might affect the cell from every angle. Then they create just the right atmosphere for the cell to exist comfortably. They provide the appropriate conditions of life for the cell to grow and multiply in its environmental culture. They constantly monitor homeostasis, and if conditions change, the team members are all clear on the process they will follow to regain balance in the culture. They understand that the fragile ecosphere of the culture must be constantly monitored and tended for the little cell to thrive.

Now, let's extend the metaphor of the research team that cared for the little cell to the organizational physiology of the university culture. The university exists within an organizational culture whereby social behaviors and norms are established and socially learned by all participants in the culture. Members of the culture interact with each other to such an extent that they come to inherit the ideas, beliefs, and values of the group. Members, in turn, share and reinforce those values with newcomers. Members of the organizational culture also act on the ideas, beliefs, and values of the group. Members in the university culture can grow, develop, and multiply just as our little cell did. Our little cell was able to flourish because the research team worked in concert every step of the way—monitoring conditions and implementing processes to sustain its life. University members at every level should also be involved with constant monitoring of the conditions that might affect the organizational physiology of the university.

University culture is as fragile as the culture the research team created for the little cell. The university culture must be tended, monitored, and have processes in place that can immediately be activated should the culture be penetrated by something that affects the homeostasis of its organizational physiology. With that in mind, it is imperative that members of the university community at every level be engaged in leadership training.

Leadership Training

The organizational physiology of the university cannot grow, develop, and multiply unless every structural unit has a leader group that monitors, tends, and has processes in place to respond to things that affect that unit's homeostasis. Therefore, it is imperative that leaders be developed within the culture of the institution. Leadership should happen at every level, and training opportunities should be offered for every member who has a functional role within the structure. Universities hire people with specific skill sets. Professors are trained to research in their academic disciplines and are evaluated on the quality of their research, teaching, and service. Professors are not trained to lead outside their discipline; they rarely have exposure to administrative tasks that do not directly affect their immediate environment. Similarly, deans and provosts are most likely selected from the ranks of the professoriate and have little to no formal leadership training. In addition, boards of regents and boards of directors are most likely made up of individuals who have little to no higher education training. This combination is unhealthy to the culture of the organizational physiology.

Higher education leaders in academic affairs should be schooled in policy development, the aspects of the age, political engagement, advancement, federal guidelines related to Title IX, innovative pedagogies, service learning and engagement, the latest technological advancements, customer management software, social media efforts that can promote the position of the university, and the difference between managing and leading. Business and financial affairs leaders likewise need to understand the aspects of the age that affect the mission of the university and plan for possible disruptions. The physical plant leaders should understand the life of the students and faculty beyond the buildings and grounds in which they live and work and constantly monitor the environment for disruptions.

Leadership training at all levels should include both the big picture and the details of university culture. All leaders need to engaged in constantly monitoring the state of affairs outside the university. Leaders from every unit at the university should come together and create a plan to sustain systems in times of penetration and imbalance in homeostasis. Leaders also need to recognize and react quickly when the first lines of defense are at risk of being penetrated. Understanding globalism, the manner in which digital technology affects the university, the changing nature of students and younger employees, the marketization and competitive nature of higher education, and the reality that access, opportunity, and participation must be equal are all realities of the age that must be constantly monitored. Sustainability plans must be created and at the ready when conditions change quickly. Good leaders plan strategically, share the plan, and constantly update the plan. In other words, the strategic plan must be a living breathing document that everyone monitors. In addition, everyone must know their role when the organizational physiology of the university has been penetrated.

The university can transcend the ambiguity caused by a complex age if the culture is monitored and nurtured. There is no denying that her walls will be penetrated by the wider society; however, strong leadership at every level will make it possible for the university to absorb the penetration into the beliefs and values inherent in the culture. If all members of the university culture respond together, understand and plan for sustainable change, and have processes in place to protect the mission of the university, it will grow, develop, and multiply within its organizational physiology and beyond.

Reference

Barnett, R. (2000). *Realizing the university in an age of supercomplexity.* Philadelphia, PA: Open University Press.

Recommended Readings

Barnett, R. (2004). The purposes of higher education and the changing face of academia. *London Review of Education, 2*(1), 61–73.

Barnett, R. (2005). Recapturing the universal in the university. *Educational Philosophy and Theory, 37*(6), 785–797.

Block, B. A. (2008). Navigating the swamp of graduate education: A principles, policies, and procedures in kinesiology perspective. *Chronicle of Kinesiology in Higher Education, 19*(1), 16–17.

Block, B. A. (2010). Cultural relational leaders: Unraveling, understanding and utilizing narratives in leadership practice. *Quest, 62*(3), 250–259.

Block, B. A. (2013). Addressing the politics of epistemology in higher education. *Chronicle of Kinesiology in Higher Education, 24*(2), 32–36.

Block, B. A. (2014). Leadership: A supercomplex phenomenon. *Quest,66*(2), 233–246.

Block, B. A., & Estes, S. (2011). Supercomplexity in higher education kinesiology. *Quest, 63*(2), 179–196.

Bloland, H. G. (2005). Whatever happened to postmodernism in higher education?: No requiem in the new millennium. *Journal of Higher Education, 76*(2), 121–150.

Bolman, L. G., & Gallos, J. V. (2011). Reframing academic leadership. San Francisco, CA: Jossey-Bass.

Dall'Alba, G. (2009). Learning professional ways of being: Ambiguities of becoming. *Educational Philosophy and Theory, 41*(1), 34–45. doi:10.111/j.1469-5812.2008.00475.x

Deluga, R. J. (1989). Employee-influence strategies as possible stress-coping mechanisms for role conflict and role ambiguity. *Basic & Applied Social Psychology, 10*(4), 329–335.

Denhardt, R. B., & Grubbs, J. W. (2003). *Public administration: An action orientation* (4th ed.). Belmont, CA: Wadsworth.

Durant, R. F., & Diehl, P. F. (1989). Agendas, alternatives, and public policy: Lessons from the U.S. foreign policy arena. *Journal of Public Policy, 9*(2), 179–205.

Gummer, B. (1998). Decision making under conditions of risk, ambiguity, and uncertainty. *Administration in Social Work, 22*(2), 75–93. doi:10.1300/j147v22n02_05

Heacox, N. J., & Sorenson, R. C. (2004). Organizational frustration and aggressive behaviors. *Journal of Emotional Abuse, 4*(3/4), 95–118.

Hecht, I. W. D., Higgerson, M. L., & Tucker, A. (1999). *The department chair as academic leader.* Phoenix, AZ: Oryx Press and American Council on Education.

Hodge, B. (2010). Oedipus and the CEO: Ambiguities of change in myth, discourse and practice. *Culture and Organization, 16*(1), 23–35.
Houlihan B., & Green, M. (2006). The changing status of school sport and physical education: Explaining policy change. *Sport, Education and Society, 11*(1), 73–92.
Huber, N. (2003). An experiential leadership approach for teaching tolerance for ambiguity. *Journal of Education for Business, 79*(1), 52–55.
June, A. W. (2013, December 2). For chairs, the seat's gotten hotter. *Chronicle of Higher Education.* Retrieved from http://chronicle.com/article/Department-Chairs-Find/143309/?cid=at&utm_source=at&utm_medium=en
Kane, J., & Patapan, H. (2010). The artless art: Leadership and the limits of democratic rhetoric. *Australian Journal of Political Science, 45*(3), 371–389.
Katsaros, K. K., & Nicolaidis, C. S. (2012). Personal traits, emotions, and attitudes in the workplace: Their effect on mangers' tolerance of ambiguity. *Psychologist-Manger Journal, 15*(1), 37–55.
Kezar, A. (2008). Understanding leadership strategies for addressing the politics of diversity. *Journal of Higher Education, 79*(4), 406–441.
Levinson, D. (1959). Role, personality and social structure in the organizational setting. In G. Salaman & K. Thompson (Eds.), *People and organisations* (pp. 223–237). London, UK: Longman.
Mathews, A. (2012). Effects of modifying the interpretation of emotional ambiguity. *Journal of Cognitive Psychology, 24*(1), 92–105.
McLain, D. L. (1993). The MSTAT-1: A new measure of an individual's tolerance for ambiguity. *Educational and Psychological Measurement, 53*(1), 183–189.
McLendon, M. K., Deaton, R., & Hearn, J. C. (2007). The enactment of reforms in state governance of higher education: Testing the political instability hypothesis. *Journal of Higher Education, 78*(6), 645–675.
Murphy, M., & Curtis, W. (2013). The micro-politics of micro-leadership: Exploring the role of programme leader in English universities. *Journal of Higher Education Policy and Management, 35*(1), 34–44. doi:10.1080/1360080X.2012.727707
Pace, J. L. (2003). Using ambiguity and entertainment to win compliance in a lower-level US History class. *Journal of Curriculum Studies, 35*(1), 83–110.
Pascale, C. M. (2001). Epistemology and the politics of knowledge. *Sociological Review, 58*(2), 154–165. doi:10.111/j.1467-954X.2011.01967.x
Pedró, F. (2009). Continuity and change in the academic profession in European countries. *Higher Education in Europe, 34*(3–4), 411–429.
Saarinen, T. (2008). Whose quality? Social actors in the interface of transnational and national higher education policy. *Discourse: Studies in the Cultural Politics of Education, 29*(2), 179–193.
Sakires, J., Doherty, A., & Misener, K. (2009). Role ambiguity in voluntary sport organizations. *Journal of Sport Management, 23*(5), 615–643.
Sherrill, W. W. (2001). Tolerance of ambiguity among MD/MBA students: Implications for management potential. *Journal of Continuing Education in the Health Professions, 21*(2), 117–122.
Schulz, J. (2013). The impact of role conflict, role ambiguity and organizational climate on the job satisfaction of academic staff in research-intensive universities

in the UK. *Higher Education Research and Development, 32*(3), 464–478. doi:10.1080/07294360.2012.680209

Skodvin, T., & Andresen, S. (2006). Part one: Negotiating international environmental regimes. Leadership revisited. *Global Environmental Politics, 6*(3), 13–27.

Stensaker, B. (2006). Governmental policy, organizational ideals and institutional adaptation in Norwegian higher education. *Studies in Higher Education, 31*(1), 43–56.

Szajnberg, N. (2011). Clarity and ambiguity in psychoanalytic practice. *Bulletin of the Menninger Clinic, 75*(1), 1–20.

Tandberg, D. A. (2010). Politics, interest groups and state funding of public higher education. *Research in Higher Education, 51*(5), 416–450.

Teles, S. (2013). Kludgeocracy in America. *National Review, 17*. Retrieved from http://www.nationalaffairs.com/publications/detail/kludgeocracy-in-america

Teoh, H. Y, & Foo, S. L. (1997). Moderating effects of tolerance for ambiguity and risk-taking propensity on the role conflict-perceived performance relationship: Evidence from Singaporean entrepreneurs. *Journal of Business Venturing, 12*(1), 67–81.

Tidd, S. T., McIntyre, H. H., & Friedman, R. A. (2004). The importance of role ambiguity and trust in conflict perception: Unpacking the task conflict to relationship conflict linkage. *International Journal of Conflict Management, 15*(4), 364–380.

Tierney, W. G. (2001). The autonomy of knowledge and the decline of the subject: Postmodernism and the reformulation of the university. *Higher Education, 41*(4), 353–372.

Tremblay, M., Vandenberghe, C., & Doucet, O. (2013). Relationships between leader-contingent and non-contingent reward and punishment behaviors and subordinates' perceptions of justice and satisfaction, and evaluation of the moderating influence of trust propensity, pay level, and role ambiguity. *Journal of Business Psychology, 28*(2), 233–249.

U. C. Berkeley News. (2003). *Former U. C. President Clark, a national leader in higher education, dies at 92*. Retrieved from http://berkeley.edu/news/media/releases/2003/12/02_kerr.shtml.

Weiler, H. N. (2005). Ambivalence and the politics of knowledge: The struggle for change in German higher education. *Higher Education*, 49(1–2), 177–195.

Welch, A. (2001). Globalisation, post-modernity and the state: Comparative education facing the third millennium. *Comparative Education*, 3(4), 475–492.

Willis, D. B., Yamamura, S., & Rappleye, J. (2008). Frontiers of education: Japan as "global model" or "nation at risk"? *International Review of Education, 54*(3–4), 493–515.

Yue, V. W. Y (2012). "Role" and "position": Job expectations and practices. *Asian Social Science, 8*(1), 12–26.

CHAPTER THREE

Building Bridges, not Blockades:

Insights into Building Healthy Campus Relationships

ANITA FITZGERALD HENCK

Introduction and Context

OVER THE YEARS, I have grown to love the academy and its transformational influence and impact on individuals, families, and communities. The work has often been exhausting, mostly exhilarating, and always energizing. And, this has never been more true than when I was able to be part of healthy collaborations that were a win-win within and between departments, as well as across a campus. Despite higher education's well-earned reputation that it is siloed and partisan, what is underreported is the extraordinary innovation and teamwork that often occurs. Collaboration through bridge building, so that seemingly intractable problems find solutions, has been central to most individual and institutional successes. Yet, falling into predictable patterns of isolated operations and poor communication within institutions can often be the default mode and is the root of blockades to progress.

After four-plus decades of employment at three institutions of higher education, I'm often teased that I've held nearly every role except for maintenance worker and president. While this jest is somewhat apocryphal, my career morphed from being hired for entry-level skills in one sector of an organizational chart into being asked to serve as a senior "generalist" over broad areas of a university. Assignments have included administrative assistant, budget and planning staff, institutional researcher, policy developer, institutional ombudsperson, speechwriter, faculty, chief student development officer, executive enrollment leader, and academic dean, among others. These were at varied levels—entry, mid, and cabinet—and have been supplemented by external roles as accreditor, consultant, and advisor to boards and senior leaders.

My work in higher education actually began as a 16-year-old freshman work-study student, hired to type a manuscript for a distinguished psychology professor at a public university in California. Typing a book for a brilliant English-as-a-second-language intellectual led me to ask clarifying questions about his document, which led to discussions where I was asked to edit the manuscript to regularize language usage. Finding this gruff but influential academic to be approachable and appreciative was the first of many times that I learned that, no matter the titled role (or not), all within the academy are persons first.

Later, as a 21-year-old newlywed moving to the Washington DC metropolitan area, I applied for work at local universities as a way to pay for a master's degree and was quickly hired as an administrative assistant at a mid-sized private university. Having been offered two similar positions at the same university, the one I chose came with a warning from human resources that the individual for whom I would work had a reputation for being "hard to fit" in placing staff in his office. A retired Navy admiral turned academic administrator, he had exacting standards and a gruff exterior. But, I was as impressed with his interview questions as I was unimpressed with those of an associate dean in the other interview. I was eager for the professional challenge my first professional role provided, and this role and its leader set a high standard. However, my experience in the long-titled role of administrative assistant to the assistant provost for academic services (APAS) was short-lived, as the APAS was soon appointed to a senior role with a federal agency in Washington DC. Five months after beginning my professional journey, he departed the university and his successor arrived, asking me to continue as her staff assistant. Simultaneously, I was invited to work for the president's office based on my daily interactions with his executive assistant as I couriered documents between offices. Completing a 15-month stint as staff to the presidential inauguration committee was followed by an offer to supervise the provost's office support staff at 23 years of age. Expanded roles as speechwriter and policy developer were followed by my request for part-time work after becoming the mother of young children. In those project-based years, I served as an internal consultant during cabinet-level transitions; in mid-level roles in budget, planning, and institutional research; and as chief of staff for an interim president during a notable presidential transition. My career trajectory was often unconventional but with interesting variety—often in "interim" and "turnaround" roles—navigating many delicate situations politically and interpersonally, with some key lessons about building bridges learned along the way.

While much of the work of higher education is transactional, it goes without saying that institutions are made up of individuals who bring their own skills, values, aspirations, hurts, perspectives, and energy to the workplace. Even more, the interplay between organizational structure and human complexity makes for interesting (and often infuriatingly oblique) ways of doing business. I've not yet heard of a new employee orientation that tells the "way we really get things done around here"; instead, policies are cited and training in procedures is the focus of most orientations. But, well-intended mentors of new employees unintentionally signal institutional values and ethos in how they model navigating the interpersonal workings of the institution.

Observations

All organizations have their patterns of operation, whether car dealerships, grocery stores, departments of motor vehicles, or institutions of higher education. Across the academy, there have been seismic shifts in recent decades from its traditional purpose and its constituency, among other changes.

Dan Berrett (2015) of the *Chronicle of Higher Education* defined February 28, 1967, as "[t]he Day the Purpose of College Changed." The speech on that date by then-California Governor Ronald Reagan redefined the purpose of college, going from "intellectual luxuries" to a focus on job preparation. The value of a broad-based or "liberal education" had been advocated as a civic good for a new nation from the time of Thomas Jefferson's development of the University of Virginia. Notably, young white males of financial privilege were the prime constituency of early collegiate public education in the United States.

Today, changes in the admissions and program delivery models, as well as vastly different demographics of college-going students have significantly transformed the collegiate experience from its historic roots. The *Chronicle of Higher Education* columnist Manya Whitaker (2018) reports that "one in four undergraduates and one in three graduate students are enrolled in at least one online course," which is one of several factors making higher education more accessible to students who are different from Jefferson's original constituency. Whitaker (2018) observes, "Since 2000 the number of low-income students enrolled in college has increased 15 percent, the number of female, Asian/Pacific Islander, and Native American/Alaskan Native students has each increased 29 percent, the number of black students is up 73 percent, and the number of Hispanic students, 126 percent. In 2015, 41 percent of college students were 25 or older."

These changes have considerable impact on institutional values and operations, with the potential for blockades or bridges to emerge. Operational patterns change when traditional institutions become enrollment driven because institutional values have gradually morphed from being defined by an established student academic profile to being defined by a steady and essential revenue stream. Often at enrollment-driven institutions, admissions standards are no longer the exclusive domain of the academic sector of the institution but are influenced by the administrative couple of finance and enrollment services executives.

It is in the context of this changing landscape that new ways of doing things redefine an institution's identity and values, providing an important lens to understanding how blockades can occur between departments, offices, and individuals in the academy.

- First, **higher education is hierarchical.** On the academic side, faculty hold "ranks" that are prescribed and competitively achieved. More similar to the military and law enforcement than to other professions, faculty advancement decisions are based on multi-tiered portfolio reviews—by peer committee, department chair, dean, provost, and the board of trustees. Further, the process of earning a doctorate hones a special identity of having developed expertise in a niche apart from the work of others, which can lead to a myopic or egotistical perspective if not self-managed well. On the administrative side, staff classifications are highly structured at most institutions (program analyst III, apprentice housekeeper, etc.), and many have a hierarchy within the hierarchy (progressions from assistant vice president to vice president to senior vice president, and, finally, to executive vice president). Hierarchies often signal an expectation of formal structures for communication, which can stymie quick responses and curtail creative solutions.

- A corollary of the hierarchical structure of higher education is that **higher education is classist.** With degrees being the institutional "product" of higher education, those who hold more degrees or degrees from more prestigious universities carry special status that can translate to a classism where staff are often bypassed as knowledge experts and treated by many as little more than functionaries. Jokingly, many senior leaders say, "I hold the title but we all know that my assistant does the work." These token words hold more importance than they are typically given. Many support staff are invaluable institutionally and can make or break the potential success of those they serve. In reality, in institutions steeped in hierarchical structures, decisions often aren't made at the best point of knowledge, but instead are bumped up the organizational chart where the senior leader consults their knowledge leader (often a junior staff member) in order to transmit an answer to another senior peer who hands it off to their staff for implementation. The combination of classism and hierarchy can breed resentment or a sense, by staff, of being devalued, create confusion for those in the middle of an organization (faculty and mid-level managers), and create blockades to be cleared, which affect the timeliness of decision-making and the potential for creative problem-solving.

- Second, **who we work for is more important than what we do.** Roles within a university are often defined by one's job classification. But, what we do is even more influenced by the character and style of our leader. Screamers and blamers, as well as absentee or unethical leaders, take a toll on their followers and all those within fallout range of their impact. Even the dream job can be a disastrous experience if the work environment is unhealthy. By contrast, transformational leaders set a baseline for success for their team. These are the leaders who invest in individuals in their span of care, model healthy communication, lead through collaboration, and respect work-life balance and boundaries. In fact, the psychological maps of institutions can often be drawn with offices "to be avoided at all costs" and "those people who make things happen and have a healthy team." These subterranean messages are never overtly shared but have considerable impact on institutions and those who serve them. While work-related stress can be significantly impacted by our personal patterns of response to stimuli, being in a high-conflict environment can spill over even to those who are typically well-balanced. Leaders' influence on their followers is profound, especially on their professional, interpersonal, and personal health. Choosing to work for a good leader is as important as finding a good job.

- A corollary of the impact of a leader on followers is that the **health of the institutional culture is a significant factor to be understood.** Much has been written on toxic cultures. And, few days pass without a breaking news story of an institution where untoward behaviors emerge under a spotlight and illegal, unethical, or unseemly behaviors come to public scrutiny. Organizations that see questions as destructive dissent, malign individuals or people groups, tolerate the misuse of power, or operate contrary to professional standards and expectations (of legislation, accreditors, financial and human resource expectations, etc.) breed unhealthiness for the institution and its members. Systemic blockades are rarely solved from within toxic organizations or sectors. These moments call for boards, accreditors, creditors, and legislators to step in to redress institutional wrongs. In unresolved toxic organizational sectors that do not value junior employee feedback, flight is often seen as the only option for innocent members of the unhealthy organization.

- Finally, **organizations have competing values and the role of a leader is to articulate commonality and move community members toward goal alignment.** While the primary role of higher education is to develop and disseminate knowledge, each sector has a different focus that can create philosophical conflicts. For example, is a measure of institutional success a large enrollment or a high graduation rate? The former might call for an open enrollment process, while a high graduation rate goal is likely reached through some level of selectivity in admissions. Without a clearly articulated institutional vision of success and defined pathway for reaching that goal, tensions can run high. The university's marketing department is caught in the conundrum of whom they target with information, admissions with whom they encourage to apply, and academic departments with whom they admit. This complexity of interests, in turn, affects who the faculty teach, who the alumni office can spotlight, and who advancement can cultivate as donors. Even more broadly, how is institutional success defined with respect to faculty scholarship versus their engagement with students? With respect to fundraising for endowed scholarships versus for new buildings? With respect to engagement in social issues versus national rankings? Lacking goal clarity, frictions increase, confusion abounds, and dissatisfaction follows.

- A corollary about institutional focus is that **each institution has competing values, internally and externally**. Healthy institutions see these competing values as important complexities that allow focus to be honed rather than us-them blockades to limit collaboration. Similarly, leaders of such institutions can model engagement across sectors by building more coalitions than by allowing each sector to operate in isolation—fiscally and interpersonally and by limiting access to people and data.

Insights on Building Healthy Campus Relationships

Present-day reality is that all within higher education feel stretched to do more and are required to change more than ever before. The *Chronicle*'s contributing editor, Jeff Selingo (2018), wrote, in the context of the changing purposes for college-going, "To remain relevant in the decades ahead, it is critical that leaders start thinking about the broad swath of students they want to serve—or need to serve—and how to appeal to their specific needs and desires."

But, if each employee or sector operates in isolation, goal alignment cannot readily occur and institutional fragmentation is likely. Higher education's historic practice of completing tasks at the expense of building cross-segment relationships results in an us-them mentality that is neither personally healthy nor professionally helpful. We often default to assuming an impasse before we even have a conversation with those across campus or even down the hall.

Because of the pervasive nature of this pattern, I've often benefitted from being invited to serve as a consultant to help organizations with a variety of projects. I often jest that I'm paid well to fly across the country to tell someone what their colleague in the office next door thinks, because the first individual never took the time to ask or to listen to their peer. A few simple questions have allowed me to find collaborations that have moved projects forward, even in siloed institutions. I'd note that, done well, these inquiries can lead to real appreciation for others—their skills, competing demands, and limited resources. Done badly, this can be inauthentic and/or feel manipulative without genuine regard for the individuals involved.

First, we can enhance our own knowledge through some basic questions designed to help us learn the perspectives of others. These may be individuals in our own suite, in an area of our institution with whom we rarely have contact, or folks with whom we regularly work but with whom we lack a baseline work relationship.

Here are three starter questions:

- **Tell me about the work you do** (or, the work of your office). All of us have preconceived notions of what particular roles and offices do. But, the perspectives can be dated, differ from a past institutional experience, or overlook an individual's unique background or expertise that enhances a particular project. Allowing people to share about their work or themselves gives keen insights into what motivates and frustrates them. And, it gives them the spotlight to share their skills and passions. It is easier to find common ground when we listen to others.

- **What does success look like for you?** (or, How will we know when we have met our goals?). In courting a possible collaboration or in learning more about another person or sector, it is good to understand the goals of different individuals or offices before alignment can occur with our sector and goals. Otherwise, effort may be expended based on assumed goals and disappointment can ensue on both sides. I've used this question several times in considering new roles that have been offered to me. I knew the title of the job and I knew the person to whom I'd report. But, starting with a common understanding of what a "win" would look like meant that I learned how the work mattered and I signaled that I wanted to understand the initial priorities of the hiring officer. Then, I routinely communicated priorities to those within my area of responsibility so there was a common understanding of organizational focus.

- **What are the greatest inhibitors to your success** (or, the success of this project)? Having established baseline mutual understanding earlier, asking this question is now less risky. Otherwise, the answers may be surprising to the recipient and require courage for the respondent. For example, sometimes we or our department may be seen as an inhibitor, and we should be prepared to hear that and not dismiss it. Names may surface of organizational members who are seen as anticipated blockades. Or, more frequently, the lack of time or resources are stated barriers. But, it is better to ask than to assume. And, this investment is worthwhile, especially if barriers can be lowered and resources combined and leveraged for success.

Guiding Principles for Building Bridges

Over time, I've developed a few principles that guide my work toward collaboration, whether in turn-around roles, as a participant in a cross-institution initiative, or serving as consultant to an institution whose projects are facing an impasse. Three textbooks and one four-day seminar have been central to my understanding and ability to articulate these as my own values and principles:

- **Institutional culture is layered and complex.** Understanding this phenomenon is key to thriving in an organization and to successfully influencing change. Edgar Schein's (2016) work, *Organizational Culture and Leadership*, identifies the importance of understanding three components of an organization's culture—artifacts (visible and feel-able phenomenon); espoused beliefs and values; and taken-for-granted underlying basic assumptions. The interplay of these three components make up the organization's culture. But, understanding that any combination of the three can be in dissonance with the other is also important. Stated values may not be experienced in all corners of the organization; the "feel good" events of the culture may not translate back to one's day-to-day work environment (or be experienced by those working overnight shifts on campus), and getting things done may be enhanced by knowing the back channels that make "done" possible when the espoused systems don't work. Organizations that face serious questions about dissonance between these components often benefit from a "cultural audit," asking someone with an outside perspective to gather data and provide feedback, allowing participants to hear what is said and what is done. Where dissonance is found, establishing clarity becomes important, with a goal toward defining the preferred reality and turning toward those practices. Moving to organizational health means cultural alignment between stated and lived experiences.

- **An organization's cultural values are a composite rather than a single perspective.** Cameron and Quinn's (2011) work, *Diagnosing and Changing Organizational Culture*, identifies four factors that interplay to define how individuals experience their organization's culture: clan (familial and relational), market (results driven and measurable), hierarchical (structured, controlled, and efficient), and adhocracy (entrepreneurial, innovative, and risk taking). Through use of the OCAI (Organizational Culture Assessment Instrument), individuals answer a series of questions that define their experienced and preferred organizational culture. Each is plotted along an X/Y axis, which provides a visual representation of which factors are more highly experienced and allows comparisons to be made between aggregated responses from staff, faculty, administrators, boards, and others. Taking the time to understand why a particular sector may value entrepreneurship more than others, for example, allows a healthy de-escalation between varied perspectives, roles, and responsibilities. This understanding is also a helpful tool to use over time, to see if progress is being made in moving toward common goals. Competing demands affect every part of the organization, which is neither good nor bad; it just "is." Understanding that sometimes a "good" outcome is all that is achievable in a given situation that has competing priorities allows us to focus on where a "great" outcome might occur in the future. Small progress is better than no progress.

And, the larger the organization, the larger the change initiative.

- **Institutions of higher education are complex, with various internal and external social responsibilities.** Bergquist and Pawlak's (2007) work, *Engaging the Six Cultures of the Academy*, identifies unique cultures within an institution of higher education that all operate within the broad definition of the academy. The first four cultures were originally introduced by Bergquist in 1992:

    - Collegial: Values academic disciplines; faculty research, scholarship, governance; and knowledge dissemination among students who are future leaders of society.
    - Managerial: Values fiscal and supervisory performance; finds meaning in the organization, implementation, and evaluation of work directed toward specific goals and purposes; and sees its purpose as shaping students into citizenry.
    - Developmental: Supports creation of programs and activities that enhance personal and professional growth for all community members; sees the institution's role as encouraging maturation of its members.
    - Advocacy: Places emphasis on fairness, equity, and advocacy within the institution and beyond; believes in the need for outside mediation to balance internal matters relative to power; and fosters systemic change of social attitudes and structures.

In 2007, Pawlak joined Bergquist in updating his seminal 1992 text on four institutional cultures and identified two other cultures within the academy. The virtual culture values the global perspective of open, shared, and responsive educational systems; assumes the connectivity it provides has a role in addressing perceived fragmentation and ambiguity in the postmodern age; and conceives that higher education is an important link in the global learning network. The tangible culture finds meaning in its roots, community, and spiritual grounding; values the concrete, face-to-face physical environment and its influence on maintaining institutional values; and believes in the institution's contributions to learning in a local perspective.

Bergquist and Pawlak's work provides important reminders of the competing values of institutions of higher education as developers and disseminators of knowledge while also being important centers for social change and fertile ground for human growth and development and also serving as employers with fiscal and operational accountability, subject to external oversight.

- In 2004, I participated in the Harvard School of Law's Project on Negotiation, Senior Executive Training Seminar as a way to learn about navigating seemingly intractable changes in my sector of higher education. Drawing from the work of Roger Fisher, William Ury, and Bruce Patton (2011) in *Getting to Yes*, I learned the concepts of BATNA—Best Alternative to a Negotiated Agreement. A simplistic view is this: It is better to be in the trenches and retain agency in finding a common ground with another sector than to have a third party require that the problem be solved as they define it. The core principles are these: Identify what the key issues are for each party. Highlight which are shared goals and values and focus on those first. Then, return to the non-shared values and determine if they are resolvable or can be put aside as less important when the points of commonality reach resolution. For 15 years, I've seen this work well in matters large and small, rarely needing a third party to engage in finding the solution. This provides both a framework and a sense of hope for me that few matters are irresolvable if we can focus on the common ground. And, within higher education, there is more common ground than we realize.

Conclusion

As I've continued to grow professionally and personally while devoting a career to the work of the academy, I have been committing to building bridges and not sustaining blockades. In that quest, I have been shaped by the academic work of Schein, Cameron, Quinn, Bergquist, and Pawlak, the Harvard School of Law's Program on negotiation and the industry newspaper, and the *Chronicle of Higher Education*. But, I've particularly been influenced by those individuals who were great mentors and supervisors, by learning together with students and colleagues, and in attempting new ways to approaching collaborative bridge building in the workplace and consulting environments.

I've learned that blockades are often unintended but are still rooted in human thinking and systems gone awry. But, even more, blockades continue when there is lack of clear communication and feedback, or the presence of systems that thwart institutional and individual success. Being willing to initiate the dialogue, respect unique roles and values, find a common vision, and work side by side for the greater good is invigorating. And, it is certainly better than continuing to be disgruntled, acting unempowered, and leaving the solutions to others.

Admittedly, present-day university relationships are more likely defined by well-intended policies set forth in consultation with the office of risk management, human resources, and general counsel than in past eras. But, I still find that leaders who are willing to do the hard but rewarding work of asking, listening, learning, and leading can advance their span of care further than those who work from a contractual ("not in my job description") or management perspective. Finding an answer is not the same as finding a resolution between two parties. And, the latter builds a foundation for future interactions because shared understanding is a new baseline.

References

Bergquist, W. H. & Pawlak, K. (2007). *Engaging the six cultures of the academy*. San Francisco, CA: Jossey-Bass.

Berrett, D. (2015, January 26). The day the purpose of college changed. *Chronicle of Higher Education*. Retrieved from https://www.chronicle.com/article/The-Day-the-Purpose-of-College/151359.

Cameron, K. S. & Quinn, R. E. (2011). *Diagnosing and changing organizational culture* (3rd ed.). San Francisco, CA: Jossey-Bass.

Fisher, R., Ury, W., & Patton, B. (2011). *Getting to yes* (revised ed.). New York, NY: Penguin.

Schein, E. H. (2016). Organizational culture and leadership (5th ed.). San Francisco, CA: Jossey-Bass.

Selingo, J. (2018, October 21). Here's what today's students want from college. *Chronicle of Higher Education*. Retrieved from https://www.chronicle.com/article/Here-s-What-Today-s/244829

Whitaker, M. (2018, January 2). The 21st-century academic. *Chronicle of Higher Education*. Retrieved from https://www.chronicle.com/article/The-21st-Century-Academic/242136

CHAPTER FOUR

From Underground Struggles to a Spirit of Mutual Concession:

Departmental Politics and the American Association of University Professors

ANDREW ADAMS

FROM THE LATE 1940S to the early 1950s, George Detmold (1917–2005) was a professor of English at Wells College in Aurora, New York. Due to declining enrollments since the end of the Second World War, and influenced by the then escalating hostilities in Korea, Wells College began to terminate some of the positions held by its instructors—Detmold's among them. In the fall of 1951, Detmold (1951) published an article entitled "Advice to One Entering the Profession from One Leaving It" in which he predicted a dark future for those "preparing for a career in college teaching" (pp. 365–371). He concluded with these observations on the "struggles" that can be part of an academic life:

> A prospective teacher should cultivate a firm moral integrity and nervous equilibrium. The profession which he is entering will make constant strong and subtle attacks upon these two qualities. Since it is so poorly paid, and its members have so keen a sense of their

> own worth, it is the scene of continual underground struggles for promotion (which means both higher income and increased prestige). Competition is no doubt a good thing in any society; it keeps all members on their toes. But too much of it can be demoralizing. When its rewards are meager and slow in coming it encourages jealousy, bitter feuds, and character assassination that can cripple the society in which they occur. A teacher should share in the work of his faculty, and yet he should avoid joining any of the cliques into which they will inevitably degenerate. He should learn to recognize and control the tension under which he will work, to avoid jealousy of his friends when they publish or win promotion more rapidly than he does, and to cultivate humility instead of pride. He can help himself on this last point by reminding himself frequently that whatever praise this country may give him for his services, it still spends more money for liquor than it does for education. First things first. Most important, he should keep his mind steadfastly on his purpose—publication (and, incidentally, the successful conduct of his classes). (Detmold, 1951, pp. 370–371)

Despite believing that his teaching career would soon end, Detmold would go on to become a distinguished dean at Gallaudet College in Washington DC. While there he inspired a generation of hearing-impaired actors, some of whom founded the National Theatre of the Deaf.

Some aspects of the passage quoted will resonate with faculty and staff in the 21st century, even if they were written when Harry Truman was president. The key words and phrases he used to describe his experiences include "attacks," "struggles," "competition," "demoralizing," "jealousy," "feuds," "character assassination," "cliques," "tensions," and "pride." In just one short paragraph, he required nearly a dozen words to describe a broad array of "struggles for promotion" that sometimes develop among colleagues in the same academic unit—struggles that can be an unfortunate part of departmental politics. Tensions, jealousy, and feuds can surface during formal processes, such as those related to promotion and tenure, or during informal departmental business, such as seeking appointment to an important committee, or simply trying to have an idea heard at a faculty meeting.

References to politics of this kind can be difficult to identify in the scholarly literature. Perhaps due to the long-standing aversion to publishing anything that may be interpreted as negative about one's home institution, much less committing to paper anything disparaging about one's colleagues, faculty members have remained largely silent on this sometimes-elusive part of campus life. The author's research has shown that references to the kinds of behavior Detmold described can be found in writings that explore criteria for faculty evaluation, in statements on ethics in the workplace, and in policies codifying the role of collegiality.

This chapter examines the ways in which policies evolved over time that sought to ameliorate the "underground struggles" George Detmold evoked. In order to focus the scope of what could have become an extensive literature survey, this study narrowed its field of consideration predominantly to sources published by the American Association of University Professors (AAUP). The six decades spanning the founding of the AAUP in 1915 to the early 1970s are of particular interest in the history of the academy and are, therefore, central to this inquiry. These are the years prior to the implementation of Title IX in June 1972, after which dozens if not hundreds of policies were adopted at institutions across the United States that offered protection from sexual harassment in particular and, by extension, from an array of other abusive behaviors. In addition, in the 1915 to 1970 timeframe, the academy began to move away from antiquated practices long marred by favoritism, nepotism, and discrimination into the modern era and dedicated to objective criteria for evaluation and clear expectations for collegial behavior.

It should be noted that the author of this article is not a member of the American Association of University Professors. This chapter was written as a historical inquiry from the perspective of an objective researcher seeking to produce independent scholarship. The author focused on publications and policies of the AAUP because they are indicative of national trends in higher education, are of uniformly high quality, and are easily accessible for research.

The New Society and an Early Statement of the AAUP's Goals

On January 3, 1915, a report in the New York *Sun* noted the founding of a national association:

> An organization of the university professors of America was perfected at a meeting held in this city yesterday. The new society is to be known as the American Association of University Professors, and it is intended to hold a position in scholastic circles analogous to that held in law and medicine by the American Bar Association and the American Medical Association.
>
> A council of thirty members was appointed to work over problems which will be discussed at the next annual meeting of the society. One of the most important of these is the new movement for academic freedom, through which university teachers hope to be able to promulgate their principles of political and economic science uninfluenced by the opinions of the boards of trustees. Another movement would allow the professors more freedom in regulating the educational policies of the various institutions. (Professors form Society, 1915, p. 13)

In late December of that year, the newly formed AAUP met in Washington to formalize its constitution, codify its rules of membership, and formulate its first statement on academic freedom and tenure.

From its inception, the AAUP articulated the highest ideals of the academy. In the first volume of its *Bulletin*, published in December 1915, the General Report of the Committee on Academic Freedom and Academic Tenure (Seligman et al., 1915) formulated many of the principles to which the AAUP is still dedicated. The following statement from the General Report upholding "the dignity of the scholar's profession" is balanced by a reference to one of the enduring realities of an academic career:

> If education is the corner stone of the structure of society and if progress in scientific knowledge is essential to civilization, few things can be more important than to enhance the dignity of the scholar's profession, with a view to attracting into its ranks men of the highest ability, of sound learning, and of strong and independent character. This is the more essential because the pecuniary emoluments of the profession are not, and doubtless never will be,

> equal to those open to the more successful members of other professions. It is not, in our opinion, desirable that men should be drawn into this profession by the magnitude of the economic rewards which it offers; but it is for this reason the more needful that men of high gifts and character should be drawn into it by the assurance on an honorable and secure position, and of freedom to perform honestly and according to their own consciences the distinctive and important function which the nature of the profession lays upon them. (Seligman et al., 1915, pp. 24–25)

The numerous references to "men" in this passage (as in many of those quoted later) are unfortunate but understandable given that the committee that wrote these words in the early 20th century was composed entirely of male academics. However, membership in the AAUP was never limited to men and, soon after its founding, an ever-growing number of women was welcomed into the organization. The AAUP would formally remove gender-specific language from its policy statements eight decades later in 1990.

Despite being in existence for less than a year, the AAUP quickly established itself as an investigative body of infringements of academic freedom; some of the cases in which it was involved made national headlines. The 1915 General Report's description of one of its first cases noted that politics can and do affect the work of the academy:

> Whether the university is dependent for funds upon legislative favor, it has sometimes happened that the conduct of the institution has been affected by political considerations; and where there is a definite governmental policy or a strong public feeling on economic, social, or political questions, the menace to academic freedom may consist in the repression of opinions that in the particular political situation are deemed ultra-conservative rather than ultra-radical. The essential point, however, is not so much that the opinion is of one or another shade, is that it differs from the views entertained by the authorities. (Seligman et al., 1915, p. 31)

The broad use of the term "politics" in this passage encompasses government and public involvement in an institution's functions. The present chapter, however, seeks to identify evidence of a much more personal variety of politics—the kind in which collegiality can degenerate into conflict and, more troublingly, in which prejudice can flourish in the absence of policy.

"Distinct Permanent Forces": Three Levels of Campus Politics

In November 1916, at the end of the second year of the AAUP's existence, President John Henry Wigmore (1916) encapsulated the broad sweep of the organization's activities in a president's report of nearly 50 pages, including an overview of the work of seventeen active committees. After acknowledging that the press had focused on the public activities of Committee A (dedicated to academic freedom and tenure), he turned his attention to the groundbreaking but largely unheralded work of Committee B (investigating methods of appointment and promotion). Then, as now, the processes of hiring and advancing faculty members required multiple levels of administrative consideration and were fraught with what Wigmore (1916) called "the operation of several distinct permanent forces, each with its own dangers of excess" (p. 17). In describing these "forces," he classified three levels of campus politics.

The first level is "the balance of force between the Board (of trustees or regents) and the President" (Wigmore, 1916, p. 17). The second is "the balance of force between the President and the faculty or department concerned" (Wigmore, 1916, p. 17). The third involves one of the many possible manifestations of unit-level politics, what Wigmore (1916) called "the balance of force between the head of a department and the members, especially the younger ones" (pp. 17–18). With almost no widely accepted or demonstrably objective methods for evaluation, faculty members at the time were at the mercy of the department head's good opinion for both appointment and promotion. Of this third and last political force, Wigmore (1916) wrote the following:

> Here the forces of jealousy, and self-will on the part of chief are the main dangers. There may be institutions in which the department-head system works well. But, in itself, it seems to me so full of

> danger that I wish to see it abolished,— so far at least as it affects selections and promotions. If it works well anywhere, the result is in despite of the faulty system. The hope of science is always in the younger men; and the department-head system is calculated to make university life dismal for the younger scholars,— to suppress originality, to fetter academic freedom, and to check scientific progress. It is a system suitable for a cotton-factory, not for a university.
>
> On the other hand, it is obvious that for promotions . . . the democratic decision of all department members is impracticable; for they cannot publicly discuss each other's merits. And so between these two difficulties the solution is not easy to find.
>
> In my opinion, not so much depends upon the government structures as upon the spirit of the institution or the group. Some systems have good or bad tendencies; but a good system may work poorly or a bad system may work well, according as the spirit of mutual concession, loyalty, and good fellowship prevails or not. (p. 18)

The "department-head system"—in which the head, unaided by a departmental review committee, wielded near absolute authority—was in place at many institutions well into the 20th century. Although multiple levels of collegial peer review now guide promotion and tenure processes, Wigmore's (1916) references to "jealousy" and "self-will" that "fetter" and "check" the faculty evoke the same negative forces that George Detmold would write of in 1951. As the next section of this chapter demonstrates, abusive and discriminatory practices of this kind were rife at institutions across the country from the early to mid-20th century and it would take decades of work to bring much-needed change to the academy.

"Little Academic Hells": Departmental Politics and the Committee B Report of 1929

As noted, in December 1915 the General Report of the Committee on Academic Freedom and Academic Tenure made reference to "the dignity of the scholar's profession" in its aspirational vision of the academy. Thirteen years later, in the spring of 1929, the AAUP's Committee B distributed a questionnaire to academics nationwide, the results of which would expose realities that were far from dignified (Craig, 1929). The first part of question B8 is innocuous; however, responses to its second part would expose the dark side of departmental politics. The question asked the following:

> Which of the following elements are operative in your faculty in cases of failure to secure promotion in rank and salary? Objectionable social and political ideas, poor teaching, lack of scholarly output, failure to show positive excellence in some direction, personal incompatibility, race, religion. (Craig, 1929, p. 199)

It is extraordinary to consider that there was a time in which evaluations for promotion considered social and political ideas before teaching and scholarship, followed closely by matters of personality, ethnicity, and religious beliefs.

Committee B's fascinating report is more than a historical relic: It as an important part of the history of higher education in the United States—even if some of its findings jar the modern reader. The committee was chaired by Stanford professor Hardin Craig (1875–1968), a distinguished scholar of Shakespeare and Milton who at that time was one of the few American fellows of the Royal Society of Literature. Craig and his colleagues noted that 92 correspondents cited one or more of the seven original reasons for non-promotion given in the questionnaire, but some respondents went further by creating a new evaluation category (shown second from last):

Poor teaching	89 times out of 92
Lack of scholarly output	61 times
Failure to show positive excellence in some direction	61 times
Personal incompatibility	45 times
Objectionable social and political ideas	10 times
Race	3 times
Sex (i.e., gender)	3 times

Religion (Craig, 1929, pp. 199–200)	Once

The first two categories (teaching and scholarship) are still at the foundation of faculty evaluation. "Positive excellence" was a catch-all phrase of the period that could reflect scholarly achievement or excellence in teaching or could be related to institutional, public, or professional service. Notably, the last five of the eight items relate solely to the personal characteristics of the candidate. It is no wonder that one respondent to the survey noted that promotion was dependent on "whim" and "pull" and that it did not matter if the candidate was "not so well equipped for the position" (Craig, 1929, p. 205). At that time, departmental politics were rampant in a way that is almost inconceivable today.

The committee's extended discussion of their findings showed that little if any progress had been made in the decade since objections were first raised in 1915 to the authoritarian department head system. Informed by the practices of institutions nationwide, Committee B described an academy in which favoritism, rather than merit, was a major factor in promotion decisions:

> This question attempted to ascertain causes of failure to secure promotion for use in the construction of a list of academic qualifications for promotion in the different ranks. The territory being vague and unknown and the information hard to get, there were many complaints to this effect from those answering the questionnaire, in reply to which it can only be said that in a job of this kind there is no use in asking questions the answers to which are already known. It is, of course, recognized by the Committee and was reiterated by those answering the question that failures to achieve promotion are almost always due to a combination of defects, and that many failures to secure promotion are due to lack of funds on the part of the institution concerned. There were several reports of "little academic hells," institutions where everything goes by favoritism and nothing by merit, where no promotions are made except under pressure of calls from the outside, or where certain enterprising department heads and deans get all the favors for those who are lucky enough to serve their groups. In several places there was such

> a lack of settled policy that persons desiring to answer the question declared themselves unable to doso. (Craig, 1929, p. 199)

In this passage, the committee suggests not only that the academy was a wasteland with regard to policy but also that this fact was widely recognized—the answer to this question was "already known." Candidates were not denied promotion because they failed to meet stated requirements; in many instances there were none to meet. Rather, their perceived "combination of defects" may well have been personal in nature and their fate could be sealed by the institutional budget.

Committee B—that was, once again, composed entirely of men—acknowledged that considerations of gender, age, and ethnicity affected appointment and promotion decisions and the writers expressed their belief that the situation required further study. Searching for what they referred to as a "sane and constructive" response to their findings, they wrote this remarkable passage:

> "Race" was mentioned three times, "religion," once. Failure to secure promotion on the ground of sex was mentioned three times, though the Committee had deliberately excluded that item from the list on the ground that it deserved a more careful consideration than it was likely to receive in this report. With reference to all four of the last-mentioned special barriers to promotion, we feel that we have nothing to contribute. The information is hard to get, and many special circumstances need to be taken into consideration before anything sane and constructive can be said or done. On the basis of what has come to us directly and incidentally, we should, no doubt, be justified in saying that in some places in this country wisdom dictates that, for smooth progress through the academic world, one should, as far as possible, be a white man of American parentage, and be endowed with certain congenial views on social matters and on matters of politics and religion. (Craig, 1929, p. 200)

With all due respect for the brilliant academics who created this report, it is difficult to believe that "wisdom" dictated such a finding. Perhaps rather than "wisdom" they were referring to "conventional wisdom," or the way things were routinely done at some institutions at that time. Nonetheless, it is astonishing from the distance of nearly a century how casually they concluded that being a Caucasian male would guarantee smooth progress through the academic ranks rather than professional accomplishments as an educator. This is the point in the report when the committee could have announced a formal investigation into the reasons why three women were denied promotion and why three other people were barred from advancement due to their race. Such an observation is, however, both revisionist and idealistic: We should consider that the committee worked just nine years after women finally secured the right to vote and more than three decades before the Civil Rights Act of 1964. The Committee B report of 1929 is fascinating as an historical document, but it is, nonetheless, unfortunate that nothing "sane and constructive" would be done about these egregious matters for decades.

As described in the next two sections, efforts to standardize criteria for promotion and tenure and to craft statements on professional ethics would gradually improve working conditions by weakening the overwhelming power of departmental politics in the years before the passage of Title IX.

"What Is Actually Done and Why It Is Done": Working Toward Objective Standards

Even as George Detmold wrote of departmental politics and the struggles they evoked, he may have been unaware that the question of how to replace the whim and pull of politics with objective standards for evaluation had been debated for decades prior to 1951. Since its founding, writers in the pages of the AAUP *Bulletin* had pondered whether the department head or a tenure and promotion committee should make these important decisions. No matter who evaluated the candidate's record, what criteria should be used?

As we have seen, John Henry Wigmore noted in 1916 of the prevalent department head system that it was "calculated to make university life dismal" (p. 18). But 13 years later, little progress had been made. While the Committee B report of 1929 observed that promotion was easiest for white American men, it also stated in gender-neutral language unusual in its pages: "We believe in a body of qualifications which should govern an appointment and promotion so stated and understood that the persons concerned may know what standards they have to meet" (Craig, 1929, p. 209).

Nearly two decades later, Lloyd S. Woodburne's 1943 article entitled "Suggested Criteria for Academic Promotion" was the first systematic exploration of standards for the evaluation of teaching, scholarship, and service published in the AAUP's journal. Later serving as dean of the University of Washington's College of Arts and Sciences, Woodburne (1906–1992) provides fascinating glimpses into the ways in which outdated and discriminatory processes were transforming into modern methods of evaluation.

While discussing the essential category of scholarship, Woodburne (1943) dismisses teaching as just one of the "services, aside from research" (p. 244). He wrote of the application process for elevation in rank:

> A test of the validity of the material usually presented in support of recommendations for promotion is particularly difficult to devise in any way which would be applicable to a group of institutions. Conferences with staff members [i.e., faculty] from a number of colleges and universities reveal, however, a vague though fairly uniform series of steps which seem traditional in most institutions. The series is initiated by the departmental recommendation to the dean of the school or college that one or more staff members be promoted to the next higher rank. This recommendation is accompanied by a vita and a bibliography of the candidate's published articles, and may be supported by reprints of the articles or copies of the books. It is sometimes possible a chairman may be able to add information concerning the services, aside from research, of a staff member whose publication record is not extensive. (Woodburne, 1943, p. 244)

Although it is cumbersome for faculty members to prepare thick dossiers of artifacts related to the full spectrum of their assignments, we can nonetheless be thankful that promotion is no longer primarily based on submitting a vita and bibliography.

The Committee B report of 1929 noted of the evaluation of teaching and its role in faculty promotion: "[T]he Committee feels sceptical [sic] about this criterion because of the fact that it knows of no way of determining with certainty whether or not a particular individual is or is not a good teacher" (Craig, 1929, p. 199). By 1943, Woodburne's report still indicated that no widely accepted approach to the evaluation of teaching had yet been found. He wrote of the ongoing issue the following:

> The most difficult aspect of university services, from the point of view of evaluation, is classroom instruction. In many respects teaching is a rather tenuous person-to-person relationship. It is difficult to determine the exact degree of intellectual ferment which has been placed in the student's mind by the instructor. In a similar fashion it is almost impossible to determine the contribution of any one course to the cumulative growth of critical ability on the part of the student. (Woodburne, 1943, p. 249)

Although he briefly reviews various approaches to classroom evaluation, he concludes: "[S]tudent opinion is at best a somewhat faulty indication of the effect of instruction" (Woodburne, 1943, p. 250).

Published just one year after Woodburne, the first exploration in the AAUP archives into the then-novel concept of student evaluations was Edward C. McDonagh's 1944 article "Let's Grade the Professors." A recently returned veteran and a sociologist at what was then called Southern Illinois Normal University, McDonagh (1944) observed the mind-set his contemporaries held: "It is suggested that every professor should be graded by his students in much the same manner he grades them" (p. 83). Dismissive of this oversimplification, McDonagh's argument sought to elevate teaching to the same level as scholarship itself. Student evaluation of teaching was one of the mechanisms necessary to substantiate the instructor's work, just as peer review and publication validate the work of the researcher. He wrote near the end of his observations that

> on some campuses, professors are rated by administrative officers in terms of how much they produce in print. This production is measured often in terms of how many lines a professor publishes each year, in a few institutions each teacher's publishing program is

> graphed and it is possible to measure the amount of thinking Professor Jones has done in print. If this type of work may be measured objectively, why not teaching? . . . Social psychologists inform us that the main reason most professors write articles is for professional recognition and status. The grading of professors would place teaching in an important achievement category and would afford recognition and status to the deserving instructor. The constant vigilance of students would tend to stimulate the professor to do a good job of the work he is paid to do, namely, teaching. . . . The grading of university professors by students would make for more objectivity regarding those teachers who ought to be raised in academic rank and salary. (McDonagh, 1944, p. 85)

Moving on to service, the third leg of the traditional faculty evaluation paradigm, approaches to its assessment vary widely from one institution to the next and even from one unit to the next on the same campus. This situation has, seemingly, been a long-standing tradition in higher education. For decades, newly appointed tenure-track professors have wondered on how many committees they should sit and which institutional service opportunities "count" the most.

Although he didn't use the modern buzzword "outcomes," Woodburne's article is notable for its forward-thinking approach. Rather than requiring candidates to provide an unenlightening list of service, he believed that an application for promotion should demonstrate what the service actually accomplished and what the faculty member's individual responsibilities were in the overall effort. Again referring to faculty as "members of the staff," he wrote that

> [a] large portion of the internal functioning of any institution of higher education is performed by faculty committees. It is not expected that all members of the staff should be perfect committee men, but, other things being equal, service on committees and boards should contribute to favorable consideration of the candidate. Here again it is not enough to say that a candidate has served on ten or fifteen committees. We must know whether the staff member has been assigned to successively more important committees,

> and whether a particular committee has made a real contribution to college policy or practice. The "appearance" of committee work is of no value whatever, but the "reality" of such services supported by evidence should always be taken into account when a man is considered for promotion. In this search after the reality of the contribution of a staff member, it may be necessary to inquire of the committee chairman and of other members of the committee concerning the candidate's real contribution to the committee report. The same distinction between "appearance" and "reality" must be made in evaluating other administrative duties performed by the candidate. (Woodburne, 1943, p. 252)

Once modern-day faculty members successfully navigate tenure and promotion processes, they may in turn serve on committees tasked with reviewing their peers for promotion and tenure and may also take part in revising criteria for evaluation. The revelation soon comes that the standards in place during their own years of candidacy were not as concrete as they once seemed. Although we have come far since the criteria-free world of 1929, methods for evaluating teaching, scholarship, and service are variable and subject to interpretation—and therefore are fodder for departmental politics. Thus we find the almost universal complaint of the assistant professor that securing tenure is more difficult for the younger rather than the older generation. We must acknowledge, however, that standards and methods for evaluation fluctuate as a natural part of the mutability of the academy. For example, the campus that formally incorporates the Boyer model of scholarship into its evaluative processes may one day find that Boyer too was a product of its time whose influence diminishes with ever-evolving trends in the academy. Similarly, debates over the effectiveness of student evaluations of instruction, and the weight they should be given in consideration for promotion, will never subside. And now many of us bob in the sometimes-murky waters of assessment, not knowing where the wave will take us or how it will affect faculty evaluation in the future.

In the end, methods and standards for evaluation must be transparent and uniformly applied to all faculty to the extent possible. To do less is to create an atmosphere of "underground struggles" in which departmental politics—"How can I please the tenured professors?"—weigh on a young faculty member's mind rather than dedication to work of the highest possible quality both in and out of the classroom.

"Active Cooperation and Encouragement": Codifying Professional Ethics

The worst aspects of campus politics—the underground struggles and the 1929 report's acknowledgement of smooth progress for white men—were all too common before the legal protections that emerged in the early 1970s. Although it did not codify an official statement on professional ethics for faculty working in higher education until 1966, the AAUP voiced its commitment to framing such standards early in its history. However, evidence of its ongoing work would surface only periodically over the first three decades of its existence.

With World War I raging in Europe and the United States a year away from entering the hostilities, AAUP President John Henry Wigmore seemed to have the conflict on his mind when he first noted the need to address ethical standards for professional conduct. Describing a campus community as an "encampment," he wrote in 1916

> [t]hat there are numerous problems of ethics peculiar to university life, the least reflection will show. But that they are susceptible of decision by any general canons of behavior might not be so apparent. Yet all other professions acknowledge the propriety and existence of a body of ethical rules; and why not the profession of teaching? Moreover, the communal life in a single encampment—an element shared with the military profession, but lacking in the medical and legal profession—adds to the need and possibility. (Wigmore, 1916, p. 32)

Without question, the Committee B report of 1929 would demonstrate thirteen years later that ethical lapses in the form of sexism and racism were evident at institutions across the country.

Published in February 1937, "A Code of Ethics for Teachers in Colleges and Universities" was written by members of the University of Michigan's chapter of the AAUP and was the first exploration of the subject published in the AAUP *Bulletin* (Vibbert et al., 1937). The Michigan committee noted of their work that it was submitted "not as a finished code for which we would ask adoption, but as a means to elicit nation-wide criticism" (Vibbert et al., 1937, p. 143). Their carefully crafted paradigm, once again written from the masculine perspective, is divided into thirty-one subsections, the five major parts of which are labelled as follows: "I. Relations of the Teacher to His Profession," "II. Relations of the Teacher to His Students," "III. Relations of the Teacher to His Colleagues," "IV. Relations of the Teacher to His Institution and Its Administrators," and "V. Relations of the Teacher to the Non-Academic World."

Vibbert and his colleagues pose a simple question in the first full paragraph of their proposal: "But why have a code?" Their answer shows that they were aware of the realities of campus politics and the negative effects of collegial tension upon both faculty and students:

> That codes may become as disastrous as the proverbial millstone, we have seen abundantly evidenced within the past fifteen years. That the absence of a code of any sort may be even more disastrous, is supported by a still larger quota of evidence, no little part of which is available in the colleges and universities. Whether or not a code would remedy the situation, it is undeniably a disgrace to the profession as a whole that the victims of academic abuses should be so numerous in these very institutions of higher learning where youth is presumed to receive its initiation into the culture of a representative democracy. (Vibbert et al., 1937, p. 143)

The third part of the Michigan code ("Relations of the Teacher to His Colleagues") is most pertinent to this examination of departmental politics. Had it been widely adopted upon publication, this section could have made George Detmold's experiences two decades later far more positive. The first three subsections on collegial behavior state the following:

> A. The teacher should give his colleagues active cooperation and encouragement in their individual development as teachers and

in measures on behalf of the objectives of his department and institution.

B. The teacher should in no case indulge in unfair competition with his colleagues for position, rank, salary, students, or other advantages of any sort.

C. The teacher should avoid indiscriminate disparagement of his colleagues. He owes to his institution and to the profession a reasonable tact, both as to content and place, in the utterance of disparaging facts. This should not restrain him, however, from an honest and timely appraisal of a colleague that is for the betterment of educational service, nor from his duty to submit to the appropriate authorities any substantial evidence in his possession concerning the unfitness of a colleague. (Vibbert et al., 1937, p. 143)

As the AAUP began to codify its first statement on ethics in 1957, the influence of the Michigan proposal would be evident; however, at no time did the AAUP's working groups cite the Michigan chapter's substantial contribution from two decades earlier.

In December 1958, the AAUP released its "Report on the Committee of Professional Ethics," the initial draft of which consisted of a "general statement" rather than a "detailed code" (Frankel et al., 1958). It outlined four main areas of faculty ethics: (a) responsibility to the subject, (b) responsibility to the students, (c) responsibility to the institution, and (d) responsibility to the profession and to the community. In 1965, the AAUP expanded the outline to five areas: (a) responsibility to the subject area, (b) responsibility to the students, (c) responsibility to colleagues, (d) responsibility to the institution, and (e) responsibility to the community. This 1965 ordering is identical to the structure of the 1937 Michigan report that it did not cite as a source.

While the Michigan proposal devoted six subsections to collegial behavior, the initial AAUP report from 1958 did not dedicate a separate section to the topic; rather, it folded references to the matter into the first section on the teacher's responsibility to the subject area. The 1958 report stated the following:

> The preservation of the integrity and vitality of their subjects also requires professors to comment on the work of their colleagues, and to advise their own or other universities about the appointment, retention, or promotion of individual scholars. It is self-evident that the scholar and teacher will best fulfill this responsibility by attempting, as far as it is humanly possible, to base his professional judgments of his colleagues explicitly upon their work and upon their contributions, actual or potential, to teaching and inquiry. (Frankel et al., 1958, p. 781)

Seven years later, in June 1965, the AAUP's (1965) overhaul of the form and content of its ethics statement dedicated a new section, part three, to collegial behavior which read

> The professor's obligations to his professional colleagues is derived from common membership in the community of scholars. He seeks to be magnanimous in his diverse relations with colleagues. In the exchange of criticism and ideas he shows respect for the opinions of others. He acknowledges his academic debts; his professional judgments of colleagues are impartial; and he accepts his share of faculty responsibilities for the governance of his institution. (p. 303)

Gone in this passage is the simpler, aspirational language of the Michigan group that suggested we give our colleagues "active cooperation and encouragement" and use "reasonable tact" in our interactions. Considered by itself, the Michigan's code's "active encouragement" sounds far more personable than the robotic injunction "to be magnanimous in [our] diverse relations" and is clearer than the vague admonition to "acknowledge our academic debts."

In March 1966, the AAUP proposed minor changes to the statement that were further refined and published in September of that year. Standing as AAUP policy for nearly two decades, in the early 1980s the AAUP published a report entitled "On the Status of Women in the Academic Profession, 1981–82" that called for important changes to the wording (Schafer, 1982). The Committee W report was written by its chair, Alice T. Schafer

(1982) of Wellesley College, who noted that members of the group "requested to amend the 1966 Statement on Professional Ethics to include explicit reference to sexual harassment and to remove all sexist references from the document" (p. 27a). While the call to delete gender-specific pronouns was honored, the revised statement on ethics ultimately published in 1987 did not include a reference to sexual harassment in particular but, rather, to harassment in general. After further editing in 2009, this is the section on interpersonal behavior from the Statement on Professional Ethics published in the 2015 edition of the AAUP's *Policy Documents and Reports*:

> As colleagues, professors have obligations that derive from common membership in the community of scholars. Professors do not discriminate against or harass colleagues. They respect and defend the free inquiry of associates, even when it leads to findings and conclusions that differ from their own. Professors acknowledge academic debt and strive to be objective in their professional judgment of colleagues. Professors accept their share of faculty responsibilities for the governance of their institution. (pp. 145–146)

Even as this paragraph neared its final form in 1987, statements on ethics were passing into the realm of historical relics. By the late 1970s, some faculty members were moving from the classroom to the courtroom. In response, university administrators sought to frame clear expectations for collegial behavior that could withstand legal scrutiny.

"Irrelevant Personal Factors": Collegiality and the Courts

In October 1999, the AAUP published a statement entitled "On Collegiality as a Criterion for Faculty Evaluation." Opposed to what it referred to as an emerging "highly unfortunate" practice, it noted that

> collegiality is not a distinct capacity to be assessed independently of the traditional triumvirate of scholarship, teaching, and service. It is rather a quality whose value is expressed in the successful execution of these three functions. Evaluation in these three areas will encom-

> pass the contributions that the virtue of collegiality may pertinently add to a faculty member's career. (p. 69)

That collegiality is an intrinsic part of teaching, scholarship, and service is a valid observation, but it is not necessarily true that it is an elusive "quality" that defies objective evaluation. Indeed, seven decades before the AAUP published its statement on collegiality, clear standards for the evaluation of teaching, scholarship, and service were rare and would take decades of careful thought to codify.

In December 2001, Mary Ann Connell, general counsel at the University of Mississippi, and Frederick G. Savage, general counsel at Johns Hopkins University, published "Does Collegiality Count?" in *Academe*, the third incarnation of the AAUP's official journal (Connell & Savage, 2001). In it they explored numerous court cases that were then transforming the academy by upholding collegiality as a criterion for faculty evaluation, even if not explicitly stated as such in institutional policy. Although publishing their findings in the AAUP's journal, Connell and Savage (2001) nonetheless disagreed with the organization's approach to the issue:

> The [AAUP] takes the position that collegiality should not be assessed independently of teaching, research, and service . . . despite such concerns within the academic community, the courts have affirmed at every turn the use of collegiality as a factor in decisions concerning faculty employment, promotion, tenure and termination. . . . Given the strength and unanimity of the case law, institutions of higher learning can feel confident from a legal standpoint in considering collegiality in faculty employment decisions, even if it is not specified as a separate and distinct criterion. (p. 40)

Institutions are now loath to leave any matter "not specified." Accordingly, by the early 21st century policies that addressed matters of collegiality began to be adopted as a matter of course both by individual institutions and statewide systems.

The author of this chapter works within the University of North Carolina (UNC) system that began to confront issues of discrimination and equal opportunity by the 1970s and, in turn, collegiality within the context of promotion and tenure decisions by the early years of the 21st century. The UNC system adopted the first version of its Policy 101.3.1, Review of Non-reappointment Decisions, in March 2003 and revised it in the fall of 2008:

> As used in The Code, the term "personal malice" means dislike, animosity, ill-will, or hatred based on personal characteristics, traits, or circumstances of an individual that are not relevant to valid University decision making. For example, personnel decisions based on negative reactions to an employee's anatomical features, marital status, or social acquaintances are intrinsically suspect. If reappointment is withheld because of personal characteristics that cannot be shown to impinge on job performance, a wrong likely has been committed. On the other hand, if personal characteristics can be shown to impede a faculty member's capacity to relate constructively to his or her peers, in a necessarily collegial environment, withholding advancement may be warranted. . . . While the terms "ill-will," "dislike," "hatred," and "malevolence" may connote different degrees of antipathy, such distinctions make no difference in applying the fundamental rationale of the prohibition. Any significant degree of negative feeling toward a candidate based on irrelevant personal factors, regardless of the intensity of that feeling, is an improper basis for making decisions. (University of North Carolina, 2008, II.B.)

Policy statements such as this have helped to end the consideration of "personal incompatibility," "objectionable social and political ideas," "race," "sex," and "religion" in tenure and promotion proceedings as were noted in the 1929 Committee B report. And George Detmold's (1951) "attacks," "jealousy," "feuds," and "character assassination" of 1951 would not be tolerated in the modern academy.

By 2010 Western Carolina University (one of the institutions in the UNC system and the author's home campus) sought to align itself with UNC policy and to address collegiality with a statement in its faculty handbook. Although, like AAUP policy, the statement did not establish collegiality as the fourth leg of the institution's faculty evaluation paradigm, it nonetheless allowed individual academic units the freedom to do so if they chose:

> Overarching expectations of all faculty include professionalism and collegiality. Collegiality is not a separate criterion upon which faculty are assessed, unless otherwise dictated within DCRDs [Departmental Collegial Review Documents] or College by-laws. Collegiality entails shared responsibility and effective cooperation to achieve common goals. Moreover, collegiality among associates must involve appreciation of and respect for differences in expertise, ideas, and background. The concept of collegiality, however, should be distinguished from congeniality; to be congenial is parallel with sociability and agreeableness, while collegiality is a positive and productive association with colleagues. A person need not be congenial to be collegial. (Western Carolina University, 2018, p. 66)

Key concepts in this statement—"professionalism," "shared responsibility," "effective cooperation," "appreciation," and "respect"—could be further defined and effectively serve as the basis for an objective consideration of collegiality, the elusive fourth leg of the evaluative stool that could further help to assure a respectful workplace for all faculty.

Conclusion

Nearly seven decades ago, George Detmold felt so demoralized by the insensitivity of his colleagues that he published reflections on his experiences. Although hopeful that reform would come in the future, he nonetheless ended his observations to his colleague on a pessimistic note:

> I would guess that the concept and practice of higher education in this country will be radically revised by the end of another twenty years or thirty years. And I don't foresee any easy living for the newcomers while that revision is under way. Tom, all things considered, don't be a teacher! (Detmold, 1951, p. 371)

It is unfortunate that Detmold felt this way, yet understandable given the totality of what he shared in his article. Thankfully, the academy has come far from the early and middle years of the twentieth century when favoritism, racism, sexism, discrimination, and many forms of non-collegial behavior flourished seemingly unchecked.

Faculty members at every rank would do well to study, or restudy, the policies and procedures in place on their campuses that seek to assure a respectful workplace. These policies, that emerged from the past experiences of human beings like us, were long needed and took decades to codify. Unless they are actively used and routinely inform our lives today, the exacting work done by our predecessors was in vain.

To move beyond underground struggles in the workplace, we should recall the sentiment from 1916 by AAUP President John Wigmore: "Some systems have good or bad tendencies; but a good system may work poorly or a bad system may work well, according as the spirit of mutual concession, loyalty, and good fellowship prevails or not" (p. 18).

By encouraging our colleagues in their careers and lives, by supporting our students in the attainment of their aspirations, by striving for the common good on our campuses and in the world, and by simply letting go of the little stuff, the darkness of departmental politics can be extinguished by the light of our shared quest to realize the highest ideals of both the academy and of human existence.

References

American Association of University Professors. (1965). Statement on professional ethics. *AAUP Bulletin, 51*(3), 302–303.

American Association of University Professors. (1990). Gender specific language eliminated from older policy documents. *Academe, 76*(3), 36.

American Association of University Professors. (1999). Report: On collegiality as a criterion for faculty evaluation. *Academe, 85*(5), 69–70.

American Association of University Professors. (2015). Statement on professional ethics. In *Policy Documents and Reports* (11th ed.) (pp. 145–146). Baltimore, MD: Johns Hopkins University Press.

Connell, M. A. & Savage., F. G. (2001). Does collegiality count? *Academe, 87*(6), 37–40.

Craig, H. (1929). Methods of appointment and promotion in American colleges and universities: Report of committee B. *Bulletin of the American Association of University Professors, 15*(3), 175–217.

Detmold, G. (1951). Advice to one entering the profession from one leaving it. *Bulletin of the American Association of University Professors, 37*(2), 365–371.
Frankel, C., Byse, C., Hullfish, H. G., Pratt, N. T., Stene, E. O., Stiemke, R. E. & Wissler, B. F. (1958). Report of the committee on professional ethics. *AAUP Bulletin, 44*(4), 780–784.
McDonagh, E. C. (1944). Let's grade the professors. *Bulletin of the American Association of University Professors, 30*(1), 83–86.
McPherson, W. H., Bevington, D. M., Christie, J. A., Denenfeld, P., Eble, K. E., Nygaard, J. M. & Yost, H. T. (1966). Statement on professional ethics. *AAUP Bulletin, 52*(3), 290–291.
Porter, K. H. (1961). Department head or chairman? *AAUP Bulletin, 47*(4), 339–342.
Professors form Society. (1915, January 3). *The Sun*, 13.
Schafer, A. T. (1982). Report of committee W: On the status of women in the academic profession, 1981–82. *Academe, 68*(6), 27a.
Seligman, E. R. A., Bennett, C. E., Dealey, J. Q., Ely, R. T., Farnam, H. W., Fetter, F. A., . . . & Weatherly, U. G. (1915). General report of the committee on academic freedom and academic tenure: Presented at the annual meeting of the association: December 31, 1915. *Bulletin of the American Association of University Professors, 1*(1), 15–43.
University of North Carolina. (2008, October 17). The Code of the Board of Governors of the University of North Carolina and the UNC Policy Manual. Retrieved from https://www.northcarolina.edu/apps/policy/index.php
Vibbert, C. B., McFarlan, H. J., McKenzie, R. D., Hoad, W. C., Shepard, J. F. & Wenger, C. N. (1937). A code of ethics for teachers in colleges and universities. *Bulletin of the American Association of University Professors, 23*(2), 143–148.
Western Carolina University. (2018). 4.04 Western Carolina University collegial review. C. University standards for collegial review. *Faculty Handbook 2017-2018*. Retrieved from https://www.wcu.edu/WebFiles/PDFs/Faculty_Handbook_2017-18.pdf
Wigmore, H. (1916). President's report for 1916. *Bulletin of the American Association of University Professors, 2*(5), 9–52.
Woodburne, L. S. (1943). Suggested criteria for academic promotion. *Bulletin of the American Association of University Professors, 29*(2), 242–255.

CHAPTER FIVE

The Politics of Newspaper Advising/Newspaper Advising as a Political Act

Melanie Springer Mock

My head felt rummy, and I walked across campus on November 9, 2016, in a surreal haze. What had happened the night before? Did our country really just elect Donald Trump to be its next president? I couldn't believe it, still, but knew we would need to discuss election coverage in my first class of the morning, Introduction to Journalism. I just didn't know what to say and worried that saying anything might initiate another crying jag, similar to the ones that had kept me awake most of the night before.

Perhaps this description of my demeanor post-2016 presidential election tells you all that's needed about my political persuasion: I've been a lifelong progressive who grew up with NPR's *All Things Considered* as an every-afternoon soundtrack. My parents participated in the civil rights movement; Jimmy Carter was their personal hero; they believed and practiced inclusivity; and refugee families, people with disabilities, and ethnic minorities often joined our dinner table. Although my family was deeply religious—my dad was a Mennonite pastor and our life revolved around the church—my parents believed that Scripture informed their political positions and denominational tradition their ardent belief in church/state separation. It took attending an evangelical Christian college as an undergraduate for me to realize that Republicans could also be good people and that Democrats were not necessarily the de facto party of those with Christian faith.

After attending graduate school, earning a PhD, and moving to the West Coast, I'm back at the same evangelical school I attended as an undergraduate, this time as a tenured professor of English whose teaching load primarily includes courses in journalism. In the intervening years, a lot has changed about my institution, though the conservative Christian ethos remains prominent on campus, especially among students. In any class I teach, it's never quite clear whether the students I'm facing have grown up with NPR, like I did, or whether Fox News predominated as their parents' go-to news source.

This is only one of the many classroom tensions I navigate while teaching journalism, especially because the two years since President Trump's election have created an even more polarized populace, and my journalism classes feel like a reflection of what is happening writ large across the United States. When politics are so incredibly divisive, as they are now, and when journalism itself is under assault by government administrators, and when my university feels it necessary to convey a sense of political neutrality to students and constituents, when all these forces are at play, teaching journalism—especially in the age of President Trump—is incredibly difficult.

But also, incredibly important.

Because here's the thing: Credible journalism is vital to the health of any democracy. We need good reporters willing to track down sources, do interviews, shed light on the darkness that can undermine a free society. Even a rudimentary glance at countries that lack freedom of the press reminds us that a robust and honest fourth estate is necessary for democracy to thrive; and if we've learned anything during the reign of President Trump, it's that truth can and will prevail when journalists do their work with integrity, authority, and good will, despite the obstacles they face.

College journalism classes—and in particular, college student publications—provide a microcosm of our larger world. Student presses also need good reporters willing to pursue stories on campus, even when doing so might contradict the narrative being built by institutional marketing and communication offices. Those universities who put limitations on student journalists, who attempt to control what stories reach their student population, are putting the health of their institution at risk, and a campus "fourth estate," one built on good reporting and writing, is necessary for universities to thrive. If I've learned anything in the past few years about being a faculty advisor to a campus publication, it's that producing strong journalism at the local level creates healthier institutions while also providing a strong foundation for journalism's future—a future that now seems unclear, given the many assaults, both literal and figurative, that journalists face.

Post-Truth Politics and Student Journalism

The accusation of "fake news" has become part of our contemporary lexicon, a handy term Donald Trump employed in the run-up to the 2016 election. Of course, fake news existed long before the Republican presidential candidate used the word to undermine negative reports about his campaign. War-time propaganda stands out as one kind of fake news that could, when weaponized, shape a national narrative about the personhood of one's enemies: Think rumors about the monstrous Huns in World War I, for example, or the misinformation circulated about the Viet Cong fighters in Vietnam. And yet, despite the evidence that fake news sometimes slipped into mainstream reporting, journalists were still seen as credible professionals. According to the Knight Foundation (2018) as recently as 1972, 70 percent of Americans surveyed said they trusted journalists to provide accurate information; that number had plummeted to 32 percent in 2016 and recovered only to 41 percent in 2017.

Exploring the many reasons *why* trust in journalists has waned in recent years is beyond the scope of this essay, though President Trump's consistent use of the term has certainly contributed to this distrust, as has his refrain that the media is "the enemy of the people," a claim he has continued to make, even after several journalists were killed in a mass shooting in Maryland; and after explosive devices were sent to several journalists, as well as the CNN newsroom; and after the brutal murder of dissident journalist Jamel Khashoggi at a Saudi Arabia embassy in Turkey. In August 2018, President Trump claimed that 80 percent of mainstream reporters are dishonest; he and his former press secretary, Sarah Huckabee Sanders, have both repeated a never-verified argument that—as he tweeted in May 2018—over 90 percent of coverage on his presidency is negative and thus fake. As Borchers (2018) reported, media analysts agree that President Trump receives negative media coverage, but also that his inability to follow protocol—to act presidential, avoid telling lies, refrain from race baiting and personal attacks—means that negative coverage might be warranted.

Students studying journalism now must navigate this post-truth morass, where credible news platforms, like the *New York Times* and the *Washington Post*, are critiqued by a president who insists they are "failing" and "gutless." Is it possible to hold up these models of journalism (their newsrooms have consistently won Pulitzer Prizes for reporting and writing) when a national leader says they only spread misinformation? How do we help students navigate this world?

As a journalism teacher, and more specifically as an adviser of our campus newspaper, I ground my instruction on the premise that credible journalism is necessary for the health of any democracy. And while a university campus is not really a democracy, credible student journalism remains a vital tool to sustaining the health of any institution of higher learning. Sometimes, campus administrators might want to cry "fake news" when my students publish something on campus that challenges the polished image our university hopes to sustain; sometimes, administrators might even believe student journalists are the enemy of the people—or, at least, an enemy of the university marketing office. Still, as a learning lab for "real world" newsrooms, the campus newspaper remains the best way to establish an informed student body. Even more than that, my idealism makes me think the work of university journalists might help us find a way through the darkness of a post-truth world to one that searches intentionally for the light.

Censorship and the Student Newspaper

This is my nineteenth year at George Fox University, my fifteenth as a newspaper advisor, my tenth year as primary instructor of our introduction to journalism courses. Like most professors at small institutions like mine, I was hired as a generalist, specializing in composition and rhetoric, which meant I would teach a wide array of writing courses. Despite having only a little training in journalism, I became immersed in on-campus journalism by degrees, and now half my load is journalism classes; the other half is courses in English. Because I am a news junkie, this transition seemed like an easy one, and as the world of journalism has undergone seismic transitions in the last decade, I've been able to reinvent my classes too, while also continuing to focus on the fundamentals of any good reporting. This includes cultivating sources, giving interviews, and navigating the ethical and legal landmines that are part of a 24-hour news cycle.

The on-campus newspaper serves as a testing ground for what students learn in introductory journalism classes, and while journalism courses do not serve as required prerequisites for being on staff, the classes can help inform the work students do on *The Crescent*. Our institution has traditionally not acknowledged a relationship between academic departments and the newspaper, and for many years publication staff operated independently, without any faculty oversight. But, after a rocky stint in the 90s when the campus newspaper, *The Crescent*, was rudderless—and all manner of humorless satire, a la *Mad Magazine*, was published—university administrators decided the publication needed an adviser, and when I was hired, it was determined *The Crescent* should be a part of my load (a small part—I receive three credit hours' release time every year).

Without much training in journalism, and zero training in newspaper advising, my pedagogical approach to leading the student newspaper has matured over time, but its essence has remained unchanged. Because I see *The Crescent* as a learning lab, I allow the student journalists under my advisement to make most all editorial decisions about the publication. They decide what articles to report, what sources to cultivate, what opinions should be expressed on their editorial pages. Section editors make choices about story selection and editors-in-chief work alongside layout editors to shape the final product. These days, that product is a small magazine the staff produces every other week; earlier iterations of *The Crescent* included a 12-page tabloid-sized paper that ran anywhere from one each week to one every three weeks. Both editorial calendars were problematic for their own reasons, but in deciding a publishing schedule, as in everything else, I let students call the shots.

Call the shots and then live by the choices they've made. As an adviser, I sit in on staff meetings that are run—sometimes inefficiently, I'll admit—by the paper's leadership team. Occasionally, when a story idea is discussed, and when I think the story idea could be more robust, I might make suggestions about angles and sources, but otherwise, students are free to pursue the stories that excite them most. I also read the content before it proceeds from copy editors to layout; and while I might provide feedback on anything from sourcing to semicolons, my students make final decisions here, too. In my 15 years as an adviser, I've only used unilateral power to pull one story: A (poorly written) satiric piece for an April Fools issue that included references to cannibalism, our dining hall, and the retirement center across the street. Given how many retired residents frequent activities at our university, this seemed like a bridge (way) too far in terms of taste.

About once a year, university administrators ask to meet with me regarding an article that has appeared in the publication, and about which they have significant reservations. I respond to these meeting requests by inviting along my editors, letting administrators know that students are responsible for publication content and that they will need to answer questions about their reporting, not me. These meetings are rarely contentious, and I have always been proud of my student leaders' ability to explain their decision making, as well as their willingness to courageously respond to administrative pressure to print only positive news about our university. Other than these occasional meetings, university administrators have refrained from editorial oversight of the student publication, even when they wished—probably especially when they wished—that I had assumed more direct control of the publication.

This has definitely not been the case at other universities, and especially at other religious institutions like mine. A May 2018 survey, reported in *Religious News Service*, concluded that nearly half of student journalists at Christian institutions believe their publications are censored by faculty advisors or by university administrators. According to Jenkins (2018), "Administrators at Christian colleges have a legal right to control their schools' newspapers, and argue they do so to safeguard the values that define their institutions." The study itself was initiated by student journalists at Taylor University who believed that faculty advisors and administrators "wield broad editorial control over school newspapers and sometimes kill stories before publication." Organizing as the Student Press Coalition, the students released the survey results with the intent of "promot[ing] a free press in higher education through research and advocacy on issues related to media censorship in Christian colleges and universities" (Jenkins, 2018).

Liberty University provides one prominent example of significant administrative oversight of the student press at a religious institution. Jenkins (2018) reported that Liberty University, located in Lynchburg, Virginia, was until this year considered the largest Christian university in the United States and in the world (that honor now goes to Grand Canyon University), with over 100,000 students enrolled, mostly in online courses; 15,000 students take classes at the Lynchburg campus. The university's president, Jerry Falwell Jr., has been a vocal supporter of President Trump, praising the president's policies, sometimes by quoting Scripture on social media and implying that President Trump is acting on biblical principle. Falwell has also exerted tremendous control over Liberty University's student publication, the *Liberty Champion*. According to Saba (2016), in October 2016, shortly after the *Access Hollywood* tape emerged—on which President Trump admitted to what was essentially sexual assault—a student editor at the *Liberty Champion* wrote an opinion piece critical of the presidential nominee, calling out the crude comments as more than what Trump characterized as just "locker room talk." Falwell would not allow the article to run, prompting the student editor, Joel Schmieg, to post about the censorship on social media. Schmieg noted the irony that one week earlier Falwell had praised the culture at Liberty University, which—according to Falwell—promotes "the free expression of ideas unlike many major universities where political correctness prevents conservative students from speaking out." Pulling a Trump-critical article from publication was, Schmieg said, "amusing and extremely hypocritical" (Saba, 2016).

Eighteen months later, Falwell's censorship of the Liberty student press again made news. In this instance, students on the *Liberty Champion* wanted to report on the unofficial visit by Shane Claiborne, a well-known progressive Christian who hoped to meet with Falwell and pray with students at the Lynchburg campus. Falwell not only refused Claiborne's invitation to meet, but also banned him from campus, telling Claiborne he would be arrested if he stepped one foot on Liberty property. Carey (2018) reported that a student journalist, speaking with *Religious News Service*, said that Falwell forbid her from covering Claiborne's proposed visit and revival meeting. "I do think that currently the level of oversight we have does make it difficult to pursue the accurate journalism that we've been taught in classes," Erin Covey told *RNS*. *Relevant* magazine reported that Covey shared an e-mail from Falwell in which he said the student paper should not "run any articles about the event," because publicity was the only thing Claiborne sought anyway (Carey, 2018).

Although Liberty University—and its president—have a much more public profile than a small Christian school like George Fox University, I imagine the student newspaper at George Fox would have handled visits from controversial figures in a much different way. Rather than feeling beholden to any one narrative about our institution, students have reported similar stories following the principles of good journalism, using multiple-sourced reporting and unbiased writing to cover lectures, chapels, and classroom visits that might conflict with the school's stated Christian values. And while administrators might feel uncomfortable with the newspaper's coverage of an event—might even ask to chat with me and my student leaders—they refrain from any kind of Falwellian overreach that might attempt to quell negative news about the university, its students, or its faculty.

For good reason too, because truth will ultimately prevail. Despite Falwell's efforts to put on a lid the Claiborne story—and, potentially, *because of* his efforts—the outcome of this brouhaha was reported in Christian publications like *Relevant* and *Christianity Today*, but also on national media platforms like NPR, *Vox*, and the *New York Times*. Jones (2018), writing for the *New Republic*, noted that the events at Liberty University reflected a broader "crisis of free speech" at Christian institutions. Her own experience as a student journalist at Cedarville University, a conservative school in Ohio, was similar to those at Liberty; at Cedarville, Jones (2018) wrote, "[T]he censorship became so strict that we eventually stopped publication of the newspaper in protest." Silencing free speech is allowable at such institutions, given the Constitution's guarantee of religious liberty, though Jones questions the wisdom of resolving these two guarantees in tension by allowing Christian expression to trump each student's right to write about their institutions in unalloyed terms.

The example of Liberty University is enlightening, showing us that a different kind of approach to student publications will, in the long term, be more positive for an institution. By allowing students (and their faculty advisers) to practice academic freedom, they are also helping nascent journalists discover the pathway to credible reporting. Places like Liberty also have the choice to side with students in giving them a free press, but when they don't, the university—and the truth—suffers. When institutional administrators force students to kill stories, rewrite stories, and spin only positive news about campus, they mimic our commander in chief, bellowing about "fake news" and suggesting that only positive stories are true ones. Those who have been awake in the last few years know how troubling this impulse can be.

Newspaper Advising as a Political Act

Several years ago, editors of *The Crescent* ran a story about the treatment of adjuncts at George Fox University. Like temporary faculty across the nation, adjuncts at my institution are paid only a fraction of what full-time professors receive for similar work in the classroom; while adjuncts don't have the same kind of committee or scholarship demands as full-time faculty peers, they also don't have the same job stability or benefits. The student who reported the story about adjuncts on our campus pointed out these discrepancies, having done multiple interviews with department chairs, adjuncts, and general education students who often receive a significant portion of their instruction from temporary workers. A week after the story ran, I got the typical e-mail: a request to meet with an administrator to talk about what was termed misrepresentations in the story. My response was also typical, in that I agreed to a meeting, but with my editors in chief along. They handled the one hour spent with an administrator beautifully, providing extensive notes to corroborate the reporter's claims. By the meeting's end, the administrator seemed to understand more clearly why the students had run the story; and while that campus leader still believed the college was treating most adjuncts equitably, s/he conceded that in some departments, temporary faculty might have a harder time of making a living wage. I remained mute for most of the meeting, proud that my students could do the work of advocating for their publication, affirming the uncomfortable truth that even a very fine institution like ours might still have challenges. The story also helped student readers see more clearly the state of some faculty members who led their classes and, hopefully, helped students have empathy for adjuncts who were overworked, underpaid, and nonetheless dedicated to helping them learn. Had the administrator compelled the editors to kill the story—or had I censored the story myself—none of these good outcomes would have been possible.

According to the Student Press Coalition survey, 88% of students believe that their faculty advisers support their right to free speech on campus and that administrators are more responsible for any censorship that occurs in student publications. This finding suggests to me that most faculty newspaper advisers also recognize the significant impact a free student press can have on their campuses, even when their administrators exert pressure to publish positive news rather than unalloyed truth. Knowing there are other faculty advisers who share my ideology about student reporting actually gives me hope that journalists will continue to do the work needed to sustain healthy institutions and, ultimately, to sustain a healthy democracy. Our campus newspapers are producing the people who will step into real-world newsrooms knowing that ethical journalism is important, and that so long as they do the hard work of in-depth reporting they will have the support of their supervisors who, despite pressure from administrators, encourage them to write the truth. This is a little different from what might happen when they land "real" journalism jobs, where the pressure to sensationalize stories—and enhance a publication's bottom line—is intense, and where they will (hopefully) encounter editors in chief who support a free press, no matter the cost.

When I feel certain despair about the state of our democracy, I hold on to this hope, that there are college newspaper advisers across the country doing work similar to my own, creating nascent journalists who value strong reporting and who are willing to call out administrators—like Jerry Falwell at Liberty—who would rather quash dissenting voices than let the truth be told. The model at Liberty is instructive because it shows that the truth will always prevail; so too is the model at places like George Fox University, where student journalists are given the freedom to pursue truth and learn that doing so might aggravate those in power but also hold them accountable. In this way, I see campus newspaper advising as a kind of political act, as we advisors stake our claim on the importance of truth, the value of democracy, the beauty of a constitution that affirms all people have a right to a voice, no matter who they are or what position they hold, be that a first-year student ranting about the quality of cafeteria food or the president of the United States.

Perhaps that all seems too idealistic. Maybe it is. After all, most of the students now working on our campus newspaper, and taking my journalism classes, will likely not enter a field where high-stakes reporting is part of their vocational efforts. In my many years as a journalism instructor, I've only had a handful of journalism majors who have entered newsrooms and stayed; many more of my students have been employed by nonprofits who need competent writers to share their mission with the world, by companies looking for assistance writing website content, and by marketing firms who want strong communicators to help them sell goods to a mass audience. Still, even though a four-year stint as a newspaper editor doesn't necessarily lead to a hard-nosed reporting job, I'm certain the principles students learn in the publication laboratory will help them navigate the post-truth world in which they've grown up. Hopefully, they will believe that any healthy democracy relies on journalists to tell the truth and to hold governments accountable. They will be discerning in their media diets, knowing that protestations of fake news cannot be accepted without question, and that multiple perspectives are necessary to fully understand the news. They will learn that the companies they work for might want them to spin narratives but that having integrity sometimes means telling the truth, even when it hurts.

Ideally, my students will also know that insisting on the truth can be hard, but necessary, in a world that longs more often for an easier road. They will affirm that some pathways might be more tantalizing, but that sensationalized reporting can lead to the disaster we woke up to in November 2016, when Donald Trump was elected president, though many people (myself included) were expecting someone else.

References

Borchers, C. (2018, June 01). The case for even tougher media coverage of Trump. *Washington Post*. Retrieved from http://www.washingtonpost.com/news/the-fix/wp/2018/06/01/the-case-for-even-tougher-media-coverage-of-trump/?noredirect=on&utm_term=.70853a7de6ea

Carey, J. (18, April 9). Report: Jerry Falwell Jr. Personally Killed a Campus. *Relevant Magazine*. Retrieved from https://relevantmagazine.com/current/nation/report-jerry-falwell-jr-personally-killed-campus-newspaper-story-shane-claibornes-prayer-rally/

Jenkins, J. (2019, January 02). Liberty University is no longer the largest Christian university. *Religion News Service*. Retrieved from https://religionnews.com/2018/04/27/liberty-university-is-no-longer-the-largest-christian-university/

Jenkins, J. (2018, May 09). Students' survey highlights censorship of Christian college newspapers. *Religion News Service*. Retrieved from https://religionnews.com/2018/05/08/students-survey-highlights-censorship-of-christian-college-newspapers/

Jones, S. (2018, April 10). The Invisible Free Speech Crisis. Retrieved November 28, 2018, from https://newrepublic.com/article/147908/invisible-free-speech-crisis

Knight Foundation. (2018, September 11). *Indicators of news media trust.* Retrieved from https://www.knightfoundation.org/reports/indicators-of-news-media-trust

Saba, Y. (2016, October 18). Falwell censored anti-Trump column, Liberty U student editor says. *Politico.* Retrieved from http://www.politico.com/story/2016/10/jerry-falwell-donald-trump-liberty-229964

CHAPTER SIX

Go Back Home:

Confronting Growing Incivility, Racism, and Bigotry on College Campuses

Amy B. Murphy-Nugen, Charmion B. Rush, Antonio M. Oakley Jr., and Carleen (Tenae) Turner

"Go back to Puerto Rico," shouted Representative Jason Smith (R-MO) as Representative Tony Cárdenas, a California Democrat of Mexican heritage, was preparing to speak on the floor of the House of Representatives (Scholtes, Emma, & Ferris, 2019). These were the words dominating the morning news cycle as we began to co-create this chapter on the increasing incivility, racism, and bigotry in many forms on college campuses across the United States. It was these words of Representative Smith's that reflected a similar racist sentiment that brought us together over a year ago to address racist comments and acts of incivility on our own campus. Almost one year ago to the day, during the Reverend Dr. Martin Luther King Jr. Day Unity March, our students were met with racial slurs and told to "go back home." Although Representative Smith claims his words were addressed to Democrats in general and in particular addressed a recent Congressional trip to Puerto Rico, like the words shouted on our campus to our students in the place they reside, *their home*, the message was clear: *This place belongs to "us," and "you" do not belong here.* Place-based hate is a phenomenon that is rooted in "perceived threats the 'outsider' poses to one's dominant identity and socioeconomic security" (Medina, Nicolosi, Brewer, & Linke, 2018, p. 1009). As demographic shifts continue to shape U.S. society and campuses continue to diversify, the frequency of place-based hate continues to increase. The result of these changes evokes direct challenges and confrontations to who belongs and who is met with increasing hostility and sometimes violence.

Like many campuses across the United States, ours has attempted to address increasing issues of incivility, racism, and bigotry. Sometimes, with student leadership often modeling the way, we are successful in moving the discussion and actions forward to strengthen equity, inclusion, and diversity. Yet too often we continue to struggle. These are deep issues, which are embedded in the fabric of our nation. Several years ago, one of us heard civil rights leader Julian Bond speak. He described how entrenched issues of race and racism are by starting his discussion explaining that the word *America* is an anagram of the phrase "I am race." Until we first find the courage to confront our history and its lingering impact on systems, structures, and institutions, we will continue to falter and fall short of the democratic and inclusive promise of our country and our respective campuses. The purpose of this chapter is to have an honest and authentic discussion about the state of incivility, racism, and bigotry in our nation and on our campuses. Once we have addressed the context of these intersecting challenges, we will offer some strategies to bridge the gap to more equitable, inclusive, and diverse campuses. These conversations are complex, and answers need to be multifaceted. With humility, we are certainly not suggesting this is a definitive, all-inclusive, final list of actions; rather, we respectfully offer a contribution to this ongoing discussion and invite you to join us in this shared call for change.

Current Context of Incivility, Racism, and Bigotry

Campus climate issues are not isolated from the larger environment in which they are situated. Every day, it seems we learn of another incident or tragedy in which incivility or hate are at the root. Before we narrow our focus to our universities, we first look at some broader, macro-level data to understand the current context of increasing incivility, racism, and bigotry in our nation. We then turn our attention to how these systemic and structural issues manifest on our campuses.

National Context: Hate Is on the Rise

Our academic institutions mirror the growing divisions, incivility, racism, and bigotry we see and experience in U.S. society. The latest Federal Bureau of Investigations (FBI) report indicates that hate crimes increased by 17% in 2017, representing the third straight year in which bias-motivated attacks have risen (Federal Bureau of Investigations, 2018). In part, the FBI attributes this increase to additional law enforcement agencies reporting bias data; however, civil rights advocates caution that hate crimes remain significantly under-reported (Eligon, 2018; FBI, 2018). Of the roughly 7,100 hate crimes reported in 2017, 59.6% were motivated by race and ethnicity (FBI, 2018). Nearly half of hate crime victims in 2017 were against black people. Approximately 20.6% of hate crimes were attributed to religious beliefs, of which, 58% of religious-motivated attacks were directed at people who are Jewish, representing a 37% increase from the prior year (FBI, 2018). Nearly 16% of reported hate crimes were against a person due to sexual orientation (FBI, 2018). The FBI defines a hate crime as a "criminal offence against a person or property motivated in whole or in part by an offender's bias against a race, religion, disability, sexual orientation, ethnicity, gender, or gender identity" (FBI, 2018, para 1).

In addition to the growth in hate crimes, a noted increase in the number of hate groups and violent acts associated with domestic terrorism is also occurring. For the fourth year in a row, 2018 marked another year in which the number of hate groups in the United States increased (Stack, 2019). According to the Southern Poverty Law Center (SPLC), a civil rights organization that documents hate groups and associated activities, U.S. hate groups have experienced a 30% increase over the past four years, with a 7% increase in 2018 alone (Beirich, 2019). Echoing behaviors articulated in the FBI's definition of a hate crime, the SPLC defines a hate group as "an organization that based on its official statements or principles, the statements of its leaders, or its activities, has beliefs or practices that attack or malign an entire class of people, typically for their race, religion, ethnicity, sexual orientation or gender identity" (SPLC, 2017, paras. 1–2). Based on this definition, SPLC identified 1,020 organizations as hate groups in 2018, representing a 20-year high (Beirich, 2019). The Anti-Defamation League (ADL) has also noted increases in behavior associated with racist and bigoted groups.

For example, in 2017, 421 documented incidents of white supremacists engaged in propaganda efforts. In 2018, those efforts increased by 182% with 1,187 propaganda distributions (ADL, n.d.a). Demonstrations associated with racist ideology also increased from 76 rallies in 2017 to 91 in 2018 (ADL, n.d.a). As the numbers of hate groups, propaganda events, and recruiting efforts increased, so too did violent acts perpetrated by extremists and terrorists. In 2018, domestic extremists killed at least 50 people in the United States, which represents the fourth-deadliest year for killings related to domestic extremism since 1970 (ADL, n.d.b).

In addition to the FBI hate crime data indicating an upward trend in bias crimes, documented increases among hate groups, propaganda efforts, and extremist violent acts, several high-profile bigoted and racially motivated events have occurred on university campuses over the last few years. One of the most notorious and traumatic hate- and race-related campus events occurred in August 2017 when approximately 100 people, who were mostly white men, carried tiki torches onto the University of Virginia's (UVA) campus in Charlottesville (Atkinson, 2018; Hartzell, 2018). The group descended on UVA's campus to protest the proposed removal of a statue honoring Confederate General Robert E. Lee. The protest turned violent when the group, shouting slogans including, "white lives matter," "you will not replace us," and "blood and soil," encountered a small contingent of counter protestors (Hartzell, 2018). Police dispersed the gathering. The next day, the so-called "Unite the Right" rally was held and included a larger group of white supremacist protestors who overtook the town of Charlottesville. Violence escalated and turned tragic when a 20-year-old white supremacist murdered a counter protester, Heather Heyer, and injured at least 19 others by driving into a crowd (Hartzell, 2018). Although there are too many examples of other campus incidents to recount here, the events at UVA and Charlottesville tragically represent the intersection of the growing expressions of incivility, racism, and bigotry in mainstream U.S. society and on university campuses (Atkinson, 2018).

Campus Context: Civic Recession and Neoliberalism

Nearly a decade ago, and within a critical analysis of the state of education, Quigley spoke of a "civic recession," in which he prophetically warned that unless we worked diligently to bridge the gap between the highest ideals of our nation and the challenging reality of everyday life for our citizens, we may be unable to fully cultivate the promise of our constitutional, democratic republic (Civic Learning and Democratic Engagement National Task Force, 2011). Quigley and other civic leaders believed our educational institutions, with a primary focus on undergraduate studies, held the most promise for strengthening civic and democratic engagement (Civic Learning and Democratic Engagement National Task Force, 2011). These thought leaders also recognized the challenges such institutions faced in rising to this occasion. Part of this nearly ten-year warning and prophesy noted "recasting people's roles from producers of public goods to consumers of material ones, gerrymandering districts and thus exacerbating the deep divides that already shape our politics, shrinking opportunities for civic alliances, and replacing what ought to be thoughtful deliberation about public issues with incivility and hyperpolarization" (Civic Learning and Democratic Engagement National Task Force, 2011, p. 5). One relevant outcome of this disconnection is educational environments shifting to focus more on developing workers at the minimization of cultivating citizens (McTighe Musil, 2011). Let us be clear—workforce development is a valuable role that universities provide to our society; however, the foundation of higher education is predicated on developing a citizenry responsive to the needs and opportunities of the greater society—that is, individuals who are equipped to think critically, question authority, challenge the status quo, and engage civically and civilly (Dewey, 1910, 1916).

One explanation concerning the current minimization of civic development on college campuses may be found in the contention that universities have increasingly embraced neoliberal approaches in their operations and structures (Donoghue, 2008; Giroux, 2002; Hamer & Lang, 2015). Giroux (2002) contends, "As society is defined through the culture and values of neoliberalism, the relationship between a critical education, public morality, and civic responsibility as conditions for creating thoughtful and engaged citizens are sacrificed all too willingly to the interest of financial capital and the logic of profit-making" (p. 427). The embrace of neoliberalism may explain why a notable amount of colleges and universities are challenged in demonstrating civic courage—and, too often, are more concerned about financial, legal, and/or public relations considerations associated with being sued or being the target of negative press coverage rather than modeling their own civic behavior by acting morally and courageously to stand with students of color and other underrepresented communities on our respective campuses. Further, considering that neoliberalism is the imposition of free-market fundamentalism within the academy, and in tandem with the U.S. socioeconomic-political history and context that is built on the near genocide of one group of people, Native Americans, and the enslavement of black people, then the resulting implication is the imposition of deeply embedded structural racism and bigotry in the academy (Hamer & Lang, 2015).

Neoliberalism replaces civic culture with a corporate one. The result is that private individual interests supersede community interests by "reformulating social issues as strictly private concerns, corporate culture functions largely to either cancel out or devalue social, class-specific, and racial injustices of the existing social order by absorbing the democratic impulses and practices of civil society within narrow economic relations" (Giroux, 2002, p. 249). In effect, for those of us who are concerned about strengthening civic engagement, civil behavior, and anti-oppressive approaches, we must refocus our efforts on increasing democratic and inclusive practices over neoliberal ones.

Solutions: Bridging the Civility, Inclusion, and Anti-Oppression Gap

As we have attempted in the previous sections, it is important to contextualize this discussion with our larger U.S. society and university campuses, and yet it may also be overwhelming to a significant amount of people. When one sees the deeply embedded injustice, racism, and bigotry in our systems and structures, people may erroneously believe their involvement will be ineffectual and retreat from engaging. Yet, "inclusive and engaged campuses are an essential component of efforts to achieve racial and social justice throughout society" (Countryman, 2012, p. 49). Although we believe structural challenges must be made to unjust systems, it is our purpose here to provide immediately accessible and effective solutions any administrator, faculty, and staff may implement. We hope that these foundational steps may serve as a catalyst for future systemic, structural, and sustainable change.

Faculty as Allies and Accomplices

> *I'm glad I understand that while language is a gift, listening is a responsibility.*
>
> —(Giovanni, 1994, p. 19)

> *My mom taught us to never look away from people's pain. The lesson was simple: Don't look away. Don't look down. Don't pretend not to see hurt. Look people in the eye. Even when their pain is overwhelming. And, when you're in pain, find the people who can look you in the eye. We need to know we're not alone—especially when we're hurting. This lesson is one of the greatest gifts of my life.*
>
> —(Brown, 2019, para. 1)

Over the past decade, college enrollment rates have been increasing for most demographic groups (American Indian: 16 to 19%; Blacks: 31 to 36%; Hispanic/Latinx: 22 to 39%; and Whites: 39 to 42%). Although it is encouraging to see an overall positive trend of growing diversity, these numbers also indicate a lingering lack of representation on our college campuses. Further, when diverse students arrive on campus, they will likely find it challenging to find faculty who look like them. As the National Center for Education Statistics (2018a) reports,

> Of all full-time faculty in degree-granting postsecondary institutions in fall 2016, 41 percent were White males; 35 percent were White females; 6 percent were Asian/Pacific Islander males; 4 percent were Asian/Pacific Islander females; 3 percent each were Black males, Black females, and Hispanic males; and 2 percent were Hispanic females. Those who were American Indian/Alaska Native and those who were of two or more races each made up 1 percent or less of full-time faculty in these institutions. (para. 2)

In an environment of growing diversity on our campuses, as well as increasing incidents of incivility, racism, and bigotry, representation matters. Systemic change relies on recruiting and retaining faculty from diverse backgrounds and experiences. Too often, the tendency toward the comfort of homogeneity results in search committees hiring candidates that "fit" their own model, which represents the dominant culture and demographics. Moving away from being satisfied with candidates who are most similar to existing faculty to considering candidates who are diverse involves more expanded and innovative ways of thinking about faculty positions. This flexibility in thinking about job qualifications is part of understanding and valuing diversity and creates the opportunity for attracting ethnic minority and other underrepresented applicants who can make significant contributions, initiate new ways of thinking, and introduce more diverse ideologies (Virginia Commonwealth University (VCU), Office of Equal Opportunity, n.d.). Career paths for ethnic minorities and other underrepresented individuals may vary in comparison to mainstream and/or white candidates. Therefore, when developing job qualifications, search committees need to identify characteristics that allow for more varied backgrounds and experiences. This consideration helps to prevent ethnic minorities and other underrepresented individuals who may have less traditional career paths from being eliminated from the pool of viable candidates.

Further, it is essential for faculty from traditionally dominant groups to reflect on their implicit and explicit biases. Implicit biases are defined by the Kirwin Institute for the Study of Race and Ethnicity (Staats, Capatosto, Wright, & Contractor, 2015) as attitudes or stereotypes that are activated unconsciously and involuntarily. In contrast to explicit bias, which are the biases a person might try to hide because they are unpopular or socially incorrect, implicit biases are activated unintentionally and without one's awareness (Boscardin, 2015; Flannery, 2015). Regardless of one's group membership, we all harbor subconscious perceptions and beliefs about other people based on a variety of characteristics. The truth is our world is more divided than ever. It is no secret that unconscious biases penetrate various realms of society (Grinberg, 2015). Influenced by social, political, and cultural forces, implicit bias affects our everyday understanding, actions, and decisions. In an unconscious manner, biases influence us when they are in direct opposition to our espoused beliefs—and sometimes in opposition to our own lived experience (Fiarman, 2016). According to research, such perceptions can start forming in children as young as six years old and are reinforced in adulthood through social settings and mass media. The encouraging news, however, is that we are not helpless to combat implicit bias.

It can be mitigated through intervention strategies, starting with recognizing where it might exist in our lives and by seeking exposure to people and experiences beyond our inner circles (Grinberg, 2015).

We can take concrete steps to build our awareness of unconscious bias and recognize the effects of our decisions with rational considerations. In a review of multiple studies on changing implicit bias, research (Staats, 2014; Staats, Capatosto, Wright, & Contractor, 2015; Staats, Capatosto, Wrights & Jackson, 2016; Staats, Capatosto, Tenney, & Mamo, 2017) recommends six areas for changes to maximize the chances of reducing implicit bias in interactions with students.

1. Educate yourself! Increase self-awareness through self-reflection; integrate chances to assess and monitor implicit bias in professional development for instructors and students; have instructors use and model reflective practice techniques for students; and, provide instruction in stress reduction and coping methods (because increased stress leads to increased chance of implicit biases affecting interpersonal interactions).

2. Recognize a response as stereotypical and remain alert to your responses. Acknowledge it may be present in any situation. Label the response as implicit bias and identify why it may have occurred. Consider alternate responses for use in the future (i.e., unbiased replacement responses).

3. Create an inclusive learning environment by creating safe and effective learning environments that promote inclusiveness and integrate informal curriculum that socializes students in inclusive behaviors.

4. Seek experiences that could provide you with ways to reverse/undo patterns that have contributed to your responses.

5. Develop empathy skills, especially by viewing empathy as a cultivated skill and not as a fixed trait.

6. Interact with people who provide experiences to counteract your responses. Increase opportunities for positive interactions with diverse people, and, seek out professional development for increased cultural awareness.

Empower Student Leadership

> *If you have come here to help me, you are wasting your time. . . . But if you have come here because your liberation is bound up with mine, then let us work together.*
>
> —(Watson as cited in Lenonen, 2004, para. 2)
>
> *In our world, divide and conquer must become define and empower.*
>
> —(Lorde, 2003, p. 27)

As the number of racial and discriminatory incidents increase at colleges and universities, students are finding themselves on the front lines of campus protests and defending their right to coexist and thrive on their respective campuses (ADA, n.d.c, n.d.d). It is important for university administration to allow students to have the space to organize and to represent their interests. Due to the growing influence of neoliberalism, we have too often ceded this physical and figurative space. Although there exist many roots to the increasing racism and bigotry on college campuses, the lack of civility is an outgrowth of neoliberalism that posits an individual is only responsible to one's self and therefore absolved of the responsibility to community well-being and the public good (Tomlinson & Lipsitz, 2013). The empowerment perspective offers an antidote to this oppressive power structure by rejecting the zero-sum underlying premise of neoliberalism that only certain individuals are entitled to society's benefits—and instead embraces the opportunity for positive potential for every individual when people are provided with "strategies to cope with a hostile world" (Gutierrez, 1990, p. 150). Solomon (1976), who developed the empowerment perspective, asserts that when people are able to strengthen their individual self-efficacy in their personal lives, interpersonal relationships, political participation, and economic activity, they increase their human capital and can more effectively respond to oppression. Therefore, empowering student leadership is an action that must co-align with the civil and anti-oppressive solutions advanced by faculty and administration. Once empowered, it is our contention that students will feel more comfortable and confident in addressing their needs, leveraging opportunities, and leading their fellow students.

In consideration of increasing neoliberalism influences in the academy, it may be reasonable to assume that many institutions of higher education will be motivated to maintain the status quo rather than to empower students to increase their personal, interpersonal, and political power. Yet if we want to transcend the traditional system of education that treats students as passive audiences (Freire, 1968), Hooks (1994) contends that we must create spaces in our university environments where we invite and cultivate student-engaged critical consciousness, constructive confrontation, and critical interrogation. In a direct challenge to the influences of neoliberalism, Tomlinson and Lipsitz (2013) specifically challenge us to reclaim space on our campuses—which they conceptualize as *insubordinate spaces*—in order to re-cultivate "democratic deliberation, mutual recognition, and collective accountability" (p. 7).

At our campus, Western Carolina University, students feel they are given space to thrive and create solutions to address incivility on campus. Situated in between the Blue Ridge and Great Smoky mountains in the Southeast United States, Western Carolina University (WCU) is a public four-year institution in the University of North Carolina seventeen-school system. In academic year 2018–2019, over 11,000 students were enrolled with a student demographic composition of 99 (.85%) American Indian/Alaska Native individuals; 129 (1.11%) Asian individuals; 683 (5.87%) Black/African American individuals; 786 (6.75%) Hispanic/Latinx individuals; 7 (.06%) Native Hawaiian/Pacific Islander individuals; 9,164 (78.74%) White individuals; with our remaining 771 students (6.63%) identifying as two or more races and/or an "other" designation (Western Carolina University, 2019). WCU has a strong commitment to serving the people and communities of Western North Carolina, a rural region with higher levels of poverty and lower levels of educational attainment than the state as a whole. Although outside perceptions of Appalachia often portray the region as homogenous and lacking in diversity, our region includes the Qualla Boundary, the home of the Eastern Band of Cherokee Indians, as well as populations of African American and Latinx individuals and families.

Building on Solomon's empowerment perspective, Gutierrez (1990) conceptualizes four key empowering changes that create a psychological and emancipatory pathway for individuals to move from apathy and despair to action: "increasing self-efficacy, developing group consciousness, reducing self-blame, and assuming personal responsibility for change" (p. 150). Our students did not wait to be invited to walk down an empowering pathway—they exemplified Guiterrez's (1990) empowering characteristics by taking an active effort in improving their campus experience (personal responsibility) by developing a call to action, *The Collective Response to Western Carolina's Racial Insensitivity* (Whee Matter, 2018). As demonstrated in their belief to act as empowered change agents (self-efficacy), our students identified and articulated how existing racist and bigoted behavior negatively impacted their lives (reducing self-blame), and through this shared awareness and experience focused their efforts on undercutting these root causes (developing group consciousness) (Gutierrez, 1990; Whee Matter, 2018). The shared identity and group consciousness of this effort was manifested in the creation of the Whee Matter Movement, which is a diverse and inclusive group of students who coalesced around a shared vision of anti-oppressive and racial justice actions. The call for action document cocreated by the Whee Matter Movement was often referred to as "a list of firm expectations" and invited collaboration with the Student Government Association and addressed the dean of students, faculty and administration, and the board of trustees. The student leadership of the Whee Matter Movement organized and facilitated an open forum attended by all governing stakeholders of the university where their list of firm expectations was presented. They asked for policy changes, curriculum development, and ultimately for the faculty, staff, and administration to listen. The list of firm expectations was punctuated by both an increasing awareness of individual and collective power as well as propelled by a shared vision inspired by Davis (2017): "I am no longer accepting the things I cannot change. I am changing the things I cannot accept" (para. 15).

In her empowerment framework, Gutierrez (1990) articulates a toolbox of techniques to further leverage power and sustain engaged action. We contend that other universities may consider how embracing such techniques can empower their respective students. Again, although we acknowledge that our campus community remains a work in progress, we are also grateful for a campus culture that is shaped by many humble and nimble servant leaders—extending from our administrators, faculty, staff, and students. This organizational characteristic should not be undervalued when navigating intractable campus issues such as racism and bigotry. These empowering techniques include: "1) accepting the individual's definition of their experience; 2) identifying and building upon existing strengths; 3) engaging in a power analysis of the individual's situation; 4) teaching specific skills; and 5) mobilizing resources and advocating for individuals" (Gutierrez, 1990, p. 152). On our campus, as representatives of the entire faculty, the faculty senate responded to the Whee Matter list of firm expectations by first passing a supportive statement, "Resolution in Support of Equity, Diversity, and Inclusion at WCU," which expressly affirmed *accepting the students' definition of their experience* by noting faculty "listened and heard our students of color and other underrepresented communities share with us their concerns and frustrations" (Western Carolina University Faculty Senate, 2018, p. 1). Further, a critical and foundational request our students included in the list of firm expectations was an unequivocal condemnation of bigotry and racism, which the faculty addressed in its resolution by "condemn[ing] in the strongest possible terms acts of bigotry and racism to intimidate members of our campus community" (Western Carolina University Faculty Senate, 2018, p. 1).

The faculty senate resolution further demonstrated an empowering framework by accepting the students' *analysis of power imbalances and structural impediments*. Administration and faculty *identified and built upon existing resources* by inviting a group of interdisciplinary professors to integrate their respective knowledge on equity and diversity issues into a five-course inclusion module for our first-year transition course. This model focused on *teaching specific skills* to incoming students, including self-awareness about one's own cultural identity; developing historical knowledge about our campus community by engaging in a campus-based sound walk; analyzing implications of racism, classism, and privilege; identifying critical interpersonal skills and qualities that are effective in engaging in challenging conversations; and practicing deliberative dialogue with one's peers.

Faculty further emphasized teaching specific skills by exploring revisions to the university's curriculum to promote cultural awareness. The result was charging the university's Liberal Studies Committee to develop an inclusive excellence requirement across the liberal studies curriculum to reach the greatest number of undergraduates at WCU (Western Carolina University Faculty Senate, 2018; Whee Matter, 2018).

The university administration *mobilized resources and advocated for individuals* by developing a plan for diversity and inclusive excellence throughout colleges and units; facilitated a leadership meeting in residential living that included discussion of the department's commitment to diversity, bias reporting, and accountability, with plans to transparently post monthly aggregated summaries going forward; and meetings involving the Orientation and Intercultural Affairs Department staff to discuss changes to orientation. Further, a revision to the university's strategic plan includes a new and extensive strategic direction focused on diversity and inclusive excellence. In fall 2019, we will welcome a U.S. Latinx minor.

As we remain a work in progress and are committed to empowering our students, there is still progress to be made. Some of our actions still in process include the development of a bias response committee on campus; revisions to the community creed; development of an African American studies minor; and consideration of an ethics statement for incoming students.

Sustaining the Effort

> *People aren't born knowing how to be citizens in a democracy. It is something they have to learn.*
>
> —(Matthews, 2017, p. ix)

> *All social change begins with a conversation.*
>
> —(Wheatley, 2002, para. 1)

In order to cultivate trust and deepen relationships that are often critical components for sustained engagement and change, we propose campuses consider supporting deliberative dialogue initiatives. The National Issues Forum (2014) defines deliberative dialogue as "long and careful consideration or discussion, a process of thoughtfully weighing options" (para. 1). Deliberative dialogue uses various methods to move dialogue to action (National Coalition for Dialogue and Deliberation, 2013). One type of intentional dialogue strategy is Study Circles, which engage diverse members of a community—crossing racial, ethnic, income, age, gender demographics, and political viewpoints—to collaborate for the purposes of strengthening their collective ability to solve problems, create opportunities, and take action. Specifically, Study Circles combine deliberative dialogue and community building strategies to "enable public talk to build understanding, explore a range of solutions, and serve as a catalyst for social, political, and policy change" (National Coalition for Dialogue and Deliberation, 2013, p. 7). Quite simply, the underlying philosophy of Study Circles is the belief that "to understand is to act" (Oliver, 1987, p. 1).

Study Circles are democratically rooted in the experiences of relevant stakeholders who are interested in exploring a topic of shared concern (Suda, 2001). The implementation of this framework should be responsive to local campus and community considerations concerning incivility, race, and bigotry. Through this intentional and guided dialogue and exchange, it is anticipated that relationships will be cultivated, trust will develop, and campus and community members will coalesce around a shared and sustainable action plan. Study Circles provide a critical bridge between civic engagement and change efforts by relying on and building social capital with the purpose of moving engaged individuals to reflect on local conditions, develop understanding through discussion, and inspiring one to act (Mattessich, Monsey, & Roy, 1997).

Conclusion

Making a real difference in addressing discriminatory behavior on our college campuses requires a fundamental understanding of bigotry and racism and a personal transformational change. In other words, with due diligence, we must "talk the talk and walk the walk." In our faculty senate resolution in support of equity, diversity, and inclusion on our campus, we articulated what we mean by walking the talk:

> We respect our students' response to address racial insensitivity throughout the university and honor their commitment to create a more respectful and inclusive campus. We value the leadership demonstrated by students of color and underrepresented communities and will continue to empower them to pursue change; however, we recognize it is our responsibility, as faculty, to cultivate an environment of diversity, inclusion, and equity. The burden of dismantling systems and structures should not be solely placed on the students, staff, and faculty who are the recipients of racism, bigotry, and hatred. Transformational change requires collaborative action that invites participation of all students, staff, and faculty. As such,

> we pledge to support significant infrastructural changes necessary to eradicate systemic racism and bigotry. (Western Carolina University Faculty Senate, 2018, p. 2)

Engaging in constructive dialogue to relieve anxiety and tensions as well as trying to combat racism and bigotry, will bring us closer to a common "home," a campus of civil unity. As diversity advocate Myers (2014) challenges us, we must look closely at some of the subconscious attitudes we hold toward out-groups, and "then we must walk boldly toward them" (9:18). Acknowledging personal biases requires addressing common emotions, behaviors, and underlying assumptions that fuel stereotypes and prejudices that are among us. As faculty, we must take a stance to look within ourselves by having the difficult conversations that separate us, our students, and our campuses.

When our fundamental understanding of bigotry and racism is transformed, so are our assumptions and resultants behaviors (DiAngelo, 2018). Intentionally, we need to build relationships to strengthen our environment, interactions, norms, and policies. Without hesitation or fear, we must take the initiative to do something. We must be willing to focus on the impact of racist and bigoted behavior and authentically repair harm and hurt. When we see something unjust, we must have the courage to confront it. When we hear something uncivil, we should engage with positive feedback and seek to repair the breach that deepens us. We should act to address our own bigotry and racism, the bigotry and racism of others, and the bigotry and racism embedded in our institutions (DiAngelo, 2018). This call to change must be more than an aspirational statement. As faculty, we should consider this call as a foundational and authentic commitment we make to one another—we make to our students—every day, on our respective campuses—which are our students' home.

As we close this chapter, we want to acknowledge and thank students of color (including two of our cocreators and coauthors of this chapter) and other underrepresented communities and their allies and accomplices who are fearlessly demonstrating what leadership and courage looks like. As faculty, it is our hope that we rise to their example.

References

Anti-Defamation League (ADL). (n.d.a). *White supremacist propaganda and events soared in 2018*. Retrieved from https://www.adl.org/news/press-releases/white-supremacist-propaganda-and-events-soared-in-2018

ADL. (n.d.b). *Murder and extremism in the United States in 2018*. Retrieved from https://www.adl.org/murder-and-extremism-2018#executive-summary

ADL. (n.d.c). *White supremacist propaganda nearly doubles on campus in 2018*. Retrieved from https://www.adl.org/news/press-releases/white-supremacist-propaganda-and-events-soared-in-2018

ADL. (n.d.d). *Campus propaganda efforts in 2018*. Retrieved from https://www.adl.org/resources/reports/white-supremacists-step-up-off-campus-propaganda-efforts-in-2018

Atkinson, D. C. (2018). Charlottesville and the alt-right: A turning point? *Politics, Groups, and Identities, 6*(2), 309–315.

Beirich, H. (2019). The year in hate and extremism: Rage against change. *Southern Poverty Law Center*. Retrieved from https://www.splcenter.org/fighting-hate/intelligence-report/2019/year-hate-rage-against-change

Boscardin, C. K. (2015). Reducing implicit bias through curricular interventions. *Journal of General Internal Medicine, 30*(12), 1726–1728. doi:10.1007/s11606-015-3496-y

Brown, B. [@brenebrown]. (2019, March 26). My mom taught us to never look away from people's pain. [Instagram photograph]. Retrieved from https://www.instagram.com/p/BveiWKNgkzT/?utm_source=ig_web_copy_link

Civic Learning and Democratic Engagement National Task Force. (2011). *A crucible moment: College learning and democracy's future*. Retrieved from https://www2.ed.gov/rschstat/research/pubs/college-learning-democracys-future/crucible-moment.pdf

Countryman, M. J. (2012). Diversity and democratic engagement: Civic education and the challenge of inclusivity. In D. W. Harward (Ed.), *Civic Provocations* (pp. 47–50). Washington, DC: Bringing Theory to Practice.

Davis, A. (2017, January 24). Activist Angela Davis urges cooperation against injustice. *Missourian*. Retrieved from https://www.columbiamissourian.com/news/local/activist-angela-davis-urges-cooperation-against-injustice/article_f77a21a0-e2b0-11e6-9d29-130699fe9e6d.html

Dewey, J. (1910). *How we think*. Retrieved from https://www.gutenberg.org/files/37423/37423-h/37423-h.htm

Dewey, J. (1916). *Democracy and education*. Retrieved from https://www.gutenberg.org/files/852/852-h/852-h.htm

DiAngelo, R. (2018). *White fragility: Why it's so hard for white people to talk about racism*. Boston, MA: Beacon.

Donoghue, F. (2008). *The last professors: The twilight of the humanities in the corporate university*. New York, NY: Fordham University.

Eligon, J. (2018, November 13). Hate crimes increase from the third consecutive year, F.B.I. reports. *New York Times*. Retrieved from https://www.nytimes.com/2018/11/13/us/hate-crimes-fbi-2017.html?auth

Federal Bureau of Investigation. (2018). *2017 hate crime statistics.* Retrieved from https://ucr.fbi.gov/hate-crime/2017

Fiarman, S. E. (2016). Unconscious bias: When good intentions aren't enough. *Educational Leadership, 74*(3), 10–15.

Flannery, M. E. (2015). When implicit bias shapes teacher expectations. *National Education Association Today.* Retrieved from http://neatoday.org/2015/09/09/when-implicit-bias-shapes-teacher-expectations/

Freire, P. (1968). *The pedagogy of the oppressed.* New York, NY: Continuum.

Giovanni, N. (1994). *Racism 101.*New York, NY: William Morrow.

Giroux, H.A. (2002). Neoliberalism, corporate culture, and the promise of higher education: The university as a democratic public sphere. *Harvard Educational Review, 72*(4), 425–463.

Grinberg, E. (2015, November 24). Four ways you might be displaying hidden bias in everyday life. *CNN.* Retrieved from http://www.cnn.com/2015/11/24/living/implicit-bias-tests-feat

Gutierrez, L. (1990). Working with women of color: An empowerment perspective. *Social Work, 35*(2), 149–153.

Hamer, J. F., & Lang, C. (2015). Race, structural violence, and the neoliberal university: The challenges of inhabitation. *Critical Sociology, 41*(6), 897–912.

Hartzell, S. L. (2018). Alt-white: Conceptualizing the "alt-right" as a rhetorical bridge between white nationalism and mainstream public discourse. *Journal of Contemporary Rhetoric, 8*(1–2), 6–25.

Hooks, b. (1994). *Teaching to transgress: Education as the practice of freedom.* New York, NY: Routledge.

Kirwin Institute for the Study of Race and Ethnicity. (2016). *State of the science: Implicit bias review 2015.* Retrieved from http://kirwaninstitute.osu.edu/wp-content/uploads/2015/05/2015-kirwan-implicit-bias.pdf

Leonen, M.F. (2004). Etiquette for activists. *YES! Magazine.* Retrieved from https://www.yesmagazine.org/issues/a-conspiracy-of-hope/etiquette-for-activists

Lorde, A. (2003). The master's tools will never dismantle the master's house. In R. Lewis & S. Mills (Eds.), *Feminist Postcolonial Theory: A Reader* (pp. 25–29). New York, NY: Routledge.

Matthews, D. (2017). Forward. In T. Shaffer, N. Longo, I. Manosemitch, & M. Thomas (Eds.), *Deliberative pedagogy: Teaching and learning for democratic engagement* (pp. ix–xii). East Lansing: Michigan State University Press.

Mattessich, P., Monsey, B., & Roy, C. (1997). *Community building, what makes it work: A review of factors influencing successful community building.* Saint Paul, MN: Amherst H. Wilder Foundation.

McTighe Musil, C. (2011, May 10). Another urgent deficit: The deficit of civic learning and liberal education. *Association of American Colleges and Universities.* Retrieved from https://www.aacu.org/leap/liberal-education-nation-blog/another-urgent-deficit%E2%80%94-deficit-civic-learning-and-liberal

Medina, R. M., Nicolosi, E., Brewer, S., & Linke, A. M. (2018). Geographies of organized hate in America: A regional analysis. *Annals of the American Association of Geographers, 108*(4), 1006–1021. doi:10.1080/24694452.2017.1411247.

Myers, V. A. (2014, December). *How to overcome our biases? Walk boldly toward them.* [Video file]. Retrieved from https://www.youtube.com/watch?v=uYyvbgINZkQ

National Center for Education Statistics. (2018a). *The condition of education 2018: College enrollment rates.* Retrieved from https://nces.ed.gov/programs/coe/pdf/coe_cpb.pdf

National Center for Education Statistics. (2018b). *The condition of education 2018: Characteristics of postsecondary faculty.* Retrieved from https://nces.ed.gov/fastfacts/display.asp?id=61

National Coalition for Dialogue and Deliberation. (2013). *Engagement streams framework.* Retrieved from http://www.ncdd.org/files/NCDD2010_Engagement_Streams.pdf

National Issues Forum. (2014). *Deliberation.* Retrieved from https://www.nifi.org/en/deliberation

Oliver, L. P. (1987). *Study circles: Coming together for personal growth and social change.* Washington, DC: Seven Locks.

Scholtes, J., Emma, C., & Ferris, S. (2019, January 17). GOP Rep. Jason Smith apologizes for telling Democrats to 'go back to Puerto Rico. *Politico.* Retrieved from https://www.politico.com/story/2019/01/17/house-stopgap-bill-1109215

Solomon, B. (1976). *Black empowerment: Social work in oppressed communities.* New York, NY: Columbia University Press.

Southern Poverty Law Center. (2017). *What is a hate group?* Retrieved from https://www.splcenter.org/20171004/frequently-asked-questions-about-hate-groups#hate%20group

Staats, C. (2014). State of the science: Implicit bias review 2014. *Kirwan Institute for the Study of Race and Ethnicity.* Retrieved from http://kirwaninstitute.osu.edu/wp-content/uploads/2014/03/2014-implicit-bias.pdf

Staats, C., Capatosto, K., Wright, R. A., & Contractor, D. (2015). State of the science: Implicit bias review 2015. *Kirwan Institute for the Study of Race and Ethnicity.* Retrieved from http://kirwaninstitute.osu.edu/wp-content/uploads/2015/05/2015-kirwan-implicit-bias.pdf

Staats, C., Capatosto, K., Wright, R. A., & Jackson, V. W. (2016). State of the science: Implicit bias review 2016. *Kirwan Institute for the Study of Race and Ethnicity.* Retrieved from http://kirwaninstitute.osu.edu/wp-content/uploads/2016/07/implicit-bias-2016.pdf

Staats, C., Capatosto, K., Tenney, L., & Mamo, S. (2017). State of the science: Implicit bias review 2017. *Kirwan Institute for the Study of Race and Ethnicity.* Retrieved from http://kirwaninstitute.osu.edu/wp-content/uploads/2017/11/2017-SOTS-final-draft-02.pdf

Stack, L. (2019, February 20). Over 1,000 hate groups are now active in United States, civil rights group says. *New York Times.* Retrieved from https://www.nytimes.com/2019/02/20/us/hate-groups-rise.html

Suda, L. (2001). Learning circles: Democratic pools of knowledge. *ARIS Resources Bulletin, 12*(3), 1–4.

Tomlinson, B., & Lipsitz, G. (2013). Insubordinate spaces for intemperate times: Countering the pedagogies of neoliberalism. *Review of Education, Pedagogy, and Cultural Studies, 35*(1), 3–26.

Virginia Commonwealth University (VCU), Office of Equal Employment Opportunity. (n.d.). *Strategies for successfully recruiting a diverse faculty.* Retrieved from http://www.ccas.net/files/ADVANCE/VCU%20Expand%20the%20Pool.pdf
Western Carolina University. (2019). *Unofficial fall 2018 census statistics.* Retrieved from https://www.wcu.edu/WebFiles/OIPE/IPE_Fall_2018_Census_Statistics_unofficial.pdf
Western Carolina University Faculty Senate. (2018). *Resolution in support of equity, diversity, and inclusion at WCU.* Cullowhee, NC: Author.
Wheatley, M.J. (2002). Some friends and I started talking. *UTNE Reader.* Retrieved from https://www.utne.com/community/some-friends-and-i-started-talking
Whee Matter Movement. (2018). *The collective response to Western Carolina University's racial insensitivity.* Cullowhee, NC: Author.

CHAPTER SEVEN

Oh God! What Have I Done!?:

What New Faculty Members Should Be Aware About the Dos and Don'ts of Academia

ELWOOD WATSON

IN AUGUST 1997, I began my academic career as a tenure track professor. It was the beginning of another chapter of my life. I was excited, yet harbored many varied emotions that many new faculty members experience:

- A sense of immense pride
- A degree of anxiety
- Envisioning what my immediate future would entail
- Wondering if my relationship with my colleagues would be harmonious or contentious
- Wondering if my students would like or respect me
- Thinking about how I would perform in the classroom
- Wondering if I would be a successful professor

- Wondering if I would be a failed professor
- Wondering if I would get tenure

The last concern is a major, if not primary, concern of most, if not all, new faculty. Anyone who tells you otherwise is not being honest with you or themselves.

The fact is, entering the academy as a fresh, newly minted tenure-track professor is undoubtedly a source of immense pride for many academics. The undisputed fact is that you have made it this far. You have hit the lottery against tremendous odds. Some would argue that literally winning an actual lottery jackpot might be more likely. This is particularly true as it relates to non-STEM fields. Indeed, the job market in the humanities and social sciences is distressingly dire.

Truth be told, whether or not you are aware of this fact, you have become a member of a select group of human beings who have managed to avoid (at least for the time being) the often less (and wrongly so) stable world of adjunct professors, many of whom live at the whims of any particular institution, are bereft of any health benefits, and often have to cobble together multiple courses (often at several institutions) every semester in the hopes that they can make ends meet. You have been fortunate enough to avoid the slightly more stable category of full-time temporary academics whose salaries on average are higher and better yet are still largely employed on an as-needed basis. When budgets get tighter and institutions engage in the process of "reassessing" and "realignment," these are the sort of positions that are often the first to be eliminated. Thus, the term "temporary" can often become a reality.

While instructors are what some would refer to as the "better served" segment of the professoriate (some academics choose to be instructors), the fact is that they still have not gained membership to that "exclusive club." Instructors are often viewed by some (certainly not all or perhaps even most fellow academics) as being on the periphery, most frequently by those on the tenure track and tenured scholars. In other words, they have not quite yet arrived or supposedly do not have what it takes to make the ranks of the potentially tenured few. Fortunately, for you, tenure-track professor, you have done so and this is where things begin to get interesting.

The fact is that far too many young (and some older) scholars who have been blessed to have the opportunity to land a tenure-track position have these preconceived and in some cases misguided beliefs they have gotten to the "promised land," so to speak. The fact that they have passed all the qualifying exams, interviews, and other requirements demonstrates their competence and validates their academic acumen. Many junior-level faculty believe that if they are extremely prolific with their publications, dazzle students with brilliant insight, garner stellar teaching evaluations, and engage in a respectable level of service activity that these factors alone will be enough for them to be rewarded with tenure and promotion after several years. The fact is that such a minor Pollyanna attitude is often misguided and potentially problematic for its inhabitants (Lee, 2015).

Those of us who have been around the academic block a few times can vouch for the fact that the academy is an often quirky, unpredictable place where unexpected events and minefields are rife in the landscape. For many junior faculty, some will soon learn, rather abruptly, that academic politics are a mainstay in the academy. Vices such as racism, sexism, antisemitism, homophobia, xenophobia, ageism, elitism, and so on are prevalent and often manifest themselves in varied ways (Thomas, 2017).

All too often, too many faculty, regardless of race or gender, assume that following the largely touted golden rules of "publish intensely" at their institutions, "teach brilliantly" at small liberal arts colleges, and/or "deeply immerse themselves" in service at vocational schools is the path to tenure and promotion. The reality is that things are not always as black and white, as many of us had been told by our graduate mentors, many of whom were often well meaning, yet less than candid with their advice.

The truth is that the journey can often be filled with potholes, dead ends, and in some cases, potential catastrophes if not handled or navigated properly, and navigating properly may look different depending on the person, the department, and the institution (Chafee, Tiernet, Ewell & Krakower, 1988). Going into the often complex environment of academia with your eyes closed or blinking too much can be potentially fatal. Getting focused and acclimated to the environment of one's department (perhaps even institution) can be challenging yet crucial to having a successful career in the academy (Tierney & Rhoads, Higher Education Reports, 1994). One way to move through the complex environment with the fewest scrapes and bruises is to find a group of people who can serve as mentors for the varying choices and challenges that you'll face. That being said, I would like to provide some examples of 20 missteps (often more) that junior and tenure-track faculty frequently make that can often derail their careers.

1. Behaving Inappropriately

While this can be interpreted multiple ways, here it means that some newly minted junior faculty tend to forget the fact that once they have signed that contract, arrived on campus, completed attending new faculty orientation programs, and been given the keys to their new office that they have now graduated to the status of professor. This means that behavior that one was allowed to exhibit in graduate school is often no longer acceptable. Hanging out at the student center, other undergraduate hangouts, telling crude jokes in mixed company, dating students, wearing explicit and brash clothing are all signs to older colleagues (and some fellow junior colleagues) that you have not yet matured enough to a degree that is considered acceptable for your peers. While they may not directly confront you on this issue(s), you can rest assured that they notice such behavior and are certainly discussing it among themselves and possibly with senior-level administrators as well. This is particularly the case in smaller, more compact departments. Such actions can easily derail your opportunity for personal and professional advancement. This is a place where a mentor can give you a quick word, allowing you to make changes as necessary.

2. Being Overly Sensitive

I am not talking about mean-spirited, over-the-top, personal attacks. No one should tolerate let alone accept vicious, nasty unprofessional comments. That being said, almost all of us, regardless of what rank we hold in the professoriate, are vulnerable to imperfections, no matter how minor, when it comes to our scholarship, and in some cases other facets of our being. When asking for any sort of assistance, you need to be prepared and mature enough to expect honest and critical feedback. There is nothing wrong with constructive criticism. In fact, it should be welcomed. Sometimes junior-level faculty, often defensive and in some cases paranoid, in an environment that can be volatile, are inclined to take such criticisms of teaching and research personally when in fact such criticism can often be accurate and may help the recipient in question to improve in such areas. If you are unsure about the advice and question whether it is genuinely meant to support your advancement, ask a colleague with whom you've developed a solid working relationship. Being seen as overly sensitive, combative, and resistant to constructive criticism can often cause potential allies to distance or withdraw themselves from communicating with you and they may refuse to offer future advice that could be invaluable in future situations, including tenure and promotion.

3. Teaching That Is Less Than Stellar

While the mantra of "publish or perish" has been deeply etched in the psyche of almost all incoming faculty, the fact is that too many faculty ignore the potential impact that student assessment can have on their chances for tenure and promotion. This is particularly true in smaller, teaching-oriented institutions. While it is highly unlikely that most colleagues, department chairs, tenure committees, deans, and other senior-level officials would consult online websites that allow students to express their comments on faculty members for decisions as to whether a faculty member should be granted tenure (e.g., Rate my Professor, though never say never), they do, in fact, pay attention to student evaluations. While one or even two semesters of mediocre to poor evaluations may not spell impending doom for a faculty member, especially in the first year or two of the tenure track, consistently less-than-satisfactory or poor student evaluations can eventually be damaging and in some cases call for dismissal even before the candidate reaches the tenure and promotion stage. Yes! Some junior tenure-track faculty have been shown the door after a few semesters of chronically poor student evaluations. It has happened. While the reasons for these factors can vary and there is no doubt that in some cases various biases such as race, gender, religion, sexual orientation, and so on come into play, the reality is no one can reasonably expect to be granted tenure and promotion with several years of less-than-satisfactory teaching. This is not to say that it does not happen; however, more often than not, especially at liberal arts colleges and other teaching-oriented institutions, the odds are not in your favor.

4. Using Social Media Recklessly

In this age of iPods, cell phones, e-mail, SKYPE, and other intensive communication, it is important for all faculty to be mindful of how they present themselves on the Internet and with all forms of social media in general. Yes, millennial faculty this applies to you as well. Posting bawdy, crude, or obscene messages on your Facebook or Twitter page, writing or posting racially or gender/sexually charged inflammatory e-mails or comments on social, political, entertainment websites, posting private or explicit pictures of yourself, and posting risqué conversations you have with friends can often land you in situations that may be hard to overcome. In fact, in some professions people have been terminated for such behavior. What may seem as acceptable commentary to one another or to people within your social group or clique can be perceived as hostile and unprofessional to others. Being seen as brash and insensitive can hamper your prospects for such success. Common sense should dictate that you think before you write or communicate online.

5. Focusing on Service at the Expense of Teaching and Research

Any competent and attentive department chair will make certain that their junior faculty will not get overextended with committee work. Eventually, you may become a department chair, and thinking this way is an important factor in strong leadership. However, the operative words here are "competent" and "attentive." As many of us who have gone through the tenure and promotion process are well aware, almost every organization on campus seeks out a fresh, newly minted faculty member to serve on its committee. This is particularly true in regard to female faculty and faculty of color who are often called on to represent their particular identity. In some cases, in an effort to want to demonstrate that they are team players and are up to the task, many junior faculty will too often say *yes* without realizing the potential ramifications that such a decision can have on their time and ability to pursue and maintain a healthy research agenda that is often needed to secure tenure and promotion. The cold, hard reality is that at most colleges and universities, particularly research-oriented institutions, one does not get tenure and promotion by serving on multiple committees, advising dozens of theses and dissertations, and deeply immersing themselves in a chronic level of service. For some junior faculty, especially women and faculty of color, by the time they recognize this fact it is often too late (Stanley, 2006). As often happens, women and faculty of color will come into a third-year review with many service points but find themselves uncomfortably close to the line of success on successfully pursuing their research agendas. While no one should reject any or every request from colleagues, it is important that in some cases you are willing and able to say *no* when you have to. If you need to solicit your department chair in such an effort, do not hesitate to do so. A strong and responsible department head will gladly step in on your behalf.

6. Being Unaware of the Environment of Your Department

Too many junior faculty are often unaware or underestimate the politics of their departments. They are under the assumption that if they just teach, research, and do their service, everything will fall into place. For some tenure-track faculty this scenario will actually be true. However, over time, for a number of others, this sort of naïve mentality can result in surprise and eventual disillusion. While no one wants to be seen "prying around" for information about colleagues, sometimes it is important to seek out people you can trust, whether it be within or outside your department, to brief you on the history of the unit you will be working in. This is a point where a solid group of mentors comes into play. Mentors can help to answer important questions. What are the priorities of your department? Does your department value research over teaching, service over teaching, teaching over service, and research over service? Are there combative and warring factions within your department? Do some faculty possess more influence than others? These are questions that should be answered. Being aware of the political, social, and cultural climate of your department is often necessary, even crucial, in that it may depend on your survival. Know what is expected of you and try to deliver accordingly.

7. Having A Combative Personality

Academia is a profession that is known to have its share of malcontents and other assorted misfits. This is nothing new. That being said, even people who are somewhat dysfunctional do not want to be around people who are always dissatisfied about one thing or another. Yes, even malcontents tend to dislike malcontents! No one wants a colleague who is constantly arguing with other faculty, fretting about some minor or insignificant issue, or gossiping about what they believe to be the shortcomings of others around them or being disagreeable in general. New faculty need to be aware of the fact that more than a few sets of eyes and ears are watching and listening to you on you. Thus, it is important to avoid appearing non-collegial (Cipriano, 2011). In some cases, even the slightest body facial or hand gestures could be perceived by colleagues as hostile. One thing is for certain, lashing out and antagonizing senior colleagues is a sure-fire way to weaken your prospects for tenure and promotion. It is always important to keep in mind how you are representing yourself.

8. Appearing Detached and Aloof toward Your Colleagues

The fact is that landing a tenure-track job in academia is difficult enough as it is. In some fields there are routinely more than two hundred or more applications for one position. In fact, some senior colleagues will not hesitate to subtly remind you of how fortunate you are to be on the tenure track on a daily basis during your first few years at the institution. In some cases, their comments are overt. Directness and subtleness aside, it is important to give the impression that you are genuinely committed to the well-being and progress of your department. Mentors you can trust will support you in this process; good intentions will also caution you if you take on too many service commitments in an attempt to show that you are, indeed, collegial. While seeming less than gracious may not cost you tenure and promotion, such an aloof attitude does not bode well for potential advancement and future support from your colleagues.

9. Allowing Yourself to Be Emotionally Distraught

Just as seeming to be less than enthusiastic about your colleagues and your department, it is also very potentially damaging to your future prospects if you are truly ambivalent about your current surroundings. More than few faculty have faced depression, burnout, nervous breakdowns, and all sorts of health issues due to the fact that the environment they were in was not conducive to their physical and emotional well-being. For junior faculty with the added stresses of meeting teaching, research, and service expectations, such issues can be magnified even more so. The fact is while no one should just up and leave a tenure-track position without weighing all the pros and cons, it is important for faculty to keep their sanity and be in control of their emotional well-being as well as the satisfaction of their spouse and children (if they are married and have children). This applies to single people as well. After a few years, if things have progressed from bad to worse, there is probably very little reason to stick it out. Even getting tenure and promotion would be a bittersweet/pyrrhic victory at best.

10. Allowing Your Personal Life to Be an Open Book

Faculty members, regardless of rank, need to be selective in how much information they share about themselves with others. This is particularly true in regard to your personal affairs. Wanting to feel included and land in the good graces of the fellow faculty, some junior faculty often expose too much information about themselves. Sometimes this can backfire in that older, insecure, envious faculty and other rivals who may not have your best interests at heart will often use such news in an effort to discredit or raise questions about you. Whether you hang out at the local bars, have an adventurous or nonexistent sex life, sleep in on the weekend, associate with professors in other departments, go to clubs, are having marital problems or mental, physical, or other related health issues, the best strategy is to keep your personal business just that—personal. If you have colleagues in your department who are close, personal friends and trusted, personal confidants, that is one thing. Otherwise, it is better to maintain a zone of privacy. There are occasionally more than a few eager beavers who all too often engage in the act of schadenfreude. Don't voluntarily give them the ammunition to do so.

11. Assuming That Academia Is an Intellectual Utopia

There are some junior faculty who are so gratified by the fact that they have beaten the odds to land on the tenure track that they soon forget that academia, while an environment that encourages diversity of thought and innovation, is filled with a number of professors who are frustrated, burned out, disillusioned, resentful of their limited successes, or unhappy with life in general. Jealousy is a vice that is rampant in the ivory tower. A young, up-and-coming, dynamic professor who teaches well and is establishing a prolific research record may very well be seen as a significant threat to older, less productive faculty as well as some fellow junior colleagues who are not performing as effectively. Your accomplishments can often serve to highlight someone else's failures and these are the very same people who will do everything they can to diminish your accomplishments or pull the ladder out from under you if they can. For women and faculty of color, this is especially true. Those persons who are not exactly in the majority in education are likely to be perceived as threatening anyway, so adding to that perception by broadcasting your accomplishments, especially when your senior colleagues don't have them or cannot share them, may simply add to their misery. The old adage misery loves company is all too often true. Thus, it is sagacious to be careful with whom you share your accomplishments and successes with (Dunn, 2015).

12. Being Too Paranoid and Defensive

Just as entering the academy with the mind-set that everyone is holding hands and singing kumbaya can be dangerously misguided, so can harboring the attitude that very few people, if any, can be trusted. To be sure, there are a number of snakes in the grass, and some academic environments are outright snake pits. That being said, most departments have a decent number of tenured senior faculty members who have an interest in helping develop and cultivate junior faculty with a desire to see them succeed and flourish. The fact is that there are a number of senior faculty who are among some the strongest supporters of junior, tenure-track faculty and have demonstrated genuine commitment to helping them promote their work. Look for and find those faculty who will strongly support your career. Use them as mentors, sounding boards, and workplace friends. Once you arrive in a leadership position, whether in your department or in your chosen field, be the kind of faculty member who supports junior colleagues. While a healthy dose of caution can be good for anyone, do not assume that everyone is out to do you harm. Such a resistant and paranoid attitude will often do a person more harm than good in the long run. This sort of myopic thinking can potentially be just as adversarial to your career.

13. Living in Denial

This is a problem that some faculty, regardless of academic rank, have. Reasons for this vary. Some are so happy to be in their current position that they fail to notice the warning signs and potential potholes down the road. Others believe that whatever problems they are currently having are merely temporary and that they will soon pass. There is a segment of junior faculty who are often in complete denial about their situation. Examples of this include: routine complaints from students to the chair and in some cases to fellow faculty; unusually poor performance reviews during the first few semesters on campus; body language and (in some cases) subtle and snide comments from colleagues indicating less-than-admirable feelings; hearing consistent comments about one's teaching and scholarship being less than rigorous; and finally, receiving a less-than-stellar third-year review. All of these are telltale signs that the likelihood of having a successful career at your current institution is unlikely, let alone being granted tenure and promotion. While the environment can change, it is unlikely to do so for any faculty member in question. A picture has been painted, whether by you or not, and it is probably best to start looking elsewhere and consider moving on if possible.

14. Being Seen as Too Unreliable and Unpredictable

The pressures of publishing, preparing lesson plans, tending to family matters (if you have children), and other factors of life can often be overwhelming for junior faculty; nonetheless, it is important for junior faculty to be seen as reliable. Therefore, it is important to do what you can to dispel such notions. Make sure to keep your office hours. Attend departmental meetings and respond to e-mail as promptly as you can. Be seen in your office on a regular basis. Make sure others can easily get in touch with you. Make sure to attend committee and all other meetings on time. While you cannot always change the perceptions that others have of you, you can make sure that the negative stereotypes they harbor do not apply to you.

15. Being Perceived as Overly Aggressive

Competition is fact of life for many of us. The academy is no exception. There are some faculty who live to be competitive with their colleagues as being among the best in their field of study. While healthy competition is good, and in some cases can even produce a healthy and productive work environment, it is important that such competition does not result in a situation where you have alienated colleagues who can be crucial to your future success. It is better to being seen as competitive as opposed to being seen as arrogant. This is particularly true for younger faculty. In fact, it is wise, if possible, to let senior faculty promote your scholarship and accomplishments on your behalf. Whenever possible, make sure to compliment fellow faculty on their achievements and, if possible, offer to assist them with a grant, article, or related project they are working on. Such a sense of collegiality can often go a long way in keeping yourself in the good graces of fellow colleagues, especially those whose votes and support you will need when it comes time for tenure and promotion.

16. Being Dismissive of Colleagues

Being a junior faculty working to get tenure and promotion is a very time-consuming experience. It can be fraught with fear, anxiety, stress and other intense symptoms. Quite frankly, it can be downright frantic! This is particularly true for junior faculty who have young children, are taking care of aging parents, or have additional responsibilities outside of academia. The demands of juggling family, academic, and personal life can be overwhelming. When all the tasks are completed for the moment, you are literally out of energy. While it is important, indeed necessary, to keep your priorities in line during those most crucial, initial years of moving through the tenure track, it may also be important to demonstrate to your colleagues that you are someone who appreciates them enough to spend some time with them. This is certainly not the case in all departments. In fact, you may very well find yourself in an environment where faculty do not associate with one another at all outside of work. The brief "hellos" in the hall and occasional helping one another on a task or filling in for a course when a college is out of town may be the extent of camaraderie. However, if you are in a department where there a high level of collegiality and faculty do frequently meet up with one another for coffee, drinks, basketball, frisbee, gin rummy, and so on, it is probably a good idea to make yourself available for such activities from time to time, especially if you are invited to do so. It certainly is not necessary or even mandatory to go out for drinks every Friday night with your colleagues. That being said, sometimes it is often in such outings where valuable information (minus occasional gossip) can be gained. It also demonstrates to your colleagues (rightly or wrongly) the perception that you are team player and are someone they would not mind making a potential 30- or 40-year investment in.

17. Disrespecting and Disregarding Students

While the majority of faculty treat their students with a level of respect that is appropriate, there are others who tend to berate, marginalize, and in some cases, outright disrespect students. Sometimes junior faculty are so eager to prove to their tenured and senior faculty brethren that they have what it takes to be a part of the academic world that they tend to believe that being extremely tough on students will earn them accolades from their more senior colleagues. This is often far from the case. If anything, adversarial relationships with students (particularly at small liberal arts colleges where faculty may occasionally teach across disciplines) will quickly get around to colleagues, your department chair, department staff, the dean, and possibly the level of provost or president. In an era where student tuition is becoming more important than ever, such a reputation can be the kiss of death for a faculty member, particularly for one who is seen as belligerent, dismissive, and confrontational toward students. For tenure-track female and faculty of color, this is always a sensitive and difficult subject given the fact that many women and minority faculty teach in areas such as race, gender, and cultural studies where some students have already come to the course with a defensive mind-set. It is not uncommon for more than a few students to pay a visit to the department chair or senior-level administrator's office with complaints about your teaching style or pedagogy. While no faculty member should shy away from speaking truth to power in the classroom, it is important to demonstrate a degree of tact and professionalism when dealing with students. It is certainly important to treat them with respect.

18. Disregarding Office and Clerical Staff

Too many faculty and graduate students underestimate the influence of secretaries, executive aides, and other clerical staff. They are often the eyes and ears of the department. Many of them have been employees of the institution for decades. In short, they know how the place operates! They often know where all the bodies are buried, so to speak. Executive aides often do all the crucial work such as filling out time sheets, ordering supplies for the department, reviewing paperwork that faculty send in for conferences, and other tedious work that keeps the department, college, or university running efficiently. Over time, they have often established strong bonds with fellow executive aides in other departments and in some cases with the executive aides of the dean of your college. They are the individuals who more than often get breaking news of what is happening before the majority of faculty such as with potential pay raises, an administrative opening in the college, and so on. The lifeblood of the department is dependent on them. They can also spread positive or negative news about you to upper administration. Junior faculty who are arrogant, combative, hostile, and disrespectful toward clerical staff or who ignore them should not underestimate the potential damage they are doing to themselves. No one is so important that they should feel that is acceptable to mistreat a person, in particular people who are so vital to the well-being of a department.

19. Lacking Political Savvy

While some junior faculty are unusually savvy in navigating the often murky and deeply entrenched world of departmental politics, others are not. Unfortunately, this is not advice that all or even many dissertation advisers give to their doctoral students. Due to this fact, far too many young, newly minted faculty enter academic departments or institutions often blind to legacies and polices that are deeply entrenched. For a career that will often span a minimum of three decades, it is unreasonable for you to think that you will never have a workplace conflict. Dissention can range from the direction of a new problem to a minor or major curriculum change. As a faculty member you will eventually find yourself in a situation where your integrity (for those who have any) requires that you stand for something on principle. Even so, it is important to proceed with caution. You should carefully consider whether your position is at odds with the institutional or departmental mission. The reason being is that in this case, you are already in the position of an underdog and need to be mindful of this fact and the potential consequences that can come from taking such a stance. If you have a problem with an individual, talk to that person as opposed to about them. You can disagree without being disagreeable. If needed, try to enlist the help of the department chair or some sympathetic senior faculty member(s) to assist you with your cause. The sad reality is that people are not going to change overnight and sometimes it is important to overlook and ignore certain comments and behaviors and to keep your eyes on the prize. While no one is saying suggesting to accept or tolerate blatantly racist, sexist, homophobic, xenophobic, anti-Semitic, anti-religious slurs and comments or outright disrespectful behavior (they need to be addressed directly and aggressively), there are times when you will have to make the decision and ask yourself, "Is their mildly insensitive comment or awkward generalization really worth the effort to go to war for?" Sometimes it may be; others it may be wiser to let fools alone.

20. Making Academia Your Entire Life

We realize the importance and virtues of being committed and conscientious, indeed. Such traits are often admired and respected, but like anything, sometimes too much can be just that, too much. We all have seen and heard about the colleague whose office light is on from 6:30 a.m. to 2:00 a.m. Other colleagues see the same faculty member's vehicle in the parking lot every weekend after 11:00 p.m. as they drive by the school. Stories abound of faculty whose marriages or relationships have dissolved and family obligations were neglected due to one partner's obsession with achieving tenure; the faculty members who never have time to stop and talk to colleagues, executive aides, or anyone else; the faculty members who have allowed their mental and physical health to deteriorate due to their dogged determination to achieve tenure. Other examples abound. The fact is that while many of us who are members of the academic profession know that achieving tenure and promotion is a significant prize and accomplishment, we are also astute to the fact that there are many other variables that result in such an outcome. Politics, academic climate, financial situation of institution, and so on all come into play in addition to teaching, research, and service. The fact is that no one is guaranteed (especially in this current climate) that he or she will be granted tenure and promotion regardless of whether they have dotted all their I's and crossed all of their t's. Nothing is a sure bet. Thus, it is important to keep some perspective on things. *Do not let academia become your entire life.* While those of us who have managed to land jobs and beat the odds are and should be grateful for our relatively good fortune, we should not allow one aspect of our life (academia) to dominate, or in some cases disrupt, other areas of our entire being. Such behavior is unwise and potentially detrimental to those in question and those around them.

Conclusion

The road from tenure track to earning tenure is one that is arduous, occasionally intense and lonely, and frequently filled with unexpected situations. Indeed, some people are unsuccessful in completing the task. Congratulations to those of you who have made it this far against the odds, likely already having weathered various roadblocks. The fact is that academia can be a vibrant, flourishing environment for those who have the drive, support, and resources to utilize at their disposal. By adhering to the aforementioned advice, tenure-track faculty can at least mitigate the extra burdens that often accompany those who are on such a path of working toward eventually receiving that all-important and gratifying letter informing you that you have sidestepped the minefields, successfully jumped all the hurdles, completed all the inaugural tasks, and have gained permanent admission to a club that only a select few are granted admission to, securing tenure and promotion. Good luck!

NOTE: Some ideas for this chapter were adapted from an earlier piece of mine (Watson, 2014).

References

Chafee, E., Tierney, E. G., Ewell, P., & Krakower, Y. (1988). Collegiate culture and leadership strategies. New York, NY: Macmillan.

Cipriano, R. E. (2011). *Facilitating a collegial department in higher education: Strategies for success.* San Francisco, CA: Jossey Bass.

Darlington, P., & Durnell, N. Y. (1996). Faculty life 101: A survival guide. *Black Issues in Higher Education*. Retrieved from http://diverseeducation.com/article/7489/ https://diverseeducation.com/article/7489/

Dunn, S. (2015, December 12). Why so many academics quit and tell. *Chronicle of Higher Education*. Retrieved from https://chroniclevitae.com/news/216-why-so-many-academics-quit-and-tell

Lee, J. (2015). Why academic politics are so vicious. *American Association of University Professors*. Retrieved from https://www.aaup.org/article/why-academic-politics-are-so-vicious#.XVrgCpNKjsE

Stanley, C. A. (2006). *Faculty of color: Teaching in predominately white colleges and universities*. Boston, MA: Anker.

Thomas, P. L. (2017, June 14). White men of academia have an 'objectivity' problem. *Huffington Post*. Retrieved from https://www.huffpost.com/entry/more-on-white-men-of-academia-student-and-self-evaluation_b_593a8204e4b0b65670e56963

Tierney, W. G. & Rhoads, Robert A. (1994). *Enhancing promotion, tenure, and beyond: Faculty socialization as cultural process: A mirror of institutional commitment*. Hoboken, NJ: Wiley.

Watson, E. (2014). 15 missteps that can derail faculty early in a career: What graduate students need to know about the push and pull of academia. In D. A. Mack, E. Watson, & M. Madsen Camocho (Eds.), *Beginning a career in academia: A guide for graduate students of color* (pp. 110–119). New York, NY: Routledge.

CHAPTER EIGHT

Tenure, Team, Inclusivity, and the Importance of Building Bridges

MARTHA DIEDE

TENURE IS A COMPLEX goal that eludes many excellent academics for reasons that vary from positions politically unpopular with committee members and university administrators to interventions in the timeline related to biology—a complex disease diagnosis for self or family member, aging of self or family member, or pregnancy and birth. Complicating the challenges of advancing in the university whether by earning tenure, promotion, or an extended contract is an insidious myth that people somehow individually merit/earn their positions (Grollman, 2014; McNamee & Miller, 2004). The people that inhabit departments with their unique combinations of dreams and foibles also contribute intricacies that require careful calculations and adjustments. No matter the position or promotion, recognizing and navigating the politics of the department and institution in which one finds oneself is a complex challenge. Processes move around and between the politics of the international and national conversation—in which, as an academic, one should engage—and between the people who work together to make or to stall changes, even on an individual level. At the point of tenure, promotion, and long-term contract, the politics become pointedly personal and pragmatic. For this reason, finding a team and working together toward shared goals can promote individual and collective progress.

First, let's consider the kinds of people that we frequently encounter in academic departments.

Barry is an eager beaver. He loves his job, loves his colleagues, and loves the students. And, everybody likes Barry. In fact, everyone asks Barry to serve on their committees. They ask Barry to be the faculty adviser for the major's club and for the club for students of color as Barry is also African American. Barry teaches a full load and advises a large number of students. And, Barry does all of it with a "this is awesome!" attitude. Unfortunately, if Barry isn't careful, he is going to let time get away from him with his publications. The clock is ticking for Barry.

Gertrude pretends to be helpful. She always has something to say in meetings, and she is very bright. A lot of what she has to say is indeed helpful. But, look out—if she is in a bad mood, she can turn on you in a heartbeat. She is the person on your campus who will try to "get you" when you make a mistake on your paperwork, and she always has the gossip. She will start a sentence with things like, "I don't know if you know this, but . . ." Gertrude can be whiny, and she is very passive-aggressive. She is a little like a middle-schooler who likes you one day and then doesn't like you the next day. She is on track for tenure, and her packet is due for review in the next year.

Jackson has tenure, and he does just enough each year to get a pretty good faculty evaluation. He skips meetings unless the committee is voting on something that can help him; he never attends functions like commencement or receptions; he shirks his duties in the department; and—worst of all—he is a poser. He pretends to be a serious researcher/teacher/scholar, but truthfully, he barely got through the tenure process himself. Yet, he loves to sit on tenure committees and judge others' work as "inadequate." There's no way to get rid of this guy, and he can't get a job somewhere else.

Tina earned tenure five years ago. She is a solid teacher, a good committee member; she presents at both state and national conferences regularly, and has a solid record of continued publication. She meets research standards and enjoys teaching. She is comfortable at the university and isn't looking for a faculty position at another university. So, Tina has begun to settle into her mid-career status, and she has lost some of her zeal for the job. Part of her thinks she would be a good administrator, but another part of her likes the flexibility of the faculty life. Tina likes having tenure and wonders if she could give that up to move into administration—even if moving up means more money.

Monique is a department head. She is decent, but she lives and dies by the political stances of the university. She crosses all her t's, but she has lost sight of the faculty as *people*. She signs up for lots of important university committees and is always very busy, yet she has no time to stop by and ask how a faculty member in the department is doing. She crosses items off her to-do list, but she rarely has time to chat. She sends directives via e-mail rather than have discussions with members of the team. In short, she is an administrator who can complete tasks, but she isn't a very nice to be around anymore.

Each of these faculty members needs partners to accomplish their goals, even if that goal is simply to maintain the status quo. While it might be easy to pretend that these faculty must be unique to a specific campus or university, the reality is that these faculty members represent types that many, if not most, academics have met, possibly with whom they have worked. As tempting as it might be to write these faculty off thinking that they have made their own challenges, that perspective leaves us missing a key characteristic: Not one of these characters makes a good partner, and they may not know how to build strong partnerships.

Challenges to earning tenure are legion, ranging from race, ethnicity, religious belief, and sexual orientation to class and the myth of meritocracy. Even if scholars can spot these challenges in other places and other fields of employment, recognizing them in the academic world seems challenging at best, impossible at worst. This is precisely the point at which partnerships should—must—come into play. Strong partnerships across disciplines, schools, colleges, inside the institution and outside of it, can make enormous differences in the ways that tenure plays out.

Briefly, let me tell you my story as an example. Before I became a faculty developer, I was a tenured professor and department head. In order to earn tenure, I first had to learn that I needed partners. Getting a faculty position, let alone receiving tenure, is not an easy process, and this larger task is often conceptualized as individual. This is to say that many institutions perpetuate the idea that they hire the best faculty for their positions and that the way these individuals prove that they belong is to leap the hurdles that stand between themselves and tenure. The system of higher education, tilted as it is toward traditional white masculinities and toward wealth, wants to stand by the idea that people earn tenure on their own merits. As Grollman (2014) rightly points out, in academia, meritocracy is a myth, and a dangerous one, as it camouflages the realities that academics may start their journeys on fields that are not level and that those inequities persist through the faculty career.

I came into graduate school believing the myths, conceptualizing my steps as the route to a faculty career, believing that my individual merits would be sufficient to move me into and ahead in my chosen career. As it had been in my undergraduate experience, my graduate work emphasized individual work and originality. Support and assistance came from friends. I'd love to say that my stellar teaching or my ability to maintain a research agenda while teaching a four-four load were game-changers, but that's not really the case. The difference maker for me was the friendships, the partnerships. I was also exceptionally lucky: My partners understood campus politics and were not shy in helping me to navigate the varying challenges I faced.

Though I should have recognized my colleagues as partners at the time, I would not have characterized my position as having a partnership with anyone to finish or to progress toward and achieve tenure. Even as I worked with my dissertation adviser to complete my dissertation, I would not have characterized him as a partner. As I started in an adjunct position and moved on to the tenure track, I developed close friends who became true partners in the teaching work that formed the focus of our collective, daily efforts. In the openly hostile environment where we found ourselves, our friendship sustained us.

My partners in this process served many different roles: cheerleaders, editors, guides through political minefields of institutional politics, sponsors, and mentors. They were also the kinds of partners who could keep me from becoming any of the faculty types characterized earlier in this chapter. Finding these partners was not simply luck. We had to agree that we needed each other and find value in our collective work. We also had to overcome barriers between us that might have potentially derailed our partnerships.

My first experiences in this department were both characteristic of the kinds of bridges necessary to achieve tenure and the kinds of blockades that frequently arise to tenure. Initially, I filled in for a faculty on sabbatical. While sitting in her office and teaching some of her classes, I completed my dissertation. Fortunately for me, my colleague in the department had excellent editorial skills and had significant background in Shakespeare, my area of focus. She offered to read my work, often providing suggestions that improved cogency and style. She built the bridge to me, however much I thought that I didn't particularly need it. And she corrected my path when I was on the way to becoming like Barry. I was far too willing to court the institution for a tenure-track position, agreeing to create classes, serve on committees, make presentations, and advise students without having any kind of assurance of permanent presence in the institution. Like Barry, I risked my own progress to focus on the aspects of my job that were immediate and came presently to mind as I saw them on a daily basis. Without the partnership that kept me from focusing too much on the immediate and insufficiently on the future, I might have spent even longer in the dissertation stage. Then I might have spent more time on student advising and on committee work and on additional requests made by the institution as opposed to the activities that moved my career in a positive direction. Unfortunately, my Barry-like enthusiasm made me myopic, and I was not a good partner. I tended to talk rather than to listen and to assume that systems where I was should be fixed rather than use my limited mental bandwidth to earn respect by treating systemic challenges as opportunities for personal growth.

I also worked with Just-Enough Jackson. Jackson did just enough, and just enough to cause trouble. He was absolutely certain that his history with the institution and his self-appointment as the wisest, most learned person in the department made him a perfect mentor for me. Every conversation about a class or a policy began with a lesson on department or university history and an explanation of how systems had come to be the way that they were. Tales of standing up to "the university" and "the college," marches into the provost's office at the front of a department "gang" in order to achieve concessions that made faculty load lighter flowed from him. Any attempt to make a change, no matter how small, was met with this kind of resistance. Jackson could also engage in publicly challenging behaviors, electing himself the department spokesperson and expressing his opinion as that of the department without ever seeking department consensus. His history and self-anointed status as the most learned one made such consensus unnecessary. He often embarrassed us as he turned his combative style on members of the department. His attitude of just enough had significantly contributed to the departmental reputation for being difficult to manage.

He turned that attitude on every colleague, eventually cussing out another faculty member, publicly, in a department meeting, for suggesting a change. Jackson also decided to announce to an accreditation visitor that I had married my partner in order strengthen my tenure case. I was embarrassed and appalled. I quickly realized that Jackson was likely to sit on my tenure committee and that, no matter how strong my packet, he would cast my work as derivative, without the appropriate theoretical underpinning that he regarded as his specialty.

Clearly, finding a way to connect with Jackson was equally important. So I began. I listened. I asked questions about changes and how they might fit into the story that he told of the department's past. I tried to keep my efforts to teach creatively limited and to suggest that Jackson need not adopt any practice that felt inauthentic to him. I drew the line at helping Jackson to lie about when he was skipping his classes. At the same time, I learned that Jackson's behaviors came from his extensive care-giving responsibilities outside of the university, some health challenges, and a sense of futility driven by unacknowledged frustration that became anger turned to the department and the university. Jackson had, before tenure, tried to make the university a more diverse, equitable, inclusive place, but no matter how much effort he applied to the problem, nothing changed. I doubted that Jackson would become a partner, but I thought that, at the very least, he would not be an obstacle. I worried about Jackson's toxic potential for me: Would I be able to withstand a consistent attitudinal barrage that cast his work as better than everyone else's, including mine? I had to keep Jackson close enough to ameliorate his challenge and far enough away to survive through the tenure process.

In such a typical position, I was fortunate that one of my colleagues became a bridge into the department. Because Jackson took a sabbatical, I stayed on an additional year. In that next year, I met a Gertrude in all of her "gotcha" glory. I faced critiques on a range of assignments, belief systems, ways of working in the department, and the standards that I set for student work. Working across my first bridge in the department, I had to learn to build additional bridges to my Gertrude in order to maintain department harmony and to achieve a position in the department, where, for family, place-based reasons, I hoped to stay. The challenge that the Gertrudes of academic departments present is that they often do not make good partners and building bridges to them can expose anyone to unforeseen risks. Because Gertrudes operate in a "gotcha" mode, their advice can be helpful and detrimental, depending on that Gertrude's mood at that moment and how it affects her perspective on individuals, events, and policy decisions.

As I quickly learned, my "Gertrude" colleague presented "gotcha" behaviors in challenging ways. My Gertrude could barely speak to me for the first seven months that we worked together. I had shared her office with three other faculty members while she was on sabbatical because there was no other space for us to work. In order to make that arrangement functional, we had to remove a chair or two from the office and to slice away some of the cartoons, papers, and other miscellaneous documents that covered her office door like wallpaper. That we had the temerity to hang sign-up sheets for students to request meetings and to make required appointments for writing classes and to move her office furniture so that our very pregnant colleague could move around the office was cause for explosive rants. She was happy to tell anyone who would listen that I was impossibly arrogant and disrespectful. Eventually, I was able to establish a strong friendship with her, and I had to learn to recognize when "gotcha" moments were directed toward department members, staff, and administrators.

In order to build a bridge to Gertrude, I had to learn that, even if I thought the door and the chairs were realistic changes for three people in a small office to make, she reacted with "gotcha" out of fear and fatigue. I had to apologize, although I felt that I had done nothing wrong. I chose to be consistently pleasant, daily greeting my Gertrude even if she did not respond. I also saw the destruction that her behaviors brought to relationships with administrators, staff, and colleagues. Even when she offered good advice, I learned to take care that my use of that advice did not possess the elements of "gotcha" that damaged relationships instead of building them. She advised that I confront, for example, the sexism in the tenure process that I observed. I had to recognize that engaging in confrontational behaviors before tenure would not earn me the tenure that I wanted, no matter how satisfying such confrontation might be.

Tina was my original bridge builder. She had been a faculty member for many years and had earned respect from students, faculty, administrators, and staff. She maintained a solid career record and had gotten used to being able to work her life around her classes and committee schedule.

Most people found her pleasant to work with, and she had built deep connections across the university. She had potential to be an administrator, to break down some of the blockades that were preventing institutional partners from collaborating and moving the institution into a sustained growth pattern. As the person who had built my first bridges into the department, I very much wanted her to support my bid for tenure, but I also recognized that she, too, presented a caution. If I decided that I wanted to do more than achieve tenure and to maintain my career as a teacher-scholar, I would have to decide how much flexibility and how much scheduling I would need to relinquish. Regardless, she also showed me that if I wanted to enjoy respect across widely varying university constituents as she did, I would have to build bridges to those persons deliberately and maintain them, even if that meant that I bit holes in my tongue.

And then there was Monique, my department head. I knew that she would sit on my tenure committee. She was a decent person who understood the university's policies and was completely committed to the university's mission. She didn't speak to us simply to speak to us as people. Unless we fit her plans or the university's mission, our needs didn't matter. In my first college meeting, I asked her a private question. Rather than allow me to remain quiet in a large, distinguished gathering, she announced to the dean that I had a question about the wording of the college's mission. Although it was not meant as a criticism, my question came across in that way. Of course, Monique avoided responsibility for this by putting me on the spot, even when I knew very little about the context in which I found myself. Additionally, Monique would volunteer weekends and holidays to support university programs, building sets for university dramatic productions voluntarily. Every time the university needed to make a change, like asking faculty collectively to renegotiate their contracts to take an 11% pay cut, she obliged and she encouraged others to do the same. Critical thinking about possible consequences of such decisions was heard as criticism, so the imminent possibility of burnout because she volunteered too much time, or the inability to recruit good faculty if everyone took an 11% pay cut, fell on deaf ears. I needed her as a partner, too. I had to recognize that I could not express my opinions about university policies and practices in her hearing. I also learned that I had to take care of myself and my own progress. Nonetheless, she would serve a crucial role in my ability to get tenure.

When the time came, I put together a strong packet. I worked with Tina to present my scholarship, teaching, and service in ways that university administrators would see as fitting the institutional mission. I leveraged Gertrude's exactitude to ensure that my packet was formatted properly and presented according to the department and university guidelines. I was unable to avoid having Jackson on my committee, and because I had worked hard not to dismiss his efforts or to puncture his ego, he did not completely dismiss my work as I thought he might, though as I had anticipated, he treated it as just barely meeting professional standards. Monique supported my bid for tenure as my department head. I got tenure.

Working with these faculty members early in my academic career provided me with an opportunity to observe the choices that faculty members can make about their positions and the ways that those choices and the determination to focus on bridges to and with others brings value to their departments, colleges, and universities. I took them as lessons, and they have stayed with me.

Building a bridge to Jackson was a tremendous challenge. He was prickly and difficult, and generally a weight to be borne. His fragile ego manifested itself in his superior attitude and his refusal to do more than the minimum required after tenure. Knowing that Jackson would never find another job, I had to consider how to manage that relationship without creating a blockade that would prevent the department from completing the very smallest curricular change. I had to learn that Jackson's bridges were built on appreciation and positive feedback, even for small things. I also learned that I could earn Jackson's respect, even Jackson's scholarly respect, by consistent effort and positive attitude. I also had to create a barrier solid enough to keep his disengagement and negativity from transmitting itself to me.

Gertrude presented her own challenges. Any bridges that she built eventually became blockades as people grew tired of being burned. Administrators and other faculty cast her perceptive observations and bright ideas aside because they came from her. Having burned her bridges one time too many, she faced blockades instead. Because she presented a barrage of information about what to fix, people had to build blockades to maintain their professional forward motion. Although I was able to turn her into an ally, I was not able fully to keep her from blockading herself in her own negative thought patterns, and neither were other faculty members. As a result, we all suffered through department meetings that involved blockading behaviors including entrenchments, yelling, and eventually the cursing of other people. Administrators took her energy and diverted it to small challenges that affected her personally, but had little impact on anyone else. She found herself arguing to teach at 8:00 a.m., a time administrators knew she wanted and other faculty did not. As she became aware that she had been set aside, she became progressively more disengaged, leaving the institution in a fit of rage and literally screaming at the dean that she was quitting in a public meeting. Once away from the university, she changed her behavior deliberately. Although she kept some of her "gotcha" attitude, she kept herself from engaging so deeply that every department and administrative decision was personal. She built bridges with her colleagues, paying attention to their scholarship, their families, and sharing her own interests. She earned permanent status at her next institution as well.

Monique presented challenges all her own. Because she didn't engage with department faculty as people, she had great difficulties getting the department to focus its collective efforts in one direction. She couldn't successfully facilitate department meetings or represent the department in negotiations for space or for faculty lines. When Jackson announced that I had married in order to further my tenure case, she had nothing to say. She wanted to prove herself as a future administrator and as a department chair, but her seemingly thoughtless acceptance of every policy change and every administrative move actually weakened her position. She thought that she was building bridges, but in effect, she built blockades. Her ineffective leadership did not go unnoticed. She needed partners in the department to advance any kind of agenda that she might have had, and by failing to treat her partners as people, focusing only on the work at hand and not attending to the human concerns of her department members, she left them thinking that she would walk across them in her career pursuits, committed more to her own success than to shared department success.

Although not in my department, Barry was another faculty member whose behavior I observed, and whose lessons about success and bridge-building have stuck with me. Barry was eager to support and help other people; in fact, he carried an extra burden—that of being an African American faculty member, and thus an important adviser to students who needed to see a person of color in that capacity. I needed to recognize Barry's personal investment in supporting students, especially students of color, and to build bridges that would allow me to advocate for Barry's kind of service as promotable, particularly when I became an administrator. Barry's "awesome" attitude brought a dose of positivity when collaboration wasn't going well or when faculty and administrators were building blockades. That positivity allowed Barry to see possibilities and to build bridges instead of blockades. So I learned that choosing a positive attitude could indeed produce positive results. I also noted that I had to be a little picky: Requests to advise a thesis, write a recommendation letter, create a course, and sponsor a student organization could not be equally important. I had to choose the ones that aligned most clearly with my values and the career trajectory that I imagined for myself. Finally, I learned that I had to be a realist. I couldn't teach my classes, maintain my research agenda, and keep all of the commitments that I made. Saying that I would write one recommendation letter meant that I might not be able to finish my article draft. Agreeing to be on a search committee meant that I might not be able to present at a faculty meeting. Barry's partnership made a difference for me. Positivity and forward thinking, I learned, are generally desirable characteristics. Still they must be coupled with a firm sense of purpose and a willingness to disappoint. This willingness to disappoint, I saw, was particularly difficult for Barry. I had the option of disappointing people, yet often, he did not because of a focus on shared success for himself and the African American students who sought him and literally lined up at his door for academic and life advice.

A focus on shared success might have benefited Tina the most of the faculty members in the department. Bridges to Tina were easy to build. She wanted to partner, knew the institution, and was willing to share her institutional knowledge. The respect that she earned was invaluable in my progress to tenure. The university tenure and promotion committee respected her and her judgment, so when she recommended me, her opinion carried weight. I learned from her that people have reasons for what they do. I learned to look for common ground and to reserve judgment. I learned how to be a partner and that I needed partners in order to succeed. Tina defined success for herself outside of the academy and did not think about what she might want to try out or where she might want to find a place in the academy that took full advantage of her skills and talents. (For a study of the devaluing of relational work, see Hanasono et al., 2019.) Had the university recognized her enviable bridge-building talents and helped her to find a definition of success that included those talents, they might have put themselves in a win-win situation that could have helped them to grow as they wanted.

The idea of shared success lies at the center of the challenge to building bridges and surmounting blockades. By sharing the responsibility for student advising, club sponsorship, and committee work with his colleagues, Barry can promote his own success, the success of the students about whom he cares so much, and the success of his colleagues. He can create spaces for them to grow, develop, and to try out their interests and ideas. Had he focused on shared successes, Jackson might have been willing to take on a little more than his bare minimum because he believed that when he needed to disengage a little, he might be able to do so. Gertrude might have been able to see that the constant fault-finding created a permanently negative feedback system and made *her* the enemy. A focus on shared success might have helped her—us—to stay away from such behaviors and to encourage each other in teaching, scholarship, and service. Like Barry, Jackson, and Gertrude, Monique's focus on herself and her own success led her to poor leadership behaviors and likely contributed to her eventual burnout and complete departure from academia. Rather than focusing on the team as humans first, academics second, Monique focused on the tasks she had to do. Department meetings eventually devolved to the point where they began with Monique's lists of duties and declarations that she wanted to step down from being chair. Because she had not built bridges to department members, no one was willing to take the risk of stepping forward to assume that responsibility. Monique experienced a mental health crisis and left academics. For Tina, a focus on shared success might have provided some intriguing direction for her career. Her colleagues might have been able to support her as she tried out administrative appointments and extended scholarly projects. Instead, without that focus, she stayed where she was, serving on important committees and building bridges but unable to attempt working in an administrative capacity within the institution that took advantage of her skills and interests. For one moment, the faculty focused on a shared goal—getting me through the tenure process. Then, project accomplished, everyone returned to their usual business.

No matter how much I declared that I could not have managed the process without them, no matter how many times they helped me to wrestle oppressive academic structures, ultimately a sense of shared success eluded us, perhaps because we also needed a shared direction. Getting tenured provided direction for me, and to some extent for my colleagues as well. Once we achieved that goal, however, we did not return to define a next step of success. We did not consider what we could do to help each other succeed, building bridges where we needed them. Instead, we focused on our own blockades. The team that helped me earn tenure broke.

So what can we learn about building bridges from my experience and the experiences of many other academics who inhabit the academy in various roles? Perhaps the first lesson is to question the myth that individual success is paramount. To succeed, we need teams with shared goals and directions. Second, we need to figure out shared successes and win-win opportunities that respect different skills supports all academic participants. Third, we can recognize and hear our partners' backstories and understand how they move us to make choices that seem strange or illogical. Finally, we can nurture the understanding that even thinking about and working in teams is a way to resist the exclusive beliefs and behaviors that lurk inside the academy. As a team, the department in which earned tenure was able to surmount the challenges in my case, but we were unable to impact the system so that the challenges we acknowledged inherent to the system—race, ethnicity, religious belief, sexual orientation, class, and the myth of meritocracy—would not impact future faculty and potentially contribute to change for higher education as a whole. If we want to dismantle those systems, we will have to build bridges, not blockades.

References

Grollman, E. A. (2014). The myth of meritocracy in academia. *Conditionally Accepted*. Retrieved from https://conditionallyaccepted.com/2014/04/17/meritocracy-in-academia/

Hanasono, L. A. K., Broido, E. M., Yacobucci, M. M., Root, K. V., Peña, S., & O'Neil, D. A. (2019). Secret service: Revealing gender biases in the visibility and value of faculty service. *Journal of Diversity in Higher Education, 12*(1), 85–98.

McNamee, S. J., & Miller, R. K., Jr. (2004). The meritocracy myth. *Sociation Today,* 2(1). Retrieved from http://www.ncsociology.org/sociationtoday/v21/merit.htm

CHAPTER NINE

The Academic Plus One

Emily E. Virtue and Drew Virtue

If birds of a feather flock together, why do so many academic couples struggle to find an academic nest to call home? The problem of dual-career couples is not new to higher education, yet when job seeking those who are in committed relationships with other academics must navigate roadblocks and red tape. While the term "dual-career couple" can refer to anyone in a committed relationship where both partners work in higher education, this chapter will discuss only those dual-career couples who both work (or hope to work) in teaching positions. In 2008, Schibinger, Henderson, and Gilmartin found that 36% of academics are in a dual-career relationship. Such relationships can be seen as either a boon or a burden for higher education institutions as employers are forced to consider additional people in the hiring process. With over a third of academics fitting the bill of "dual career," it might seem as though institutions would put forth considerable time and effort into recruiting, hiring, and retaining dual-career couples. But Wolf-Wendle, Twombly, and Rice (2004) found that most efforts have been on an ad hoc basis. Nationally, the lack of consistent policy suggests that institutions might not see the long-term value of dual-career hires or, at the very least, find the process of dual-career hires cumbersome or risky. Conversely, dual-career couples find the job search process a confusing maze of politics to navigate. This chapter will explore historical traditions of dual-career hiring, the politics of being hired, and the politics of being an "academically accommodated" (Loeb, 1997) partner or what we refer to as "the academic plus one." We'll share our own stories of being in a dual-career relationship as well as strategies to navigate some of the issues that academic couples may face.

Research on the concept of dual-career hiring began in earnest the 1980s and 1990s as researchers reported findings of partnered academics (Astin & Milem, 1997; Bird & Bird, 1987; Burke, 1988). Historical records and accounts show that almost as soon as women first earned PhDs (and perhaps before), academic couples filled the ranks of faculty members at institutions of higher education (Wolf-Wendle, Twombly, & Rice, 2004). Many predicted that the number of academic couples seeking jobs would increase, but it appears as though the number has remained steady. Yet, the problem of couples finding adequate and fulfilling jobs at the same or nearby institutions remains difficult. Though researchers predicted that there would be a shift in the academic labor market due to retirement (Finkelstein, Seal, & Schuster, 1998), the 2009 economic recession changed this prediction (PBS News Hour, 2013). Indeed, there are highly qualified academic couples clamoring for positions, but vacancies that at one time seemed imminent are now harder to find (PBS News Hour, 2013). The results of job searches often end up unequal as one partner may be offered a job commensurate with his or her qualifications while another may need to adapt expectations, take on a new position, or accept a position for which he or she is overqualified. In these cases, the academic plus one may feel less valued than his or her partner—and may not be the only one. Often the portrayal of the "plus one" goes beyond the mental perception of the individual but filters into the new academic community and may have lasting effects.

Perception Is Everything

At a gathering at the president's house before the start of the fall semester, Janet introduced herself to two men standing at a cocktail table, stating that she was a new lecturer in the Economics Department. Her new colleagues beamed, "Oh wonderful! You must be here because of your husband's job! He teaches for the Accounting Department, doesn't he?"

After deciding to go back to school full time to pursue a doctorate, a lecturer was told she could still adjunct for the department. She would no longer be allowed to have her own office. Instead, the department chair informed her that she would have to occupy a small table in the corner of her husband's office.

In a department meeting during the spring semester, the chair updates ev-

eryone on the search process for the vacant tenure-track position. "We were able to offer the job to our first-choice candidate. Her partner is also a teacher in our discipline and we've been able to fund a new position for the spouse as well. This means we'll be able to serve more students in the department next year."

These vignettes reflect personal experiences as a dual-career academic. The practices highlighted are not uncommon in higher education: People make assumptions about others' value based on who they are partnered to or what they might have to offer the university. What each of these stories has in common is that the value of a spouse is assigned to them, sometimes even before the spouse has interacted with others on the campus. While some are lucky and are immediately viewed as a new asset for the university (as demonstrated in the third vignette) others are treated as part of a package or are physically pushed aside.

The Politics, Policies, and Procedures of Hiring

Perhaps the most important element of the dual-career or spousal-hire process concerns the nature of a couple's relationship itself. Couples may go on the job market at the same time or their job searches may be separated by a number of years; however, couples should consider the nature of the job search process and, ultimately, what it means for them to have a "successful" search. Some items to consider for a dual-career search include the type of job and its expectations, the type of institution, the location of the institution, the level of permanence associated with a job search, and the level of happiness between both individuals in a couple.

While institutions may offer multiple types of teaching positions, potential dual-career academics need to decide if the positions will fulfill their professional expectations. Individuals can teach in adjunct positions that include a partial course load, lecturer positions that include a full course load but typically no service or scholarship requirements, instructor positions that include a full course load with minimal service or scholarship requirements, postdoc positions that include research expectations, visiting professor positions that have varying responsibilities depending on the institution, and tenure/tenure-track positions that incorporate a full course load with service and scholarship expectations. In addition to these roles, potential job candidates can also seek administration roles in which they may still teach, though the primary focus of the position may be on administrative tasks or nontraditional teaching roles with responsibilities that vary (e.g., directing a center that is focused on providing pedagogical resources to other faculty, staff, or administrators). While there are a number of different roles associated with teaching, the roles themselves vary significantly in terms of pay, benefits, title (and its perceived prestige), and the duration of contract (e.g., nine months versus twelve months).

In addition to the different types of teaching jobs, the type of institution also presents different variables that dual-career couples should consider when applying for jobs. Some institutions place more emphasis on research whereas other institutions place more emphasis on teaching. Similarly, the degree of focus on research will typically affect the course load an individual has to teach, whether it be two, three, or four or more courses per semester. Dual-career academics should also determine whether they want to work at two- or four-year schools or public or private schools. Institutions also vary in the size of the student population, the geographical location of the institution, and the level of specificity of programs—each of which should at least be considered during a job search. For example, an English department includes literature courses, but does it also contain professional writing courses if a candidate's background is in technical writing? Or does an institution offer a rarer program, like marine biology? Job candidates are most likely familiar with the types of teaching jobs and the types of institutions and have considered them while applying for jobs, a task that includes setting priorities and making challenging decisions. However, the task becomes more challenging when two people are navigating through all these choices at the same time. Each is trying to reach an endpoint that complements both individuals' academic pursuits, while also ensuring that both individuals are content with the outcome.

The following sections describe different strategies for an academic couple to find jobs that meet both of their needs. Ultimately, academic couples are in a unique situation in which it becomes more challenging to separate their professional and personal lives, especially as it pertains to that couple's relationship. To that effect, we have spent a lot of time working to define what it means for us as a couple to be content in both our personal relationship and our professional goals.

Communication

From the outset of the job search process, the couple needs to communicate their needs and desires with one another. While this may seem obvious, it represents an important foundation for the job search process. We suggest that the couple identify where they are both willing to compromise and what points are nonnegotiable. For example, we found that we both had strict geographic parameters related to where we would and would not consider living. Since one of us was further along professionally in terms of the tenure process, we agreed that we would not consider any positions that seemed a step backward. To accomplish this primary goal, we also recognized that we may have to return to the "nonnegotiable" list to reconsider: If there were good jobs in an area outside of our geographic preference, would we be willing to give up a desired location in favor of two jobs we'd be pleased with?

Communication should be honest and daily—it should happen just as often as your opinions, preferences, and opportunities change. For us, this meant taking a walk every day at lunch to assess where we were in the process and what new factors we might need to consider. Bird and Schnurman-Crook (2005) note that successful dual-career couples engaged in "couple's talk" and found that most couples encouraged open communication.

Playing the Best/Worst-Case Scenario Game

The job search, negotiation, and moving is a process that can only be described as evolving. One day you may have had an excellent phone interview and feel confident you know where you'll land. A week later, you may find yourself without a request for a second interview and wondering how you will make ends meet if nothing works out. While there is not a survival guide for academics who find themselves lost in the job hunt, playing a simulation of your possible outcomes may help.

We found that at the beginning of the job search process it was best (and fun) to play the "if you could go anywhere and do anything" game. It allowed us to think expansively and wondrously about all of the possibilities before us. We could identify dream jobs, institutions, and locations. From there, we narrowed down our ideas into stepping stones that seemed appropriate for those big goals. Finally, we pragmatically thought about how to accomplish this search from a logistical standpoint (we'll cover resources later in the chapter). All our dreaming out loud allowed us the freedom to consider the best for ourselves and one another.

But what do you do when those big dreams seem unreachable or at least unlikely in the immediate future? We have found that it is helpful (and emotionally and mentally healthy) to play "worst-case scenario." What if one of us gets an offer six states away? Do we live apart? Where do the kids go? What if we're both given offers at different institutions? What if we have to stay in our current jobs for another year? How do we develop professionally in that time? There are no easy answers, so we will not try to offer any. However, we have found that playing the game (which of course, relates back to communication) has been key to our relationship and our respective professions. We have been able to draw boundary lines for what is and is not acceptable in our lives and reconsidered possibilities as they arise. At times, our personalities and visions for the future have been challenged, but ultimately we have learned that flexibility is an invaluable skill for dual-career couples to possess.

Number-One Defender

In addition to the need for communication, we also recognize how vital it is to be certain you have one another's back, both on and off the court, so to speak. When the time comes to actually negotiate for a job (or two), it is vital that academic couples remember their roles as both potential employee and number-one defender. Negotiations can be stressful and time consuming, which can sometimes play into the employer's favor. Even when your own job offer sounds like a dream, it cannot come at the cost of your partner's livelihood and happiness. It is always appropriate in a job negotiation to ask for a bit of time to talk with your partner.

Once you have made it through the negotiation process and have arrived on campus, it is still vital to remember your role as defender. As exemplified earlier in the chapter vignettes, being a spousal hire can carry with it preconceived notions and assumptions. While we do not mean to suggest that an atmosphere could be hostile, academic couples should be deliberate in how they talk about their partner's professional careers. Rather than accepting the common comment, "You're here because of your partner's job" you might say, "We were both hired at the same time." Even if one partner is hired at a higher rank than the other, academic couples and institutions benefit from moving the conversation away from who "belongs" at an institution to a more productive conversation about what both people have to offer.

Greer and Poe (2005) state that traditionally couples have used the "I will follow him" approach wherein one spouse (usually the female in a heterosexual couple) will move when the male partner has a better offer elsewhere. Though gender seems to be less of an issue today, the notion of one spouse "following" the other is still prevalent. Schibinger, Henderson, and Gilmartin (2008) note the hiring stigma in which "less good" partners attach themselves to the primary hire. This stigma is unfounded as second hires are not less productive than their peers (Schibinger et al., 2008). Nevertheless, because of the niche interests of many academics, candidates must apply when a position is available and often that means a partner must move to a new campus as well. To address this issue, the American Association of University Professors (AAUP) recognized that supporting dual-career couples benefits both candidates and hiring institutions. These "defender" roles are particularly important as the academic plus ones continue to navigate their roles at an institution.

Politics of Promotion: Moving up After a Step Back

In an ideal world, each candidate will find a position that is commensurate with their experience during their job search process. But, for many dual-career couples, one of the members of the couple may accept a part-time, temporary, or non-teaching position. Through informal research, conversations with dual-career couples, and various news outlets, one theme remains constant: Patience is a virtue.

When Drew accepted his tenure-track position, the institution was not able to offer Emily any accommodations. However, quickly after arriving in our new home (two months before the start of the semester), Emily was offered an adjunct position. While not ideal, this allowed Emily to get to know the department chair, other faculty members, and administrators. Over time, Emily's previous work experience and research interests became known to the college dean who suggested she apply for a fellowship with the provost's office. Taking on the fellowship position allowed Emily to transition into a full-time teaching role and develop professionally by coordinating academic initiatives on campus. This process transpired over three years, and while that certainly can seem like a long time to many, patience is often what is required as an academic plus one. Patience and support from one's partner is also key to navigating the long and winding road to full-time employment.

As Emily continued to wait for a full-time position to open up, at times she found it difficult not to feel undervalued by colleagues, administrators, and even students. It is not uncommon for professionals to be protective of their career-related identity and want to be fulfilled by it. Bird and Schnurman-Crook (2005) found that individuals in their study had all invested in their professional identity and committed to maintaining this identity. Yet, when the academic plus one feels as though they are not being adequately challenged or supported in their role, their professional identity may suffer. It is vital that partners continue in their role as defender (and encourager) during the periods when the academic plus one is continually job searching or more realistically job waiting.

Waiting Is the Hardest Part: The Politics of Hiring the Academic Plus One

While the goal of each candidate search is to hire the most appropriate person for each position, consideration should be given to factors that may impact whether a candidate will accept a position. Three factors that should be considered in the hiring process are family matters, career following, and financial impact.

A candidate is not merely a list of accomplishments on a curriculum vitae. While those in the hiring process may fall into the habit of thinking only about what a candidate brings to campus professionally, we must remember that many candidates bring family with them. In the case of dual-career academics, family dynamics may extend not only to a spouse or partner but also to children. Institutions should try not to interfere with a candidate's personal life, yet an awareness of how family dynamics can impact the hiring process is crucial. Magner (2006) argues, "If 'the best possible faculty member' seeks a partner accommodation, then the primary purpose of the search is best served by trying to meet that request." This assertion rings true for both hiring managers and candidates, yet concerns from others on campus about such considerations are often voiced.

The benefits of working with dual-career couples extends not only to the couples themselves but also the institution. When both partners are gainfully (and happily) employed, turnover rates decrease and longevity at an institution can increase. Solidifying new hires as long-term employees will reduce budgetary expenses for filling the position after a short amount of time (this may occur when the new hire's spouse does not find employment at the institution or elsewhere locally).

Conclusion

As institutions seek to fill faculty vacancies, they should employ policies and programs that will aid candidates' partners. Programs should include supporting partners in terms of finding available positions, building partnerships between hiring entities (such as department heads and human resource directors), and avoiding "quick fixes" (such as hiring partners as contingent or adjunct faculty). Both the AAUP and leading scholars in the field of higher education note the importance of these guidelines (Jaschik, 2010; Loeb, 1997; Wolf-Wendel, Twombly, & Rice, 2004).

June (2009) notes that institutions that already have policies or officers in place to aid dual-career couples are invaluable and often have better access to potential jobs. Such resources may lead to temporary positions that can help partners get their foot in the door, increasing access to future full-time positions. While temporary positions are not ideal (and some have argued against them), these positions nevertheless can serve as both a career and financial placeholder. In addition to resources on campus such as human resource personnel, department heads, and career services staff, partnerships should also include businesses outside of academia in the surrounding community. West Virginia University (Dual Career Program, 2018) and the University of California, San Diego (2018) each have successful partnerships with local business and combine these partnerships with coaching and résumé consultation to aid the job search process beyond the campus.

Ultimately, the goals of both candidates and hiring managers overlap in myriad ways that suggest all institutions of higher education should create policies and procedures for dual-career academics. In institutions where shared governance is a priority, those on faculty and staff senates may advocate for increased consideration to dual-career couples. Finally, hiring managers may find the best candidates for their campus positions if they recognize how broadly reaching experience in higher education can be. Those with teaching experience may very likely have additional strengths in advising, counseling, event management, curriculum development, or academic support. When dual-career couples apply to a university, an attitude of "how can our university benefit from these skills" may open the door to long-term benefits for both employees and employers alike.

References

Astin, H. F., & Milem, J. F. (1997). The status of academic couples in US institution. In M. A. Ferber & J. W. Loeb *Academic Couples: Problems and Promises* (128–155). Urbana, IL: University of Illinois Press.

Bird, G. W., & Bird, G. A. (1987). In pursuit of academic careers: Observations and reflections of a dual-career couple. *Family Relations*, 97–100.

Bird, G. W., & Schnurman-Crook. (2005). Professional identity and coping behaviors in dual-career couples. *Family relations, 54*(1), 145–160.

Burke, R. J. (1988). Some antecedents of work-family conflict. *Journal of Social Behavior and Personality, 3*(4), 287.

Finkelstein, M. J., Seal, R., & Schuster, J. H. (1998). New entrants to the full-time faculty of higher education institutions. 1993 National Study of Postsecondary Faculty (NSOPF-93). Statistical Analysis Report. *National Center for Educational Statistics*. Retrieved from https://files.eric.ed.gov/fulltext/ED424831.pdf

Greer, R. M., & Poe, R. E. (2005). Developmental aspects of dual-career relationships: Reflections and issues. *College Student Affairs Journal,* 24(2), 162–169.

Jaschik, S. (2010, September 1). Doing "dual career" right. *Inside Higher Ed*. Retrieved from https://www.insidehighered.com/news/2010/09/01/dual

June, A. W. (2009, March 6). Employment for spouses gets harder to find. *Chronicle of Higher Education, 55*(26), A1. Retrieved from https://www.chronicle.com/article/Employment-for-Spouses-Gets/6950

Loeb, J. W. (1997). Programs for academic partners: How well do they work? In M. A. Ferber & J. W. Loeb (Eds.), *Academic couples: Problems and promises* (pp. 270–300). Champaign-Urbana, IL: University of Illinois Press.

Magner, D. (2009, March 6). The fairness of partner hiring. *Chronicle of Higher Education, 55*(26). Retrieved from https://www.chronicle.com/blogs/onhiring/the-fairness-of-partner-hiring/899

PBS News Hour. (2013, March 18). College see older workforce holding on to coveted positions [Video file]. Retrieved from https://www.youtube.com/watch?v=2LGLYoyPjgE

Schibinger, L., Henderson, A. D., & Gilmartin, S. K. (2008). *Dual career academic couples: What universities need to know*. Michelle R. Clayman Institute for Gender Research, Stanford University. Retrieved from http://gender.stanford.edu/sites/g/files/sbiybj5961/f/publications/dualcareerfinal_0.pdf

University of California, San Diego. (2018). *Partner opportunities program*. Retrieved from https://aps.ucsd.edu/services/pop/index.html

West Virginia University. (2018). *Dual Career Program*. Retrieved from https://careers.wvu.edu/career-opportunities/dual-career-program

Wolf-Wendel, L., Twombly, S. B., & Rice, S. (2004). *The two-body problem: Dual-career couple hiring practices in higher education*. Baltimore, MD: Johns Hopkins University Press.

CHAPTER TEN

Training for Academic Leadership in the 21st Century:

It's All About the Group

STEVE ESTES

> *The reason that university politics is so vicious is because stakes are so small.*
>
> —Henry Kissinger (Good Reads, 2019)

ONE OF THE WELL-KNOWN aspects of the contemporary university is that academic life can be quite "political." Why is this so? It would seem that the ingredients for a highly functional political culture are all in place: a well-educated and motivated workforce, administrators who are dedicated to fulfilling the mission of the organization, wonderful working environments, and a highly regarded profession. What could be the problem with university politics?

Kissinger's maxim is interesting. Faculty and administrators see it as a humorous rendition of campus culture that both groups agree with when we are not in the spotlight. But it is also an uncomfortable reality when legislators or trustees—outsiders—are being critical of university life. An anonymous saying supports Kissinger's sentiment and adds perspective: "The politics inside the Washington, D.C. beltway are *nothing* compared to the politics of a small, midwestern liberal arts college."

By "political" it is meant that the discussion of "the common good" too often devolves into acrimonious and non-functioning debate, where the debate participants are the faculty on one side and the university administration on the other. To paint with a broad brush on these suffering campuses, faculty do not see their campus administrators as good leaders, and campus administrators do not see faculty as good followers. This is a far cry from what "political" can be in the best of circumstances. When relations are good the discussions of the campus community, faculty, and administration alike, head toward what is best for *all* of the community.

In contrast, politics in the idealized campus community are representative, functional, and inclusive. Members of high-functioning campuses have a shared sense of values; there is an implicit agreement regarding the nature of campus culture, a set of agreed-on goals, and the leaders of the body politic are seen as "the best and brightest" of the group. Leaders are trusted to represent the community and are seen to carry out what is in the community's best interests.

A sense of trust too often is missing on the contemporary university campus. Too often faculty who become administrators are seen as having gone "to the dark side" and appear to be something alien from what they once were. And, conversely, administrators operating with good intentions come to see their former faculty colleagues as lazy, naïve, isolated, selfish dilettantes with little regard for what it takes to make a university run well. The split between the leader and the led is complete when faculty begin to "wait out" incumbent university leaders, and university leaders stop listening to the faculty senate in making decisions.

Some universities are very well led. Professionals on both sides of this relationship fortunate enough to have worked in a high-functioning environment enjoy a healthy relationship between faculty and administration. But when asked, these fortunate colleagues often have a hard time explaining just *why* their experience is a positive one. This chapter focuses on the dynamic between university leaders and followers and suggests that there may be a misunderstanding of how leadership works. What we *think* is working well may not be, in fact, really what is going on. And our potential solutions to bad leadership may in fact lead to the very problems that we are trying to solve.

One scholar who has studied culture and moral behavior is Alasdair Macintyre (2007), and his insights into the problems of contemporary culture provide insights into the nature of leadership. Macintyre's (2007) *After Virtue* is one of the most well-known moral treatises of the 20th century, and he explains that how we behave and think about right behavior is a complex, contingent process that operates at a cultural level. Without going too deeply into this excellent work, Macintyre argues that the quest to live a moral life in our times is enhanced by understanding the problem of *emotivism*. "Emotivism" as a philosophy of our times is one where *characters*, the idealized role that exists in the postmodern world, are understood to come in one of three types: rich aesthetes, bureaucratic managers, and therapists. Each *character* (not to be confused with someone who has good or bad character, but the *role* one plays on a campus) interacts with the others, and the prevailing sentiment of this philosophy is the following dictum: "I think this is good, so should you" (Gibson, 1993, p. 20). In Gibson's (1993) analysis, "the individual suffers the manipulations of the bureaucratic manager, while being sustained by the therapist, to chase the dream of the lifestyle of the rich aesthete" (p. 23).

What a cynical description, especially when applied to university life. Yet it seems accurate when one focuses on the non-functioning university. According to Gibson (1993): "The individual [faculty] suffers the manipulations of the bureaucratic manager [university administrator], [and] is sustained by the therapist [one's disciplinary colleagues], to chase the dream of the rich aesthete [the idealized scholar]." We may not like the interpretation or explanation, but it seems to fit on poorly led campuses. Administrators fulfill the role of Macintyre's "bureaucratic manager," and faculty fulfill the role of the "rich aesthete."

How accurate is this criticism? Too often this condition seems to be the case, and the incidence of this condition seems to be increasing (Barnett, 2000; Block & Estes, 2012). Faculty complain of university administrators making bad decisions that occur without consultation: Raising enrollments to increase the budget, promoting intercollegiate athletics to market the university, using university property to bring commerce to the college campus, and a host of other decisions seem at odds with the values of the faculty. Faculty in these situations feel like pawns on the chessboard, doing the bidding of administrators and simply serving as labor in the university marketplace. In such an environment the word "politics" seems appropriate: Administrators (read Macintyre's "bureaucratic managers") make decisions on the basis of "I think this is good; so should you." Faculty cynically use the "mushroom theory" to describe the knowledge they have of how decisions are made: Faculty are kept in the dark and are fed a diet of "waste" information—just enough to provide a patina of plausibility to justify whatever decision is made. Conversely, administrators see faculty as concerned primarily with parking, raises, and minimizing teaching loads. *Emotivism* seems to explain this situation well.

Not all universities are led by bureaucratic managers, of course. And not all faculty are accurately described by these observations and analysis. But enough faculty and administrators will admit to living in such an environment that the relationship of university leadership and faculty culture is worth studying. In these academic environments it is fair to say that administrators have lost the trust of the faculty. Specifically, administrators in these environments no longer enjoy the trust of faculty, that feeling that the administration shares the *values* of the academy. And what values might I be referring to? The value of the lifestyle of pursuing knowledge for its own sake and having as a goal the sharing and dissemination of knowledge so that the world is a better place for having the contemporary university in it.

This chapter takes the position that the differences between university administrators and faculty—the "politics" that seem to get worked out by the bureaucratic managers of the university who say "I think this is good, so should you"—is a failure of leadership. This is not to say that it is *only* university administrators who fail in this leadership situation; it is *also* to say that university faculty do not understand what leadership *is*. A good, contemporary understanding of what good leadership is and does will help both sides of this relationship and will help by changing Macintyre's emotivist dictum to read something like, "*We* think this is good, and so should the world."

If this rendering of the contemporary university is accurate, how did we get to this place? Others have chronicled the evolution of the modern university better than can be done here (Barzun, 1993; Bok, 2003; Bok, 2006; Rosovsky, 1991). It seems entire wings of libraries are dedicated to the study of the modern university. Is it possible that this emotivist condition is a failure of leadership, of followership, or a combination of both? It follows that the culture of the academy will produce *both* faculty and administrators who share the same characteristics. We spend years in training to become faculty; one might even say that we indoctrinate. The selection process is rigorous, the training is long and focused, and only a fortunate few (hopefully the deserving) earn permanent positions on a faculty. The characteristics of the faculty are incredibly varied, but a majority of faculty share a common set of values regarding research, teaching, and service. One thing faculty are not trained in, though, is *followership*. Indeed, it is arguable that faculty are trained to be "independent operators," pursuing a line of inquiry that is unique and distinct from that of our peers. Outside of the generalized description of being a "member of the academy," we have little in common with one another. We are, in short, not trained to be members of a group who "follow."

Nor are we trained to lead. Indeed, a common lament among academic administrators is that we do not train for faculty for their role of administrator. It appears that when one moves from faculty to administrator one "hits the ground running" and mostly tries to keep one's head above the water. In such a state, the administrator adapts by conforming to the environment rather than carrying forward the values of the academy. The article "8 Deans Share" in the *Chronicle of Higher Education* (2019) summarized the experiences of eight deans, and common among their observations was that some aspect of their leadership was lacking, for which they could have been better prepared. In other words, they had not trained to lead as well as they would have liked. Comments included, "Training would have helped me to understand how information that is essential to the college's operations flows both among staff members and between the staff and the dean"; "What was new to me—and for which I received little formal training—was my leadership role during times of crisis"; "A course for new deans that offers insights on workplace culture would be valuable"; "I quickly discovered that the scope of pulling together necessary meetings of constituents in my division . . . made effective organization, and indeed simply initially scheduling such meetings, a challenge that most are unprepared for before becoming dean"; and "All new deans should take a leadership course during their first year" (*Chronicle of Higher Education*, 2019).

Given that every dean in the article voiced the same need for leader training, it would seem that training for academic leadership would be commonplace. But, of course, it is not; were leadership training commonplace then the observation of these deans would be positive toward their training. The failure to train for academic leadership is seen in both traditional academic units as well as those that are highly specialized. For instance, Allan Detsky, a division head and chief of medicine, offers a possible explanation as to why academic leaders continually underprepare: Academic leaders "are often chosen on the basis of success in the core activities in research, education and patient care rather than on the basis of demonstrated leadership and management skills. Indeed, most academic leaders in the past have 'learned on the job'" (Detsky, 2010, p. XX). **[AU: Please add page number for quote. Reference citation uses 2011. Please reconcile]**

These academic leaders have a point: Training for their leader role will help them as leaders. But all of these leaders also have in common an implicit agreement as to what leadership *is*: These administrators see themselves as the *cause* of good leadership—each in his or her own way is the focal point of leadership. This chapter argues, though, that focusing on the *leader* dismisses the important other half of the equation—the *led*. All of the leaders discussed would agree that getting the communities they lead to *follow* is their goal, and in doing so they will be more effective in their leader roles. But just what each would to do to "achieve" leadership was a mystery to them until they actually began their job.

These administrators are not alone in their quest to understand leadership and to train for it and just what "leadership" is subject to immense effort and scholarship. Recent literature in leadership has begun to focus on followers. A short summary of the history of leadership scholarship provides a context for this perspective and provides some insights into how good academic leaders might view their units, their universities, and their role in them as leaders. Perhaps one of the best summaries of this recent approach to understanding leadership was developed by Alexander Haslam, Stephen Reicher, and Michael Platow (2011) in *The New Psychology of Leadership: Identity, Influence, and Power*. Haslam and colleagues (2011) argue that the traditional means of understanding leadership—one that is implicitly assumed by the academic leaders cited—takes the position that the leader in some mystical way *causes* followers to think and act in ways that help an organization achieve its mission.

This understanding of leadership is very old, so old in fact that leadership scholars throughout the 19th and 20th centuries accepted this basic relationship of *leader* and *led* without questioning its validity. One of the first attempts to understand leadership in this way was Plutarch (2001) where, in a series of 23 paired biographies of famous Greeks and Romans who lived during the first and second century AD, he explored the influence of character on the lives and destinies of celebrated leaders. Plutarch was most concerned with capturing his subject's common moral virtues and failings, trying to understand just what made these leaders successful and, implicitly, offering a model of leadership that could be copied.

Retired Army General Stanley McChrystal (McChrystal, Eggers, & Mangone, 2019) and his team of leadership researchers has picked up on this thread, but has, in a sense, flipped it on its head. Rather than focus on the leader as Plutarch, and untold numbers of leadership researchers have done, McChrystal focuses on the *follower*. He does so because it appears that leadership is much more dynamic and contextual than was previously understood. Formerly leadership scholarship focused on the traits that can be identified in leaders. As the thinking went, if one could emulate these traits then one could also become a successful leader.

McChrystal agrees with this formula, but only in part. Successful leaders are, McChrystal argues, a *reflection* of what followers value. Good leaders embody the values of the led, make them come alive, and represent that community's values to the world. In the end, McChrystal argues that leaders are a reflection of what makes us human in the first place.

McChrystal and colleagues note that leadership has historically been construed as "a process driven, action-oriented practice" (p. 369). In this sense, leadership is the process of influencing a group toward some predefined outcome. Leadership is something that is designed and executed by the leader, and his or her effectiveness is determined by how well the community of followers were influenced by that leader to achieve the desired result. But McChrystal argues that this definition is the outcome of a *mythology* of leadership—a widely believed but unverified and unverifiable set of understandings that, while seemingly coherent, in fact takes us off track and does not yield an understanding of what leadership really is. The nine deans, and most of the leadership literature to date, follow the outlines of these myths. A summary of these myths and how we interact with them explains their popularity, and both their successes and limitations.

McChrystal and colleagues (2019) describe the three myths as the "Formulaic," the "Attribution," and the "Results" myth. McChrystal and colleagues (2019) use "myth" in a sophisticated way, and his argument is persuasive. Myths are powerful cultural tools that explain much about cultural attitudes, beliefs, and values:

> Myths are stories; they are attitudes extracted from stories; they are "the way things are" as people in a particular society believe them to be; and they are the models people refer to when they try to understand their world and its behavior. Myths are the patterns; of behavior, of belief, and of perception which people have in common. Myths are not deliberately, or necessarily consciously, fictitious. They provide good, "workable" ways by which the contradictions in a society, the contrasts and conflicts which normally arise among people, among ideals, among the confusing realities, are somehow reconciled, smoothed over, or at least made manageable and tolerable. (quoted in Estes, 1990, p. 47)

Understood in this way, the contemporary understanding of how leadership and followership relate to one another can be explained as one based on popular myths. It is important to note that myths are not *necessarily* false; they just happen to be so. What is key in this definition is *belief*. The theme embodied in a myth is *believed* to be true, and that is what gives the myth its power. This definition can therefore explain our belief and faith in the scientific method, mathematics, or any method we use to operate in culture. We *believe*. Myths explain to us and others how the world (read leadership) works, and we *believe* in this understanding. So just what are these myths, and how do they have an impact on how faculty and administrators relate to one another?

The formulaic myth "reflects our desire to tame leadership into a static checklist, notwithstanding the reality that leadership is intensely contextual and always dependent upon particular circumstances that change form moment to moment and from place to place" (McChrystal et al., 2019, p. 371). Much of the leadership literature to date, for example Plutarch's *Lives*, but also much of the biographical leadership literature, takes this perspective.

If one can just determine the traits a leader possesses that make up his or her character, then one can simply emulate those traits and a leader will be made. The nine deans discussed earlier in this chapter rely on (and believe in) this myth in their quest for training. If they can just study the subject enough, and follow the exercises in the lesson plan, then they can acquire the skills and traits needed to be successful in their administrative duties. Once acquired then, they will know how to do the work necessary to accomplish college and school goals.

The attribution myth "misrepresents leadership as little more than a process directed by the leader and, in this view, outcomes are attributable mostly to that leader" (McChrystal et al., 2019, p. 376). In a sense, this is the flip side of the formulaic myth. The nine deans discussed earlier are willing to work hard in, and take responsibility for, their administrative duties. The consequence of doing so is that they will be considered "good" deans, having delivered on plans made, and their colleges and schools will reap the benefits of having executed strategic plans. In such a universe, faculty would attribute the success of the college or school to the leadership of the dean, and all is good with a good administrator at the helm. As McChrystal and colleagues note, however, the myth of the "heroic" leader is often embellished, while at the same time incomplete. No leader is ever as heroic as the myth makes one believe, and no myth is detailed enough to explain all of the facets of the leader's life so that one has a comprehensive understanding of the interaction of the leader and her followers.

McChrystal's third myth is results, the idea that the outcome of the work of the leader is the measure of the leader's ability. McChrystal and colleagues argue that this myth is a "falsehood," the idea "that the objective results of the leader's activity are more important than her words or style or appearance. The truth is that when we look closely, we see leadership as much in what our leaders symbolize as in what they accomplish" (p. 378). Again, one can see that there is an overemphasis on the leader relative to followers. More importantly for this argument, though, is that this myth reduces what faculty as *followers* often look for in a university administrator. If we believe that leaders "deliver" only results, then we are likely to be disappointed because leaders are implicitly expected to do something quite different. Much, even most, of the "results" work of the university is done at the department level by faculty doing research, teaching, and service and is measured by publications, student outcomes, and service projects.

If the formulaic, attribution, and results styles of leadership are myths, then what should we be looking for on the well-led campus? To answer that we need to retrain ourselves as to what *leadership* really is. Doing so is a reality check, and both explain what is going on at the well-led campus and what can be turned around at the poorly led campus.

McChrystal and his group set out to understand *how* and *why* any group follows the leader and how leadership gives meaning to the follower and the group. McChrystal and his group (2019) came up with the following guidelines that help us understand what leadership really is:

1. Leadership is contextual and dynamic and therefore must be constantly modulated and therefore cannot be boiled down to a formula.
2. Leadership is more an emergent property of a complex system with rich feedback and less a one-directional process.
3. The leader is vitally important to leadership but not for the reasons we usually ascribe to him or her. It is often more about the symbolism, meaning, and future potential leaders hold for their system and less about the results they produce.

In sum, "Leadership is a complex system of relationships between leaders and followers in a particular context that provides meaning to its members" (McChrystal et al., 2019, p. 379). In terms of the problem of the contemporary faculty, what faculty *want* is a university administrator who *represents* and *symbolizes* the life of the faculty.

McChrystal's analysis is similar to that of Haslam and colleagues (2011): Leadership is a much more nuanced and complex relationship than it is usually understood to be. Haslam and colleagues and other social psychologists define leadership as a social activity that provides a number of tangible outcomes all of which *focus on the group*:

- Leaders fulfill the function of serving as an in-group prototype—a model of behaviors, values, and attitudes that are seen as typical of what "one of us" would do and be.
- Leaders are seen as in-group champions; they represent the "best" that

we can be in our environment.

- Leaders craft a sense of social identity; followers *want* to be like the leader, to possess the values that they believe that the leader lives by.

Using the guidelines that McChrystal and Haslam and their colleagues developed, one might see university administrators and faculty in a different light. Anecdotally, at universities that are well led it *does* seem that the administrators are one of the faculty, and good faculty are appreciated and cheered by administrators as excellent representatives of the academy. Substitute "administrators" for "leaders" in Haslam's outcomes and one can see how the distinction between the leader and the led begins to fade away.

From the faculty side of the equation, it becomes easier to identify just what it is about good administration that we look for. Faculty want an administrator to be a "model" of behavior, values, and attitudes—in short, a representative of faculty culture. Faculty want administrators to be an in-group champion, to represent the faculty "at our best." Finally, we want administrators to craft a sense of what it means to be a member of the academy. While faculty are doing the hard work of university business, we expect administrators to "have our backs" by telling the world just what the academy is all about, why it is good for the world, and how to sell this image to the larger culture.

Changing how we understand leadership is going to be a heavy lift. Telling someone what good leadership is, or what good followership is, is easy. Getting that same person to believe what good leadership and followership are is another matter. Old habits and thoughts die hard. But it must begin somewhere, and McChrystal, Haslam, their colleagues, and others doing current leadership scholarship seem to be making inroads as to what we expect in our best leaders and telling that story. One can hope that many will hear the message and make that understanding the "new mythology" of leadership.

References

Barnett, R. (2000). *Realizing the university in an age of supercomplexity.* Philadelphia, PA: Open University Press.

Barzun, J. (1993). *The American university: How it runs, where it is going* (2nd ed.). Chicago, IL: University of Chicago Press.

Block, B., & Estes, S. (2011). Supercomplexity in higher education kinesiology. *Quest, 63*(2), 179–96.

Bok, D. (2003). *Universities in the marketplace: The commercialization of higher education.* Princeton, NJ: Princeton University Press.

Bok, D. (2006). *Our underachieving colleges: A candid look at how much students learn and why they should be learning more.* Princeton, NJ: Princeton University Press.

Chronicle of Higher Education. (2019, January 27). *8 deans share: What I wish I had known.* Retrieved from https://www.chronicle.com/article/8-Deans-Share-What-I-Wish-I/245551

Detsky, A. S. (2011). How to be a good academic leader. *Journal of General Internal Medicine, 26*(1), 88–90.

Estes, S. G. (1990). *Sport myth as lived experience* (Unpublished doctoral dissertation). Ohio State University, Columbus, OH.

Gibson, J. (1993). *Performance versus results: A critique of values in contemporary sport.* Albany, NY: State University of New York Press.

Good Reads. (2019). *Henry Kissinger quotes.* Retrieved from https://www.goodreads.com/author/quotes/28442.Henry_Kissinger

Haslam, S. A., Reicher, S., & Platow, M. (2011). *The new psychology of leadership: Identity, influence, and power.* New York, NY: Psychology Press.

Macintyre, A. (2007). *After virtue: A study in moral theory* (3rd ed.) Notre Dame, IN: University of Notre Dame Press.

McChrystal, S., Eggers, J., & Mangone, J. (2019). *Leaders: Myth and reality.* New York, NY: Portfolio/Penguin.

Plutarch. (2001). *Plutarch's Lives/ the Dryden translation (Volume 1).* New York, NY: The Modern Library.

Robertson, J. (1980). *American myth, American reality.* New York, NY: Hill and Wang.

Rosovsky, H. (1991). *The university: An owner's manual.* New York, NY: Norton.

CHAPTER ELEVEN

Living on the Edge:

Embracing the Corners Where We Meet

LAURA M. PIPE, PHD

You can't be on the edge if there is no edge.

—Thrasher (1997)

IN FAMED SKATEBOARDING LITERATURE *Thrasher* magazine, there often exists sage advice for the would-be leader. One important piece of collaboration advice came in the description of building a skatepark: "You can't be on the edge if there is no edge" (*Thrasher*, 1997). This statement offers a very clear view for a skateboarder—without edges there would be nothing to skate. This is true of teaching and learning centers: Without the academy and all of its silos, bunkers, boundaries, and walls (Kretchmar, 2008), there would exist a void of a different sort that would limit the truly beautiful outcome of collaboration that bridges, traverses, and sometimes dismantles barriers. What if the point of all those edges is to find the corners—the places where the edges meet, where work and innovation happen?

At the University of North Carolina at Greensboro (UNC Greensboro), the Teaching Innovations Office (TIO) within the University Teaching and Learning Commons (UTLC) oversees pan-university faculty and educational development. The TIO supports the university's 1,200 full-time tenure and non-tenure-track faculty, along with varying numbers of adjunct faculty and graduate students. This is done with a staff of three full-time developers, who teach a minimum of one course annually. The reality of modern fiscal demands and the shifting direction of the academy is often manifested in teaching and learning centers that are supported disproportionally, in staff and resources, in comparison to the volume of faculty that they are expected to serve. This reality demands innovative and collaborative approaches to faculty support, often in the form of partnerships across division lines.

Partnerships, though essential, are not easy to form and in some instances can be perceived from a space of political paranoia and discord as encroachments into someone else's area—or kingdom, depending on the level of political challenge. However, there is a value in standing back and asking the questions "Why are we here?" and "Whom do we serve?" from which it will likely become evident that these political boundaries are limiting the strategic deployment of talent and resources, not to mention limiting the overall potential for innovation and support that benefits students.

The aim of a teaching and learning center cannot be to change the political climate of campus. That task would most likely be unobtainable or extremely costly for any center. Though as the *Thrasher* magazine quote alludes, what if centers began seeing the edges created by campus politics as skateboarders see edges in the world? Known as the skater's eye, skateboarders have an ability to look at any given space and see the skateable lines throughout (Carr, 2010), making every space a masterful edge that can be used. What if developers cultivated their own eye, one that allowed for edges, bunkers, and silos to become masterful structures that can be used for advancing the work of teaching and learning?

Setting the Stage for Collaborations in the "Wild West" of the Academy

As noted, collaborations across the academy can be easy, queasy, or sometimes downright "let-me-zy" (or "let me do that"). The ease or difficulty in developing collaborations are often the direct result of organization—of the institution and of the center. At UNC Greensboro, the TIO follows the work of David Logan on leadership and has structured the center in ways that promote innovation and collaboration through trans-departmental partnerships.

In the early 2000s, Logan made a splash with his work on group dynamics and work environments that looked toward team development for innovative product design. Logan and his colleagues (Logan, King & Fisher-Wright, 2011) outline five stages of work environments that either prevent, hinder, or cultivate innovative approaches to product design.[1] In these five stages of work environments, academic institutions typically fall into two stages—stage two: "Working for the Weekend" and stage three: "the Wild, Wild West."

Stage two, "Working for the Weekend," is the stage where employees have very little engagement. They are literally working for a paycheck with no desire to innovate or engage beyond the requirements of the job description. Stage three, "the Wild, Wild West," is defined by the cultivation of individual success, dyad relationships, and sometimes the language of "we" with the meaning of "me," or the "let-me-zy do that." Both stages are detrimental to progress and collaboration and serve to reinforce the traditional power structures that maintain the bunkers and silos of the academy. Though both stages can have drastic impacts, stage three can be downright deadly to collaborations. The philosophy in stage three is defined by the collecting, hoarding, and protecting of resources in such a way that information becomes a currency that bestows power (Logan, King & Fisher-Wright, 2011). This is the anthesis of the collaborative work that our faculty and students need from faculty and educational development.

Stage four and five of Logan and his colleagues' work are the foundations of where collaboration can truly happen and be innovative and engaging. The arrival at stage four requires an epiphany that stage three is just not working. Stage three is marked by intentional dyad-based relationships, where a power broker is the connecting point that keeps people, talent, and resources under the broker's control. Stage four, on the other hand, moves to triad (or more) relationships and focuses on bringing people, talent, resources, and problems together to address the needs of the institution. Logan and his colleagues (2011) reference organizations like Apple, Google, and Zappos in their description of stage four. However, in the academy, this stage looks different than in corporate America. In the academy, stage four is marked by a massive organizational change—one in which the traditional understanding of boundaries, silos, and hierarchies is reimagined to focus on tasks, projects, talents, and outcomes. This requires a fundamental change in how individuals see the institution. Instead of seeing insurmountable obstructions, such as organizational charts, individuals see talent and potential—a new edge. Stage five is project specific and cannot be sustained for long periods of time. Stage four sets up the environment for innovation; stage five becomes the transforming moment of putting a project into action. Logan and his colleagues describe this as the Apple team creating the iPhone. They moved to stage five to create a product that no one had ever attempted and returned to stage four when it was complete. Stage five moves beyond edges and transforms the academy into an innovative incubator.

What does this look like in when deploying a center? It looks like this: Each job function is a task, including supervision. The team is organized around the talents of the individuals, with a focus on mission and values of the center. At UNC Greensboro, the TIO is organized around projects that align with individual members' experiences and goals. For example, the director is tasked with supervision of the unit but is only the team manager on projects regarding equity and inclusion. The assistant director takes on the role of the team manager for all programming that involves technology-enhanced pedagogy. And the coordinator takes on the role of team manager for all programming involving course design and learning outcomes. In essence, the team manager changes as the project and needs change to best align talent with outcomes.

This philosophy then leads to new ways of looking at partnerships. Instead of creating boundaries that emphasize yours- and mine-type collaborations (where what is mine is clearly visible), the partnerships with other units takes on a task and talent alignment. For example, the TIO at UNC Greensboro has a strong partnership with the Information Technology Services (ITS) Department. The ITS: Learning Technology unit is embedded with the TIO and many of the resources and talents are seamlessly shared between the two units. No longer is it necessary to divide up who covers the photocopier costs when the task, the advancement of teaching and learning, becomes the focus. The aim is shared and understood, and so resources in both offices are organized and dedicated to that goal.

Defining Collaboration: Know Your Aim in Any Lane

None of this collaborative work would be possible without clearly defined goals and values. This includes defining what collaboration is and what it looks like in the context of the institution and the center. Collaboration on many campuses—whether one will admit it or not—is still in stage three with an emphasis on reaping individual accolades in clearly defined credit categories. Individuals are often reminded to "stay in their lane" and remember organizational chart boundaries. However, it only takes a few individuals and offices willing to change the dynamic to regain focus on the institutional aim. For UNC Greensboro, this institutional aim is student success, which—as it is in many institutions—is an evolving indicator.

By regaining a focus on the institutional aim, such as student success, the center is able to create programs and opportunities for collaboration that target key institutional initiatives. For example, the TIO has a significant focus on equity, diversity, and inclusion as it relates to creating inclusive learning spaces that support student success. The aim of inclusion is not only present in almost all TIO-generated programming, but it is also the guiding catalyst for collaborations with the faculty senate, the Office of Intercultural Engagement (Student Affairs), and the Residential Colleges Office. The partnership with the Office of Intercultural Engagement (OIE) is a strong example of how the aim of student success paired with inclusive learning environments is driving a partnership through intentional outcome-driven projects.

VOISES

In 2018, the TIO began working with the OIE on bringing student voices to the forefront of conversations with educators about their practice. The university had been named a minority serving campus in recent years; however, many faculty members believed the "serving" needed more support and attention. From conversations and dialogues, the VOISES (viewpoints of inclusive student experiences) program was born. The VOISES program allows student volunteers to serve on a panel about their experiences on campus. The panels are typically organized around key identity groups into which the student participants self-select. Topics have included the experiences of students identifying as LGBTQIA+, Indigenous/First Nations, Latino/Latina/Latinx, veterans, having disabilities, and being first generation. Three questions are asked of students: What has been/was your journey to college? What has been your greatest experience in the classroom? and What has been the most challenging experience in the classroom? Audience members are allowed to ask students questions after the first three, but they must write these down so that they may be asked by the moderator (a faculty or staff member who is identified by the students as an advocate or ally).

One of the greatest assets of VOISES is the partnership with OIE. OIE identifies and recruits students and the moderator. TIO recruits faculty and staff participants and handles the logistics. This partnership has allowed for authentic student voices to be present in faculty practice and still maintain a high level of protection and support for the student panelists. The greatest impact has been in institutional change coming from the conversation with students that empowers student participation in campus cultural transformations. Faculty participants have noted that VOISES brought more awareness for things such as the use of pronouns, the significance of seeing oneself in the narrative, and the role of faculty as mentors.

Outlining the "Why"

For the TIO, all work and projects are sifted through a rubric of gatekeeping questions (figure 9.1). These questions define why an activity or program is aimed in the support of student success. The questions also allow the TIO to outline resources, justify resource allocation, and advocate for new resources when necessary. The questions are at the core of the TIO developing its own version of the skater's eye by asking, "Where can we partner and with whom can we partner?" In many ways, the questions help generate a forward motion past any bunkers or silos. More importantly, these questions were developed by the TIO team as a whole—not the director or upper administration—and are used to govern all programming and collaboration decisions. The process of using gatekeeping questions promotes a clear understanding for all campus partners. Partners come prepared to the collaboration conversation with clear and thoughtful understandings of why and how the collaboration is being approached from the perspective of TIO.

The first question, "Does this activity support the advancement of teaching and learning?" is arguably the most important in all projects and collaborations. The advancement of teaching and learning is the sole purpose of the TIO at UNC Greensboro, as it is for most centers. Framing work and collaborations around the advancement of teaching and learning is directly tying TIO practice to UNC Greensboro's larger goal of student success. As noted in the recent work of Sorcinelli, Berg, Bond, and Watson

(2017), pedagogy and curriculum development have an impact on student involvement and learning. This creates an indirect but incredibly significant route for faculty and educational development to engage with student success. The connection between faculty and educational development and student success is further demonstrated in the work of Tinto (2012) in which it was determined that faculty-to-student contact has a dramatic and significant impact on whether a student is successful (followed by peer-to-peer contact). Thus, by framing TIO's goals through advancement of teaching and learning, the activity or partnership is shaped and directed by the larger UNC Greensboro aim of student success.

Any project or partnership that does not meet question one with an affirmative is immediately tabled: either documented and concluded or shared with a more appropriate unit. For example, TIO oversaw the faculty mentoring program that focused on career preparation for tenure-track faculty. The aim was on research and writing support. Though writing and research are significant parts of the faculty life, they are not necessarily directly tied to advancing teaching and learning. Upon reviewing the goals of the program, it was determined that the program would receive better support and focus if it was overseen by the associate vice provost of the University Teaching and Learning Commons. The mentoring program was moved to that office and has been provided with a direct line to the Office of the Provost, promotion and tenure committees, and more resources.

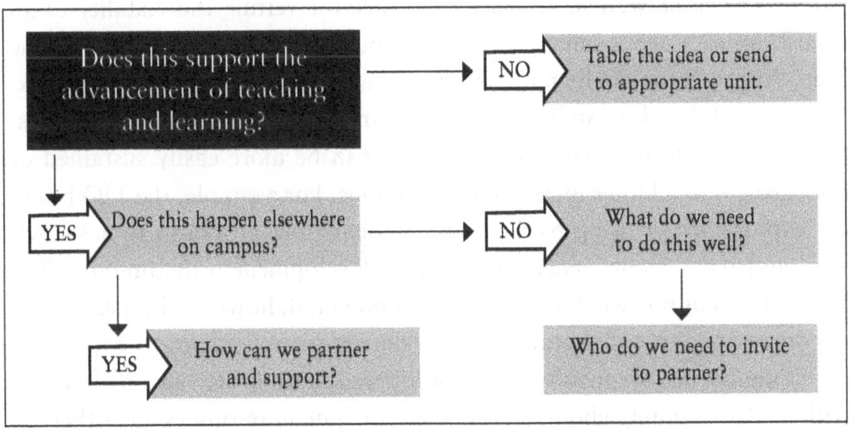

Figure 9.1: TIO at UNC Greensboro's question matrix for projects and collaborations

The remaining questions are guiding for resource and talent allocation. As budgets and financial climates change, a center must be equipped with a justification of how resources and talents are being stewarded toward the greater aim of the institution. The questions are as follows: Is this work being done elsewhere on campus? If so, who do we need to contact to better support this work? If not, what resources (monetary and talent) will we need to accomplish this work well? Who should we invite to help us think through this work and begin to develop this work?

By asking questions about work already in progress on campus, the center is able to address the political challenges that may arise from starting a new project that could be considered "competition" by another department or office in a stage three mentality. The center can reach out to that department and office to offer support, resources, talent, and data. For example, the TIO was asked to develop an online learning peer-review process as part of a grant. Another office on campus, UNCG Online, had been working toward the use of a specific standardized rubric for course review. The TIO was able to partner with UNCG Online to expand the work already being done while collecting data on faculty needs and desires for a peer-review process. The standardized rubric is currently being altered and tested by both groups in an effort to better support the culture and needs of campus.

On the other hand, if the proposed idea is not currently happening on campus, the question about what resources and partners are needed for the work to be done well serves as a key space for vetting the viability of an idea. If an idea needs intensive resources but can only be supported by the center, the director can better assess how the project would alter other work. Moreover, if the idea can be supported by multiple offices and departments, there is a significant chance that the idea can be more easily sustained or even grow into a larger innovation on campus. For example, the TIO began the exploration of using badging and credentialing programs to acknowledge and track faculty engagement with development programming. The initial stages of this work presented great potential; however, by asking others on campus to collaborate in using the software, badging is expanding in its significance for faculty as a tool for recognition. TIO again partnered with UNCG Online, who had been asked by human resources and others to explore credentialing software, which has allowed for the conversation on badging to expand to other offices. Additionally, the use of badging became a resource for the advising centers on campus, as the TIO partnered with several student success offices to incorporate badging into the campus-wide Advising Institute.

By having very clear but easy-to-remember questions, the center is able to quickly assess all new ideas for viability. Moreover, the use of the rubric allows for every team member in the center to be able to quickly ascertain the alignment of any request presented to the center with the center's goals. For example, the TIO is often asked to promote workshops and programs happening on campus. The application of question one—Does this support the advancement of teaching and learning?—allows every member of TIO to make a quick decision on whether TIO is the best avenue for that promotion. Thus, the director does not have to be involved in the evaluation of every partnering request presented to the center.

Finding Partners: Doers over Hierarchies

One of the greatest challenges to deploying a stage four (Logan et al., 2011) culture is that the remainder of the institution is likely not operating in a stage four space. This is when it becomes critical for the director to serve as a go-between for the campus culture and the stage four center. The director serves as the lead code switcher, who can translate the work being done or the work needing to be done to upper administration and other partners on campus. It is essential that protecting the culture of the center becomes its own task and priority. This can be done in a number of ways but is often done through the process of making goals, tasks, and successes as transparent as possible to others.

With that staging in mind, the center is set up to do the labor of innovations—finding other doers on campus. Stage three (Logan et al., 2011) is marked by the need to have hierarchies and to maintain those hierarchies. The idea that "only directors talk to directors" is one that is limiting but is still regularly deployed in many environments. However, doers are scattered throughout the hierarchy and are often not in positions like directorships. It is essential to traversing the edges that teams are able to partner with the talent that can support the aim or goal. For the TIO, this means that the director may have to reach out to other directors as a courtesy to keep them abreast of partnerships between TIO and their office. However, the team manager for the project (which can be the director or another team member) will focus communication with the doer in the partnership. For example, the TIO partners with OIE (Intercultural Engagement) and the Residential Colleges Office (RCO) on an equity, diversity, and inclusion project related to the work of the Sustained Dialogue Institute on campus. The Sustained Dialogue Institute (www.sustaineddialogue.org) is an international organization that helps campuses set up dialogue groups and networks focused on equity and inclusion.

The TIO sponsors an annual Equity, Diversity, and Inclusion Institute for faculty focused on the principles of the Sustained Dialogue curriculum. OIE organizes and supports a program called Spartans in Dialogues, which is a Sustained Dialogue model for students. The Spartans in Dialogue program is organized by the assistant director of OIE. The director of RCO serves as a faculty mentor for one of the student dialogue groups.

These three areas have come together to develop a larger equity and inclusion curriculum that supports faculty, staff, and students. The hierarchy of each office is not directing who participates in the development of this curriculum; it is the talent needed for this curriculum to be successful that is targeted. The three offices are currently developing a model of Sustained Dialogue groups for faculty and staff, which would not be possible without the individuals outlined. The TIO and RCO directors are responsible for navigating the campus political structures as a task. The directors are better situated for communicating upward and outward the transparent aims and goals. However, it is the expertise of all of the individual partners listed that is cultivated and needed to develop, organize, and deploy this work.

Attention, Focus, Work: Cultivating a Campus Reputation

The key to all of the collaborative work that allows for teaching and learning centers to traverse the edges of the structures of the academy is in the cultivation of the center's reputation on campus. The center needs to be seen as a go-to partner for all things teaching and learning, but also as a space that makes partnering and collaborating easy and productive (and maybe fun). The cultivation of a reputation on campus as a productive collaboration space is essential to calming stage-three fears of kingdom building that are pervasive on many campuses. As productive partners, the center becomes a space for innovation where credit is equally shared and mutually beneficial.

In order for this reputation to be cultivated, the director has to take on the task of transparently championing all partnerships with a focused message on the outcome of the partnership. This means that every time the project is mentioned, the director ensures that all partners are credited, but also that all partners have the same message about the project. Additionally, directors should be tasked with championing the successes of their campus partners on projects in which the center is not involved. For example, the TIO is not directly involved in the deployment of OIE's Spartans in Dialogue program. The program is focused on student dialogue groups, which is outside the parameters of question one (i.e., advancement of teaching and learning). However, OIE is a key partner in a number of programs and the success of Spartans in Dialogue is essential to those programs. It is the TIO director's job to champion Spartans in Dialogue, as the director has access to spaces that the assistant director in OIE does not.

The reality of this work is one that requires significant dedication and attention. Collaborating across academic boundaries and edges is not for the faint of heart. There will always be individuals so encamped in stage three that collaborating with them can be an arduous task. It becomes essential that the center has established a strong culture dedicated to the power of collaboration. Otherwise, the momentum of collaboration can quickly be halted by the stage-three power broker environment. Every team member has to pay particular attention to the goals and aims of the center and the institution so that when these moments of struggle arrive, there is no desire to turn back. This dedication is what is required for developers to cultivate their own "development eye," the one that allows for the edges, bunkers, and silos to become masterful structures for advancing the work of teaching and learning.

Notes

1 When Logan wrote the book *Tribal Leadership*, the term *tribe* was big in organizational development. However, it should be stated that the use of the word *tribe* is problematic as it appropriates an indigenous way of knowing without any connection to indigenous communities or an indigenist perspective. The term *dynamics leadership* or *staged leadership* would be more appropriate.

References

ACE and POD Network. (2018). *A center for teaching and learning matrix*. Retrieved from https://podnetwork.org/content/uploads/ACE-POD-Teaching-Center-Matrix-2018.pdf

Carr, J. (2010). Legal geographies—Skating around the edges of the law: Urban skateboarding and the role of law in determining young peoples' place in the city. *Urban Geography, 31*(7), 988–1003.

Kretchmar, S. (2008). The utility of silos and bunkers in the evolution of Kinesiology. *Quest, 60*(1), 3–12.

Logan, D., King, J., & Fischer-Wright, H. (2011). Tribal leadership: Leveraging natural groups to build a thriving organization. New York, NY: Harper Business.

Sorcinelli, M., Berg, J., Bond, H., & Watson, C. E. (2017). Why now is the time for evidence-based faculty development. In C. Haras, S. Taylor, M. Sorcinelli, & L. von Hoene (Eds.), *Institutional commitment to teaching excellence: Assessing the impacts and outcomes of faculty development* (pp. 5–16). Washington, DC: American Council on Education.

Thrasher. (1997, September). How to build a skatepark. San Francisco, CA: High Speed Productions, Inc. 200.

Tinto, V. (2012). Completing college: Rethinking institutional action. Chicago, IL: University of Chicago Press.

CHAPTER TWELVE

It Worked for Me:

The Golden Rule

Rochelle L. Ford, PhD

One of the principles I have lived by to the best of my ability is the Golden Rule: Do unto others as you would have them do unto you. This principle has helped me to develop healthy relationships where ever I have traversed. From my family, friends, social organizations, faith-based groups and higher education institutions where I have worked and studied, this Golden Rule has helped me to develop long-lasting mutually beneficial relationships even in highly political environments. Developing mutually beneficial relationships has helped me to excel as a higher education leader at multiple levels.

In order to understand how the Golden Rule has worked for me, it's important to understand how I want to be treated and how I believe mutually beneficial relationships operate.

I always want to be treated with respect, no matter how I look, sound, or may appear. As an African American woman from upper middle-class suburbia, and often one of the younger leaders in the room throughout my professional life, some people have prejudged me to think that I would not bring value. Some people have thought that I would be too narrow in thinking, too inexperienced, too ethnic or too unconventional. Before I spoke, they would question me and begin conversations doubting me and make me earn their respect. As a result, I often would feel like I was starting at a deficit and lacked the respect that I believe all humans should have. Therefore, I try very hard to show people respect regardless of who they are or how they may dress, sound, or appear.

When I meet administrative assistants, deans, custodians, executives, bus drivers, delivery people, professors, presidents, graduate assistants, chancellors, faculty members, and students, I greet them in a positive manner, with a smile, with a genuine interest in who they are as people and what they hope to accomplish.

My smile is not disingenuous; I love smiling. It makes me feel better, and it is contagious. I have too many blessings; therefore, I try to not to frown and be cast down. Instead, I smile because I am thankful for the opportunity to meet new people who each have a story and contribution to make to society. Therefore, I try not to prejudge and discount people. Instead, I listen to people. I try to discover who they are as people and what they want to contribute or what their role is within an organization.

Learning about people inspires me and leads to discovering ways we can help each other. This discovery paves the road to increasing my ability to be empathic and appreciate who people are and the possibly the struggles they have overcome.

Everyone has a journey, a road that only they have traveled that gives them perspective. Such different perspectives enable organizations to solve problems creatively. However, if we don't listen to each other, we don't learn, and we miss those opportunities to creatively solve problems.

Just as I want people to give me the benefit of the doubt, I try to do the same. I want people to listen to me and trust that I am acting in a sincere, positive manner. Of course, people should verify what I say and should look to see if I am acting in the best interest of others. I want people to understand what I am saying and ask clarifying questions if they don't.

Now, I am not naïve; I know that some people are only out for themselves, and if that is what motivates them, I need to know that and use that knowledge to bring them along. If their receiving the glory will get the project moving along, then I am willing to take a back seat. Their participation in a project based on their motivation helps me to succeed. Instead of fighting against them, I can better incorporate them or find a way for them to see that our success is their success. Listening, respecting them, acknowledging them, and cheering them on is what I hope others might do for me too.

Finding a place where we can help each other means that I have to get up from behind my desk and meet people where they are. Go to their offices.

It means serving them whether it is getting a cup of coffee, making a photo copy, or taking a package to them myself. There is never a task that is beneath me. If the trash needs to be emptied, then I can empty it.

Showing others that I am willing to walk in their shoes helps me to empathize with them and shows a level of humility.

I prefer people to be humble, and so I try to be too. At the end of the day, we are people deserving respect just because we are human, created equal, and hired into an organization to help achieve a common goal—the mission of the organization.

Therefore, I try to keep that Golden Rule in mind: Do unto others as I would want them to do unto me.

CHAPTER THIRTEEN

Professional Development:

A Process in Progress

DAVID A. SHAPIRO, PHD

Boyoo dze kiwo-oh kimo-on kikur kifah'
"One hand cannot tie a bundle."

—Translated from the Lamnso dialect, one of 250 spoken in Cameroon
(J. Lukong, personal communication, 2005)

THIS CHAPTER, INDEED THIS book, is about the importance of building bridges within the academy. Such bridges are not a luxury; they are integral to university culture. They are the fabric, the language, the medium of exchange. Building bridges requires a necessary skillset not only to survive, but to thrive within a university context. Building bridges also enables individuals and the collective university to achieve their most positive potential.

What Are Bridges?

For me, bridges represent both a commitment to mindful communication that considers and values the viewpoints of others inside and outside of our discipline and an aspect of human nature the compels us toward new experiences, those that are challenging, unfamiliar, and lead toward learning, growth, and development. Note that our inclination to communicate with others, our manner of communication, and our inclination toward what is new and different represent choices. For some, our nature might be to work in isolation, to create our own silo. If the university is to function as a well-oiled, integrated machine, however, all diverse dimensions must work in concert.

Every stage of our professional development invites us to encounter new bridges and new challenges. For example, as I write this chapter, I am crossing a bridge to a place I have never been before. Four months ago, I officially retired from my position as a university professor and speech-language pathologist, sources of nourishment I have cherished over the last 41 years. This new context is most unfamiliar and, at times, uncomfortable. Nevertheless, I know it is right and it is time. Only by electing to talk with one of my colleagues could I better understand what I am experiencing. She put into words what I could not. She explained, "Retirement is inextricably combined with issues of how to age with grace and plan in a balanced manner for an uncertain future" (K. Lunnen, personal communication, November 14, 2018).

This transition affords me an opportunity to reflect on the lessons I have learned about professional development that may help other university faculty as they embark on and pursue their own careers. In doing so, I will discuss a few of the many opportunities and challenges I have experienced over my career, both personally and professionally, and share insights and positive solutions. Throughout, I will emphasize the lifelong nature of professional development and the limitless and exciting possibilities facing every university citizen. While focusing primarily on university faculty, I am hopeful that the lessons and solutions discussed will have implications for others within the university community (e.g., students, staff, and administration) and allied contexts (e.g., healthcare, social service, business, politics, and more) where people are called together to serve the greater good.

What Is Professional Development?

For me, professional development and personal development are intricately related. Professional development is not only about what you *do*, although keeping abreast of advances in your chosen discipline, often involving specialized training that may lead to credentials and degrees, is essential. Even more, professional development is about merging the person you are with the professional you are striving to become, the decisions you make, how you conduct yourself—particularly when nobody is looking, and your relative openness to learning, growth, and change. It is about believing that nothing is impossible when you choose to focus on common interests that can bridge any divide, inviting and genuinely considering alternative points of view—not only yours but the perspectives of others, and remaining committed to your individual and shared goals.

To address professional development further, I will focus on three topics—my professional development and your professional development. Then I will conclude with a few take-home messages. You will see that reviewing my professional development will be a foundation to offer insights and suggestions for your professional development. My objective is for you to consider and perhaps apply one idea that you might not have considered previously that could facilitate your individual and collective goals—and to challenge you.

My Professional Development

In order to discuss my own experience, I first need to share the personal and professional significance of stuttering.

What Stuttering Is and Why It Matters

Stuttering is a universal disorder of speech fluency. Stuttering interferes with the most human element of all—being able to tell one's story and using the words one wants when one wants: "I do," "I love you," "I'm sorry." In the United States alone, there are over three million people who stutter. In the world, there are over 70 million. Think of how often and how casually we share our thoughts. If using speech and language uniquely distinguishes us as human, being unable to share one's story can render that person feeling other than, or most often, less than human. Feeling less than human creates an unimaginable sense of isolation, which can lead to a host of negative emotional consequences (Shapiro, 2011).

James Earl Jones, an American stage and television actor, whose career spanned over 60 years, has one of the most distinctive baritone voices. His is the voice of Darth Vader in *Star Wars* and Mufasa in the original production of *The Lion King*. Jones is also a person who stutters. Poignantly sharing the significance of stuttering, Jones was quoted as saying, "One of the hardest things in life is having words in your heart that you can't utter" (BrainyQuote, n.d., Jones, 2005; Jones & Niven, 1993).

My Personal and Professional Story

I too am a person who stutters. There was a time, nearly my first 20 years, when stuttering consumed me. Stuttering was the basis on which I defined myself. Stuttering affected my relationships, my sense of my abilities, and what I thought I could become. My dog, Buddy, was the only living thing to which I could communicate. Oddly, people who stutter can speak fluently with a pet or when alone, just as they can sing without stuttering. I had a grandfather who, when I stuttered severely, while walking with him hand in hand, said to me, "I love you just the way you are." I swore an oath that if I could find a way to talk, I would do my best to help others find their voice.

While I had several good clinicians, I also had clinicians who, discouraged with my continued stuttering, threw in the towel. They stopped believing in me. I had teachers who told me that, because of my stuttering, I should not plan on going to college. I had professors who told me that, because of my stuttering, I should not enter the profession of communication sciences and disorders. They were wrong! Sometimes just believing in yourself can be heroic. *Never* say never. *Never* even think never. I am convinced that when one says "the sky is the limit," that only reflects the limitations in one's own thinking.

I must add that the day that changed my life was meeting the most wonderful girl in the world. I learned from her that when you have one person who believes in you, there is nothing you cannot accomplish. She has been my best friend and girlfriend throughout our 35-year marriage.

As mentioned earlier, I recently completed my 41st year as a speech-language pathologist, a specialist in fluency disorders, and a professor at Western Carolina University. Honestly, not a single day passes when I have not felt thankful for the privilege of teaching, learning, providing clinical service to people who stutter and their families, and engaging in research—on six continents. At one time in my life, I had hoped that I could change the world. Knowing better now, optimistically rather than in defeat, I feel fortunate to have been a part of helping my students and people who stutter and their families change their own world. As a result, I feel a connection to the human condition that transcends any conceivable limitation and an internal satisfaction in what I have done, with whom I have done it, and the ultimate importance of the process and products of communication.

Over these years, I have worked with many people. A man who never ordered a meal at a restaurant for his wife in their 40-year marriage *now* does so and communicates independently. A young woman who looked away and spoke little so that her boyfriend would not see her stutter *now* looks him in the eye and says, "He's going to hear what I have to say whether he wants to or not." A child who stuttered severely and was bullied *now* speaks without hesitation and is an advocate for others.

I have traveled to interesting places. With a colleague from France, I worked with people who stutter from 20 different African nations. I have met indigenous healers in huts with smoke and herbs and bones and learned about diviners and herbalists. I hear you thinking, "Why did he meet with these people?" Because I wanted to learn about *their* assumptions and *their* interventions for people who stutter. Most importantly, I learned that our own view of the world is not necessarily shared; it represents *a* view, not *the* view.

I have served as the president of the International Fluency Association. We coordinated the eighth World Congress on Fluency Disorders where professionals and people with disorders of speech fluency gathered in Lisbon, Portugal, from over thirty different countries across six continents. We also brought current information and clinical service to countries where it had not existed previously. I am so pleased that two young professionals I met in 2001 while I was working in Japan became leaders in my profession and coordinated the ninth World Congress in Hiroshima, Japan, during summer 2018. I know it is their time to step up, just as it is my time to step back.

Your Professional Development

Having shared my own experiences, I now offer a few observations that you can apply to building bridges within your own discipline across your professional development. To help you do so, I offer cases in point and food for thought.

What Do You Profess?

Most of you reading this book are university professors. All of us have had many professors. I have always thought it a fair question to ask a professor of any discipline, "What do you profess?" What I am looking for is the central tenet, the higher-order theme, that at once guides and integrates one's teaching, service, and research. You see, what I am about as a professor and speech-language pathologist is far more than correcting speech errors. You can tell that the message of stuttering is significant to me both personally and professionally. However, the true meaning of what I do emerges when the message of stuttering becomes a medium for a larger message, that of harnessing and realizing positive human potential. *That* is what I profess. In other words, what I do, who I am, and the values I hold are directly connected to my conviction that it is the universal birthright of every person to be able to use speech and language freely and to experience communication freedom.

Furthermore, I profess that by focusing on a common purpose, the differences that are viewed by some as potentially divisive (e.g., theoretical, political, geographic, economic, religious, ethnic, etc.) simply drop away. What we are left with are diverse people working together for a common purpose, growing and learning together, as *one* people, as *one* family, setting an example for how insoluble problems can be addressed by constructive and positive means, indeed by communication. For me, there is no clearer avenue for achieving harmony on a university campus or any other dynamic community—or for achieving peace across the world.

Too often, faculty focus on what they need to *do*, rather than on *why* they are doing what they are and the larger purpose being served. I would argue that "publish or perish" misinforms faculty, creates unnecessary fear that interferes with productivity, and provides little reminder of the honor it is to be a professor and to serve the academy and the larger world. I suggest that "profess or perish" reminds faculty to articulate and to live their larger mission within and across their teaching, service, and research pursuits. It is when these "legs of the stool" relate directly to one's ultimate mission and are so integrated as to be indistinguishable but for the surface form, that one is a PROFESSor and a member of a PROFESSion. Without such cohesion, one's effectiveness and sense of personal satisfaction are reduced to frustration and conflict, yielding products that may be disjointed without relevance to each other.

Case in Point

I served for many years on the Tenure, Promotion, and Reappointment (i.e., Collegial Review) Committee at the department, college, and university levels. I also have been an external reviewer for such actions at other universities both nationally and internationally. Faculty across disciplines meticulously chronicle their productivity with evidence of their teaching, service, and research. As a reviewer, however, occasionally I am left wondering, "What does this person profess? What do these products mean? How do they relate to each other? What is the significance to the candidate, to the university, to the discipline?" I recommend that what one professes be clear and explicit (rather than implicit), thereby integrating one's mission, bringing satisfaction and a sense of accomplishment to the candidate, and guiding one's ongoing professional development.

Food for Thought

So, what do *you* profess? What is your ultimate mission in life? What are your central tenets? What truths do you hold dear? How does what you do as a teacher, service provider, and researcher relate directly to what you profess, to who you are, to your larger purpose? How does your teaching, service, and research relate to each other? What is the significance of your work to you, to your university, to your discipline? What does your work mean? Why does it matter? How is it serving the world? Do you deliberately bridge to others within and outside of your discipline to gain the benefit of their perspectives, however divergent? How do you invite alternative perspectives? Do you listen to others—really listen? How do you utilize other points of view? How does what you *do* relate directly to what you *know*, to the knowledge and values that you hold as true? In what ways do you think about your own thinking? How does your work both invite and express a sense of cognitive creativity and intellectual freedom?

Learn Something and Dialogue Every Day!

Just as we implore our students, I charge you, as I charge myself, to learn something and to interact with others every day. In T. H. White's novel (1958), *The Once and Future King*, Arthur, who was king to be, sought counsel from Merlin, his mentor. Merlin said to Arthur,

> The best thing . . . is to learn something. That is the only thing that never fails. You may grow old and trembling in your anatomies. You may lie awake at night listening to the disorder in your veins. You may miss your only love. You may see the world around you devastated by evil lunatics or know your honor being trampled in the sewers of baser minds.
>
> There is only one thing for it, then: To learn. Learn why the world wags and what wags it. That is the only thing which the mind can never exhaust, never alienate, never be tortured by, never fear or distrust, and never dream of regretting. Learning is the thing for you. (p. 140)

Essential to learning and scholarship is dialogue. Dialogue is not just talking, although dialogue may look like talking. Dialogue is interaction involving listening and hearing, with all parties identifying the perspectives of each other in addition to one's own. Dialogue requires considering alternative perspectives and talking with people whose worldview is different from our own. Dialogue is at the heart of building bridges.

It is true that birds of a feather flock together, but it is also true that opposites attract. Will I apply the perspective of indigenous healers in my work? Not directly. But when I embrace differences, when I seek to understand distinctly different perspectives, what I learn informs what I do by realizing that there are many ways of knowing; mine is only one. And there is value, humility, and humanness in that. Our open-mindedness is only as authentic as we are willing to accept those who seem closed-minded. In fact, understanding and accepting, if not nurturing, divergent truths—that is, conflicting world views—is at the heart of diversity and an enlightened society. In my mind, that is what a university represents and what is a reasonable expectation for a PROFESSor.

When I see faculty and administrators presenting their own perspective without considering that of others, I am reminded of Albert Murphy's (1974) admonishment of "two monologues in search of a dialogue" (p. 29). Too often, such unilateral assertions lead to incivility and behaviors that are both unbecoming to the larger academy and inappropriate models of professionalism for students and faculty. Such blockades are incongruous with the goals and objectives (i.e., the larger mission or the PROFESSion) of the university. In contrast, I am most impressed when I see people inviting divergent perspectives and striving to see and understand the world through the eyes of others.

Case in Point

As elected president of the International Fluency Association (IFA), I quickly realized that the organization never had an official strategic plan within its 25-year history. Early in my term, therefore, I constructed and distributed a survey that was completed by the general membership literally throughout the world. The resulting 2013–2020 Strategic plan (International Fluency Association, 2014) was reviewed and approved by the IFA's executive board, board of directors, and general membership. It articulates IFA's mission, vision, guiding principles, core values, and priorities, each with measurable objectives, assignments for completion, and a timeline. It is a living, breathing document that is guiding tremendous accomplishments by diverse professionals, all of whom are bridging divides across countries and cultures as we commit to a common cause. Importantly, there is "buy in" from all stakeholders; we all own it and, as a result, we are all committed to completing it.

However, one of the board members protested that I should not have invested the time and effort to receive input from the international membership. He thought that I, as president, should have acted more decisively and constructed the strategic plan based on my own experience and priorities. He asserted that I did not have the necessary skillset to be president. Surely, I could have constructed the strategic plan far more quickly from my own perspective only. Having heard and considered his perspective, I was reminded of the old expression that "Haste makes waste." Quality takes time and there is no replacement for working, dialoging, and learning together. Working alone would have made it mine to be imposed on others; now it is ours and we own it collectively.

Food for Thought

How does your teaching, service, and research promote learning and dialogue every day? How do you distinguish between monologues and dialogues? How can we transform monologues into dialogues across university settings? How might dialogue be promoted to reflect value, humility, and humanness on the university campus? How do learning and dialogue build bridges to understanding? Notwithstanding our best efforts and intentions, how do blockades form and what might be appropriate intervention in these instances? Have you encountered "closed-minded people?" In such instances, what do you recommend from the perspectives of open-mindedness and an intention to understand and accept, if not to nurture, divergent truths? How are your goals and objectives as an individual faculty member consistent with those of the university? What can be done when the two sets of goals and objectives are at mismatch? Is it always appropriate to consider alternative perspectives before acting decisively? Are there some perspectives that are not deserving of consideration (e.g., those that are in violation of cultural norms, civil rights, due process, etc.)? If so, how are those boundaries determined?

Question and Speak Truth As You Honestly See It

Question

The open invitation to question that we enjoy in the United States is something that I have never taken for granted. Here we are, ready, willing, and able to question. Yet, too often, university citizens are reluctant to question or to challenge, particularly when interacting with authority figures. In my own career, particularly when others hold contrastive perspectives and I am genuinely trying to see through their eyes, I have found it helpful to ask them to explain (i.e., not to defend) why they hold their perspective and how they have come to this viewpoint. I have asked others to help me by relating their perspective to their underlying assumptions. I have found that *how* we inquire is at least as important as *what* we say. Usually a genuine spirit of inquiry leads to establishment of a colleagueship and a bridge to understanding. It is when we attend to the message (i.e., what) without consideration of the medium (i.e., how) that blockades are erected, which can only interfere with shared learning and growth (McLuhan, 1964; McLuhan & Fiore, 1967).

Truth

What is truth? For me, truth is an informed perspective that has withstood not only the test of time, but the deliberate challenge from diverse and alternative perspectives. What does that say about a person—and one's commitment to professional development—if one does not speak truth as one honestly sees it? On campus, faculty often comment that they cannot speak truth until they achieve tenure (i.e., relatively permanent job security, wherein just cause is required for dismissal). Students often feel reluctant to talk with a professor about a controversial subject or a challenging perspective. Clearly, I wonder why anyone would be on a college campus—or any other enlightened context—if it weren't for the opportunity, the expectation, the freedom to speak truth. You see, for me, speaking truth is not optional.

Case in Point

Some years ago, I was in a long meeting on a Friday afternoon with a former chancellor and all the vice chancellors—my superiors. Not only do I hate challenging authority, I also still experience reluctance to speak out because of my history of stuttering. Nevertheless, I felt I did not have a choice. I spoke against the motion being supported by the entire administration, which had to do with university-wide program review (i.e., identified programs that were being slated for termination). Indeed, I was uncomfortable, but, as I said, speaking truth is not optional and is related to integrity. Afterward I was miserable and stressed all weekend. However, I was pleased to find an e-mail Monday morning from one of the vice chancellors thanking me for the lesson in civility. What does this mean? Speaking truth is essential. How we present ourselves is no less important.

Food for Thought

As university faculty, our primary responsibility is to speak truth—in a civil, respectful manner—as we honestly see it and as it relates to our chosen discipline. We call it intellectual freedom. That freedom of expression is maintained and preserved by a cornerstone referred to as "university tenure." Why then are some faculty reluctant to exercise these responsibilities, these freedoms? Why do some call for the abolishment of university tenure? How might our manner of expression impact the likelihood that our message is received and considered as intended, rather than rejected? In what ways are we mutually responsible for the course and outcome of a conversation, of a meeting, of a vote, and so on? What place does the "art of persuasion" have within an authentic, genuine dialogue? Why do some interpret that our society, our academy, has descended into incivility? How might we be contributing to this state of affairs? How might we preserve civility? What are the roles of questions and truth in civility? What might you do in a situation where you must express truth as you honestly see it, knowing that your truth will be unpopular and difficult for others to accept?

Do Something That Matters and Do It Well

I indicated previously that, after 41 years, I genuinely believe what I do matters and I have served, taught, and researched to the best of my ability. When I have the opportunity, I recommend to university faculty to do something that matters to them and their discipline and to do it to the absolute best of their ability. What you do should keep you up at night; this is a good thing. Are you passionate about it? Here is my mantra: *Do it, be it, love it.* If you are not passionate, become passionate or find something else to do. Most people think that life is determined by the presence of a pulse. For me, life is determined by the passion we hold about what we do and the world we inhabit. A career may seem like a long time, but life is so very short.

I recommend faculty to quit looking over their shoulder to see how they are doing in comparison to others. To learn and be mentored by others is one thing; to compare is another. Don't strive to be better than others. Strive to be *your* absolute, authentic best. This is where one needs to assess one's own commitment. Years ago, one of my senior colleagues explained to me that there is a clear distinction between interest and commitment. With an apology to vegetarians, he said that those who enjoy bacon and eggs in the morning are reminded of that difference. According to him, the chicken was interested; the pig was committed (J. Pearce, personal communication, 1995; see also Google, n.d.).

I have been an interviewer and reviewer many times. Too many applicants for admission, employment, promotion, and more list what they have done. I am looking for who they are, the value of what they do, to whom their experience is important and the relative impact it has had. Less frequently addressed is the fourth "leg of the stool" (i.e., colleagueship). I am looking to see if one can work collaboratively or only in isolation.

Case in Point

Frequently, I hear junior faculty asking what "counts" as they anticipate being reviewed by the Tenure, Promotion, and Reappointment Committee. This invites "bean counting." I have always felt that they are asking the wrong question. More appropriate would be, "To my profession and to me, what matters?" In other words, *what matters counts*. Asking this question would prevent well-meaning faculty from putting routine, unnoteworthy materials and activities forward for consideration. Similarly, I often see files where a candidate has numerous presentations but so few publications. Expressions of scholarship need to be regular, varied, and ongoing. If one's teaching, service, and research (and one's life) all integrate directly as expressions of what one PROFESSes, there would be greater balance and no rush to the finish line.

Food for Thought

How does what you do reflect what you and your discipline are striving to become? How does what you do matter? What does it mean? Are you passionate about what you are doing? How is what you do related to what you profess? How does what you profess guide what you do? Do your scholarly presentations and teaching lead up to regular publications? If not, what is interfering with your publication schedule?

What If My Ideas Are Rejected?

Who isn't afraid of rejection, particularly as we are encouraged to speak our truth, however divergent? Faculty often think about rejection. "Publish or perish" reverberates, but combating fear of rejection is part of the necessary skillset for an effective faculty member.

Case in Point

I arrived at Western Carolina University directly from my doctoral program at Indiana University. I sent my first draft manuscript to many friends and colleagues for review and comments. I heard essentially that I had written a wonderful paper and that I was brilliant. Then I sent it to a scholarly journal. The review was scathing. The only thing the journal reviewers did not ask me was, "Why were you ever born?" It was rejected; I was rejected. I realized that all of the people to whom I submitted the paper did not tell me the truth. I was heartbroken. It took me nearly two years to benefit from the journal reviewers' feedback and to send it out again. It is now published as two papers in major journals.

Time passed. I received another scathing review for another manuscript. This time I reflected on the reviewers' feedback and did not take it as personally. Rather I considered all of their feedback and then responded point by point, justifying and accounting for my arguments with numerous citations. Here is how things change. That paper went from being rejected to being the lead article in the next issue of the journal.

I am not rejecting the value of feedback, however unsettling. The point is to keep learning from every experience. Do your homework. Be civil. Move forward. Steve Jobs' 2005 commencement address at Stanford University reminds us that the dots in our lives always are connected. We just cannot know in foresight how they connect, but we surely can see the connection in hindsight.

Now I review for most major journals related to my discipline. As a result, I never send out a review the day I write it. I always sleep on it, remembering that a very sensitive person is at the other end, waiting to receive the review. Communicating in haste risks creating a blockade—resistance, defensiveness, rejection. Respectful, considerate communication invites and builds a bridge to understanding. It is as if we reap what we sow: Usually we receive respect and consideration when that is what we give. I think I am a better reviewer from my experience receiving reviews. I have learned from positive and negative examples. The responsibility of a good reviewer is to communicate thoughtfully, respectfully, and accountably, even when the feedback provided may not be what the author wishes to receive. Civility and respect must be paramount; we in the academy deserve no less.

Food for Thought

Scholarship is the business of testing and challenging ideas in order to move a discipline forward. Such forward movement requires interaction with others inside and outside of one's discipline and the consequent ambiguity if not disequilibrium that results from challenge to one's own constructs. As a scholar, how do you embrace such disequilibrium while tempering the fear that your ideas will be rejected? Reluctance to challenge one's own ideas can only cause cognitive blockades—impediments to learning and change. As an author and as a reviewer, how can you maximize the benefit of diverse perspectives, which are necessary to move beyond the status quo? How can such perspectives enable you to build bridges that lead to greater understanding within your discipline, thereby enhancing your own career?

Remain Balanced and Open

What is balance; what is openness? For me, balance is about responding directly to two voices—internal and external. If you respond only to your own priorities (internal), you will get yourself fired. If you respond only to the external priorities and not to your own, you will experience burnout. I would argue that it is possible and necessary to respond to both voices. It is ideal when the internal and external priorities are directly compatible. Openness has to do with our willingness to consider that which seems different and our inclination to embrace if not celebrate human diversity in all of its forms.

How do I remain balanced? There is a difference between a job and a career. My career reflects the lens through which I view the world. Indeed, professional development is a continuum over time and experience. There are stages. Too many people want to start at what they consider the top. I have been asked what others can do so they might live the life I have. I think they are asking the wrong question. One cannot skip stages in the continuum. Achievement is not only on the basis of what one does, but who one is and how and what one strives to be and become. Balance and achievement have to do with internal motivation and what one professes in life. Peter Yarrow (2018), a folk singer and social activist, recently stated, "If you're part of a movement that you believe in, then you're committed to it for life. It becomes a part of you. You don't need external inspiration. This is what your life becomes" (p. 8). Balance, then, is building bridges throughout life that reflect one's passion, purpose, and PROFESSion.

Case in Point: Balance

I routinely ask my graduate students, as I have asked my faculty colleagues, what their priorities are. Often, I hear that family is first and career is second. Isn't it possible to have two nearly top priorities? Why do so many students and faculty view home and work as mutually exclusive? My wife and I have two adult children who are successful, educated, independent professionals. They seem to have benefitted from an example, however imperfect, of two parents who focused on home and career.

Case in Point: Openness

The only speaking invitation I declined for safety reasons was that of l'Association Libanaise des Orthophonistes, the organization of Lebanese Speech-Language Pathologists, in Beirut, Lebanon. Although prospective hosts assured me personal safety, the official Lebanese government website warned against visitors of my demographics (i.e., Jewish, Caucasian, and of Middle Eastern descent). My hosts would not allow me to decline. Rather, they scheduled me to provide a workshop that was fully transmitted by distance technology. Even though the start of the conference was delayed because of roadblocks and traffic diversion due to a bombing, we interacted face-to-face in real time, as if we were in the same room. The point is that both the Lebanese professionals and I were not only able to remain open to differences, we celebrated and nurtured those differences within the context of our many commonalities. This openness is the essential tool that builds bridges.

Food for Thought

How do you remain open and balanced, given the demands of your chosen career and life? Does your investment of time reflect your priorities? Does your work accommodate both your internal priorities and external expectations? What adjustments might increase a sense of balance? How can you maximize your openness to difference and change, knowing that both are essential to scholarship? How might you benchmark your own progress? In other words, how are you evaluating your accomplishments (in teaching, service, research, and colleagueship) on the basis of specific objectives and implementing change as needed?

Summary and Conclusion

In summary, this chapter has addressed the importance of building bridges as a cornerstone for professional development across academic disciplines. Among the points made are these:

- Know what you profess and live a life and a career that reflect your mission and values.
- Learn something and dialogue every day.
- Shift perspective and invite contrastive points of view.
- Question, speak truth as you honestly see it, and embrace and nurture diversity.
- Do something that matters and do it well.
- Embrace rejection as an opportunity to learn and to grow.
- Remain balanced and open.

Here are a few closing thoughts:

First, it is often true that as one door closes, another opens. However, why wait for a door to close? It is also true that if you remain committed, do and be your absolute best, and mind your manners, one door opens and then another door opens, and so on. I have seen this all over the world.

Second, *never, ever, ever* put a cap on one's potential—yours or anyone else's. One never can know. Miracles and the "impossible" happen every day.

Third, it is an honor and a privilege of the highest calling to be a university professor and a member of the academy. To enable each to become all he or she is capable of and to serve the larger community, near and far—*that* is a PROFESSion.

Fourth, I wish for everyone reading this book to have the confidence to feel equal to and as good as any person past or present, and the humility and civility to feel better than not a single one.

Finally, find someone to love and love that person as if there is no tomorrow. That is the one thing, the North Star, the light that brings you home.

References

BrainyQuote. (n.d.). *James Earl Jones quotes.* Retrieved from https://www.brainyquote.com/quotes/james_earl_jones_125784

Google (n.d.). *Chicken and pig make breakfast.* Retrieved from http://www.agilejedi.com/chickenandpig

International Fluency Association. (2014). International Fluency Association strategic plan 2013–2020. *Journal of Fluency Disorders, 39*, 54–63.

Jobs, S. (2005, June 14). You've got to find what you love [Commencement address]. *Stanford University.* Retrieved from https://news.stanford.edu/2005/06/14/jobs-061505/

Jones, J. E. (2005, June). Finding my voice. *Time Magazine*, F14.

Jones, J. E., & Niven, P. (1993). *Voices and silences.* New York, NY: Scribner's.

McLuhan, M. (1964). *Understanding media: The extensions of man.* New York, NY: McGraw-Hill.

McLuhan, M., & Fiore, Q. (1967). *The medium is the massage.* New York, NY: Random House.

Murphy, A. T. (1974). The quiet hyena: Two monologues in search of a dialogue. In L. L. Emerick & S. B. Hood (Eds.), *The client-clinician relationship: Essays on interpersonal sensitivity in the therapeutic transaction* (pp. 29–44). Springfield, IL: Thomas.

Shapiro, D. A. (2011). *Stuttering intervention: A collaborative journey to fluency freedom* (2nd ed.). Austin, TX: PRO-ED.

White, T. H. (1958). *The once and future king.* London, UK: Collins.

Yarrow, P. (2018, November 16). Yarrow concert melds '60s activism, songs and current issues. *Asheville Citizen Times*, 8.

CHAPTER FOURTEEN

How Shall We Then Proceed?

Martha Diede and Gayle Maddox

This book started with three examples demonstrating the need to build bridges, not blockades, within and—frankly—without the academy. Many of us believe that working in higher education is one of the best jobs a person could have. Most academics went into this type of work because we believed in something higher than ourselves—a "calling" of sorts. Some of us arrived in the academy through love of discipline. Others got a first job in student affairs and fell in love with the idea of guiding students through an academic experience. Some of us got into the academic project because we saw the tremendous potential of working with young adults as they navigate adulthood, and we wanted to be leaders in that endeavor. Faculty, staff, or administrator—no matter how we got into academics, we are now invested in the academic endeavor. We are now part of an experience that—when done well—can transform students' lives—and our own.

Unfortunately, in higher education, sometimes we forget our purposes when day-to-day frustrations—politics—creep in. In an effort to protect what we have, we often build blockades around ourselves. Sometimes, we've been known to take the relational "bridges" built around and across campus and burn them down, which creates blockades not only for us, but also for our colleagues and students. Essentially, we forget the four basic tenets of navigating university politics:

- Empathy for others—even people we don't like

- Jobs—and e-mails—on campus are attached to real people with real concerns, fears, hopes, dreams, responsibilities, and all of the other complexities that make for humanness.
- Context matters—whether you know it or not, whether you like it or not, a reason exists behind what people do, say, and write. Leaders keep the "big picture" in mind and help others to relate the everyday details to that bigger picture.
- Forgiveness is an essential practice because every human being makes mistakes (Luskin, Ginzburg, & Thoresen, 2005).

In heated moments, these tenets are extremely difficult to keep in mind. Nonetheless, taking an empathetic stance, reminding ourselves that we work with real, complex people daily, keeping our eyes on the big picture, and practicing forgiveness are essential leadership practices—at any organizational level—for building bridges.

These four tenets come into play rather frequently. A few months ago, we had a meeting with a university administrator. The 30-minute meeting had been scheduled to talk about adjunct faculty needs. An hour into the meeting, we found ourselves in a disputatious situation that had devolved into discussing issues from six months prior. Our colleague was angry, and we felt stress levels rise. The administrator sat upright in his chair and asked us if we wanted more fights on campus. And, then, he sat back in his chair, sighed, and said, "I'm just tired."

Our first inclination when we left the meeting was to be angry, disempowered, and vengeful. Most of us in academe have probably experienced these feelings. Those feelings translate into mental phrases that waffle between "this university is going to regret treating me/us this way" to "I/We won't forget how you treated me/us" to "I/We should probably just disengage from the university and do my/our own thing for a while."

None of those responses was or is the right answer. It took us a few days to process that the most important thing said in that hour-and-a-half meeting was that we were tired. It was a Friday afternoon on the last day of the semester. Of course, we were tired!

If we take that situation and apply empathy, a real person, context, and forgiveness, then we can walk away and say, "That was a bad meeting. The next one will be better. I understand that we are all trying to do our best for our colleagues and our students. I choose to forgive." I don't have to burn a bridge and build a blockade to make my point. If possible and/or appropriate, we can verbalize similar sentiments to our colleagues to build and encourage a culture of bridge building. Leadership—of self and others—is about knowing when to step up to a challenge and find a way forward as well as when to step back and take a deep breath.

Without these four foci, the daily struggles take a toll on the people, the campus, and higher education in general. Heated discussions and daily slights that can be taken out of context often lead to battles that detract from what is really important—making sure our campuses continue to educate college students through academic pursuits, critical thinking, and creative ideas.

For those of us of ascribed or avowed identities—African American, Indian, Chinese, LGBTQIA, Jewish, Muslim, Hindu—that do not fit the "norm" of higher education, this burden is even greater. Given the kind of behavior we experience, we may ask, "How often do I forgive? How can I keep my focus on the real person when that real person behaves in ways that are simply repugnant?" These questions are also essential to the project of bridge building. They highlight the need for bridge-building leaders at every institutional level who know that partnerships are essential to success in higher education at every level, from individual to institutional. These partners need to build supports so that when one person or institution needs the time to step back, the partner can step up. These partners can encourage—literally fill with courage—ourselves and our colleagues in continuing excellent work in contexts that have additional blockades not of our own making. And as partners, we can also work to dismantle the blockades so that everyone can thrive.

Regardless of demographic, ascribed or avowed identity, transcending blockades is essential to anyone's success. Students succeed better when surrounded by partner groups that provide senses of belonging in various ways at different times in the journey, from student to graduate. These partners, who provide belonging, support students in transcending the blockades to completing their degrees. Partner groups also support faculty at every level by providing senses of belonging throughout the faculty journey, whatever trajectory that journey may take.

Faculty members survive and thrive when they also have support from peers. The same is true for administrators at every level, even university presidents and chancellors. Anyone listening to a room full of provosts and/or chancellors hears comments about the loneliness of top positions while in the presence of people facing similar challenges. The knowing glances, nods, and sly smiles reveal both the immediate community and the need for one.

Complicating barriers and blockades—within and without higher education—are demographics. The landscape of and for higher education is changing. Rapidly. The confounding influences are many, and include but are not limited to the following:

- While the professoriate and administrative ranks remain in the hands of white men (National Center for Education Statistics, 2018), students are more often from one or more minority groups, often concurrently (Herrmann, Bager-Elsborg, & McCune, 2017; O'Shea, 2016).
- At state and federal levels, support for higher education is waning (Fabricant & Brier, 2016), even as industries lament the lack of appropriately skilled workers (Hanson & Slaughter, 2018; Kerr, 2013; Kochan, 2012; ManpowerGroup, 2018).
- Public safety nets are eroding (McNicholars, Shierholz, & von Wilpert, 2018; Mobley, Kuo, & Bazzoli, 2011; Potts, 2016).
- Wages are stagnant or dropping (Desilver, 2018; Reich, 2019; Smith, 2019).
- College costs are increasingly passed on to students and their families (Barr & McClellan, 2018; Mitchell, Leachman, Masterson, & Waxman, 2018).
- This confluence of events and attitudes leaves many agencies and schools requesting ever more money from donors and running campaigns on a near-continuous basis (Gawor, 2018).
- Institutions of higher education are also targeted as "too liberal," castigated for indoctrinating students into liberal thinking, even while those in higher education worry that students learn to think at all.

To respond to these changes, institutions of higher education must become nimble, able to respond to new stimuli on their horizons without becoming mired in the detritus of thousand-year-old patterns, and those institutions must have sufficient resources to absorb mistakes. Central to this ability to make new choices collectively, the people who lead these institutions at every level must determine that they will support surmounting blockades, engaging in partnerships with an operational vision for seeking mutual benefit rather than winning at all costs. That attitude means exceptionally difficult choices, made more so because those decisions affect people: faculty positions created or eliminated; staff hires or lay-offs; site openings or closures; maintenance issues addressed or postponed (Lippens, 2017). In such a thin-margin environment, bridge-building leadership is essential.

The thin economic margin on which many institutions of higher education operate becomes even thinner when interpersonal and intra- and inter-institutional challenges complicate fulfillment of mission, vision, and goals. Such complexity results in a bandwidth challenge for administrators as well as faculty, staff, and students. Considered from this vantage point, such scarcity is more than a lack of monetary resources (Mullainathan & Shafir, 2013). Money is easy: Someone can give money or raise money. Time, however, is a fixed constraint; no one can generate more than twenty-four hours in a day. Every minute people choose what they will do with the resources to which they have access. Choices about how, where, with, and for whom to spend time fall heavily on leaders in higher education. Do they spend time on policies to create opportunities for more, different kinds of people with different intersecting identities to engage with higher education? Do they spend time with people, building relationships that may benefit the students, faculty, and staff that they serve? One of the most pressing questions is this: Do they spend time building bridges into and out of higher education, or do they spend their time building blockades, hoarding opportunities for themselves, those like them, or like the people that they wish themselves to be? Do they have the time to think deeply about how their choices create or hoard opportunities? The answer is clear. In higher education—the academy—we cannot afford to spend our time, energy, and talents in the pursuit of projects that benefit us alone. Educational leaders do not have sufficient resources for that kind of thinking or operation. Instead, educational leaders must choose to spend time and energy on pursuits that make the most difference: building bridges; tearing down blockades.

This attitude is essential to anyone involved in higher education, whether that person leads from the front, the middle, or the bottom. As each of these chapters has shown, the barriers to and within the higher education environment are many; similar blockades to advancement may exist in varying institutions. Faculty positions are often encoded in policies that imagine the professor as a person with few to no connections outside of the academy, perhaps with a partner who will manage everything about daily reality and thereby free up brain bandwidth for deep, complex thought but who has no networks or allegiances beyond the partner (Reed, 2018). This frequently unexamined bias translates into challenging behaviors that add to institutional blockades. Finding an appropriate position for a partner is treated as a challenge to operation, not as an opportunity for enhancement. The challenge is so pervasive that faculty have begun to study, write, and argue for institutions to change their thinking about faculty hires (Zeliadt, 2016). Staff positions are frequently blocked in by policies that envision staff persons to have only minimal degree preparation, perhaps a bachelor's degree. The result is that staff members who have advanced degrees and academic pedigrees of their own have few, if any, places to use their substantial talents to benefit their offices or their institutions. In what is perhaps the most insidious blockade of all, these challenges are frequently treated as local to each individual who faces them. Institutions with support maintain the idea that the partner is a "problem," speaking of the partner as a kind of necessary factor to consider in recruiting "top talent."

Given this landscape, how shall we then proceed? What do we do when the institutions in which we operate, the units where we work daily, treat us as barely human and descend into what feels like near battle? First, we can keep in mind that we can lead no matter our institutional positions. Depending on the circumstances in which we come to this book, leading may seem impossible. It isn't. We can lead ourselves if no one else. We can give ourselves the time to process tough situations and circumstances. Few people turn down requests for a little time to consider our options before providing responses, and if that fails, fewer people still turn down requests for a biological (bathroom) break. We can choose to be empathetic and look at the real people involved in our interactions. We can take deep breaths and consider our contexts and the ways that those contexts may be impacting us. We can choose to forgive because we know that people make mistakes. We have gaps in knowledge. We have unexamined biases and have learned behaviors that do not serve us well. Most importantly, we can build bridges inside and outside our institutions with those who will remind us that we can tear down blockades.

References

Barr, M. J., & McClellan, G. S. (2018). *Budgets and financial management in higher education.* San Francisco, CA: Jossey-Bass.

Desilver, D. (2018, August 7). For most U.S. workers, real wages have barely budged in decades. *Pew Research Center.* Retrieved from https://www.pewresearch.org/fact-tank/2018/08/07/for-most-us-workers-real-wages-have-barely-budged-for-decades/

Fabricant, M. & Brier, S. (2016). *Austerity blues: Fighting for the soul of public education.* Baltimore: Johns Hopkins University Press.

Gawor, B. (2018, February 16). The future of higher education fundraising campaigns according to fundraising leaders [Web log post]. *Education Insights Blog.* Retrieved from https://www.ruffalonl.com/higher-education-fundraising-campaigns/

Hanson, G. H., & Slaughter, M. J. (2018). High-skilled immigration and the rise of STEM occupations in US employment. In C. R. Hulten & V.A. Ramey (Eds.), *Education, skills, and technical change: Implications for future U.S. GDP growth* (pp. 465–500). Chicago, IL: University of Chicago Press.

Herrmann, K. J., Bager-Elsborg, A., & McCune, V. (2017). Investigating the relationship between approaches to learning, learner identities and academic achievement in higher education, *Higher Education* 74(3), 385–400.

Kerr, W. R. (2013). U.S. high-skilled immigration, innovation, and entrepreneurship: Empirical approaches and evidence. *National Bureau of Economic Research.* Retrieved from https://www.nber.org/papers/w19377

Kochan, T. A. (2012, March). A jobs compact for America's future. *Harvard Business Review.* Retrieved from https://hbr.org/2012/03/a-jobs-compact-for-americas-future

Lippens, A. F. (2017, May 26). Tackling the deferred maintenance crisis. *Executive briefing for higher ed leaders.* Washington, DC: EAB.

Luskin, F. M., Ginzburg, K., & Thoresen, C. E. (2005). The efficacy of forgiveness intervention in college-age adults: A randomized controlled study. *Humbolt Journal of Social Relations* 29(2), 1163–1184.

McNicholas, C., Shierholz, H., & von Wilpert, M. (2018, January 29). Workers' health, safety, and pay are among the casualties of Trump's war on regulations: A deregulation year in review. *Education Policy Institute Report.* Retrieved from https://www.epi.org/publication/deregulation-year-in-review

ManpowerGroup. (2018). *Solving the talent shortage: Build, buy, borrow and bridge.* Retrieved from https://go.manpowergroup.com/hubfs/TalentShortage%20

2018%20(Global)%20Assets/PDFs/MG_TalentShortage2018_lo%206_25_18_FINAL.pdf

Mitchell, M., Leachman, M., Masterson, K., & Waxman, S. (2018). *Unkept promises: State cuts to higher education threaten access and equity.* Washington, DC: Center on Budget and Policy Priorities.

Mobley, L., Kuo, T. M., & Bazzoli, G. J. (2011). Erosion in the healthcare safety net: Impacts on different population groups. *Open Health Services and Policy Journal,* 4(1), 1–14.

Mullainathan, S. & Shafir, E. (2013). *Scarcity: Why having too little means so much.* New York, NY: Times Books.

National Center for Education Statistics. (2018). *The condition of education 2018* (NCES 2018-144), Retrieved from https://nces.ed.gov/programs/coe/indicator_csc.asp

O'Shea, S. (2016). Avoiding the manufacture of "sameness": First-in-family students, cultural capital and the higher education environment, *Higher Education* 72(1), 59–78.

Potts, M. (2016, October 13). The American social safety net does not exist. *The Nation.* Retrieved from https://www.thenation.com/article/the-american-social-safety-net-does-not-exist

Reed, M. (2018, January 31). The two-body problem revisited [Web log post]. *Inside Higher Ed.* Retrieved from https://www.insidehighered.com/blogs/confessions-community-college-dean/two-body-problem-revisited

Reich, R. (2019, June 4). *The gig is up.* [Web log post.] Retrieved from https://robertreich.org/post/185372914705

Smith, N. (2019, February 14). Wage stagnation is one disease with many causes. *Bloomberg Opinion.* Retrieved from https://www.bloomberg.com/opinion/articles/2019-02-14/u-s-economy-wage-stagnation-is-one-disease-with-many-causesaqszXWz

Zeliadt, N. (2016). Academic couples see upsides to the "two-body problem." *Spectrum News.* Retrieved from https://www.spectrumnews.org/news/academic-couples-see-upsides-two-body-problem/

CONTRIBUTORS

Andrew Adams—Dr. Andrew Adams is the associate dean of the David Orr Belcher College of Fine and Performing Arts and professor of piano at Western Carolina University in Cullowhee, North Carolina. He earned his bachelor's in music in piano from the Kansas City Conservatory and his master's in vocal coaching from the University of Illinois. He completed his doctorate in piano performance at the University of Colorado. For over a decade, Dr. Adams has served on the editorial board of the *Journal of Singing*, the official publication of the National Association of Teachers of Singing. He has published numerous articles and reviews in *Piano Professional* (England), the *American Music Teacher*, the *Journal of the International Alliance for Women in Music*, and the *North Carolina Music Educator*. Adams serves on the board of the American Conference of Academic Deans (ACAD) and is the editor of their online newsletter, *ACAD Leader*.

Betty Block—Dr. Betty Block is currently a professor in the Department of Health and Human Performance at Texas A&M University Commerce and Texas A&M system regents professor. She has over 30 years of experience in higher education including undergraduate and graduate coordinator, department chair of three departments, and associate provost and vice president for academic affairs. While a faculty member, she served as a member of the executive committee and the chair of the university senate, chair of the university institutional review board, and chair/compiler of accreditation and strategic planning committees. Dr. Block has held multiple state, regional, national, and international leadership roles in professional societies, including president of the National Association for Kinesiology in Higher Education. Her research focus is higher education leadership, super-complexity, ambiguity, and politics.

Martha Diede—Dr. Martha Kalnin Diede directs the Center for Teaching and Learning Excellence at Syracuse University. Her publications include *Spirit of Adoption* (2014) and *Shakespeare's Knowledgeable Body* (2008). She has over 15 years of experience in higher education including department chair of two departments and director of two faculty centers at two different universities. She has served as a member of the Chancellor's Leadership Council, the Inclusion and Diversity Committee, the Information Technology Leadership Council, and committees focused on classrooms and institutional space use, community engagement, and first-year experience, and as a member of accreditation and strategic planning committees. Her research focus is the future of higher education and the effect of that future on faculty.

Steve Estes—Dr. Steve Estes is a professor in the Department of Health and Human Performance at Middle Tennessee State University. His administrative appointments include director of the Center for Technology in Education at Cortland, department chair at East Carolina University and Middle Tennessee State University, and dean of the College of Professional Studies at Missouri Western State University. He has served as president of the National Association for Kinesiology in Higher Education, faculty senate chair at SUNY Cortland, and as the keynote speaker at academic and professional conferences in his specialty areas. Dr. Estes's research interests include leadership and the relationship of mind and body in sport and physical activity.

Rochelle Ford—Rochelle L. Ford, PhD, APR, is dean of the Elon University School of Communications and a leading public relations professional, researcher, author, and international speaker. An expert in diversity and inclusion, she has authored more than 100 articles and four books. A frequent contributor to several national publications including the *New York Times*, she has executed funded award-winning research for such organizations as the PRSA Foundation, Carnegie Foundation, Plank Center for Leadership, and Arthur W. Page Society. A 2018 PR Week Hall of Fame inductee and Fulbright scholar, she has received numerous accolades including the PRSA's National D. Parke Gibson Multiculturalism award.

Anita Henck—Dr. Anita Henck is dean and professor in the School of Education at Azusa Pacific University. She was previously chair of the Department of Leadership and College Student Development at APU while serving as program director of the MA in leadership, with a joint appointment in the PhD program in higher education. She has served in faculty and leadership roles in higher education for more than 30 years, including previous roles as vice president for student development and retention at Eastern Nazarene College in Quincy, Massachusetts, and assistant to the president and provost at American University in Washington DC, as well as in faculty roles at both institutions. Her areas of specialty in consulting and publications are transformational leadership, effective leadership teams, leadership transitions, organizational culture and change, and generational differences in the workplace.

Gayle Maddox—Dr. Gayle Maddox is a tenured faculty member at Western Carolina University where she has served in various leadership roles at the undergraduate and graduate levels. She teaches integrated public health courses as well as health pedagogy classes for future teachers. In addition to serving on the faculty, she has also worked in student affairs and student success programs. She has authored articles on critical thinking in health, student engagement, and the politics of higher education.

Melanie Mock—Dr. Melanie Mock is a tenured faculty member in the English department at George Fox University in Newberg, Oregon. Melanie is the winner of George Fox's 2009 Faculty of the Year award and recipient of the 2014–2015 Undergraduate Faculty Achievement award for research and scholarship. Melanie has published a number of books, including *Worthy: Finding Yourself in a World Expecting Someone Else* (2018); *If Eve Only Knew* (2015); *The Spirit of Adoption: Writers on Religion, Adoption, Faith, and More* (2014); *Just Moms: Conveying Justice in an Unjust World* (2011); and *Writing Peace: The Unheard Voices of Great War Mennonite Objectors* (2003).

Melanie is also an accomplished essayist in both popular and academic presses. Her essays have appeared in *Christian Feminism Today*, *The Nation*, *The Chronicle of Higher Education*, *Inside Higher Ed*, and *The Mennonite World Review*, among other places. Much of her work focuses on her experiences with parenting, feminism within a Christian context, and evangelical culture.

Amy Murphy-Nugen—Amy B. Murphy-Nugen, MSW, PhD, is an assistant professor in the Department of Social Work at Western Carolina University. Her research intersects issues related to community advocacy and social justice. She teaches community and organizational practice, human behavior in the social environment, social policy, rural community advocacy, and a specialized course on financial capability and asset development. Dr. Murphy-Nugen's asset-building, empowerment, and anti-oppressive practice and policy experience focuses on affordable housing and housing loss, community building and engagement, community economic development, and not-for-profit management/leadership. She has facilitated community building and engagement processes for groups with five key stakeholders to neighborhoods with 40,000 residents, as well as county-wide planning efforts and everything in between. Her professional experience spans providing team leadership; analyzing and advocating for socially and economically just local, state, and federal legislation and administrative policy; and delivering capacity-building technical assistance to not-for-profit community-based development organizations and local units of government.

Antonio Oakley Jr.—Antonio Oakley Jr. is from Charlotte, North Carolina, and is a recent graduate from Western Carolina University. Antonio has found a passion for helping students in any way possible. He has worked with first-generation students as a peer academic leader with the Mentoring and Persistence to Success Department, a cat camp counselor, and a project care mentor. He has shown a passion for diversity and leadership by speaking up for underrepresented students on campus. During his college career, Antonio joined Alpha Phi Alpha Fraternity, Inc., and has been a part of the Whee Matter Movement, a movement that allows the voices of underrepresented individuals to be heard. He had the pleasure to be the commencement speaker for the 2019 graduation ceremony. Having the opportunity to be a part of this process was humbling and rewarding for Antonio. He hopes to be published again in the future.

Laura Pipe—Dr. Laura Pipe directs the Teaching Innovations Office implementing pan-university faculty development initiatives. Throughout her career, Laura has developed academically enriched programs that promote integrated learning, teaching innovations, and faculty collaboration. Her expertise is in inclusive teaching and integrated learning, and she serves on the editorial board of the *Journal for Learning Communities Research and Practice* and is a consulting editor for the journal *College Teaching*. Laura completed her BS in journalism (Texas Christian University), her MS in higher postsecondary education (Syracuse University), and her PhD in kinesiology (UNCG). Her scholarly and teaching interests focus on action sports (bicycle motocross, skateboarding, stock car racing) and Native health and center on the construction and regulation of public and private space. Laura's research continues to have exciting resonance with her philosophies in interdisciplinary and application-based learning.

Charmion Rush—Dr. Charmion B. Rush is an assistant professor of inclusive and special education at Western Carolina University. Dr. Rush's teaching, research, and service focus on preparing educators to teach diverse populations, emphasizing the ethnic/minority students enrolled in special education. Her areas of research include culture responsive pedagogy, disproportionate representation, implicit bias, inclusion, and literacy practices.

David Shapiro—David A. Shapiro, PhD, is a speech-language pathologist, specialist in fluency disorders, and the Robert Lee Madison distinguished professor emeritus at Western Carolina University. He has presented workshops and papers, provided clinical service, and conducted research on six continents. His book, *Stuttering Intervention: A Collaborative Journey to Fluency Freedom* (2011, 2nd ed.) continues to find a wide international audience. Most recently, Dr. Shapiro received the Oliver Max Gardner award (2016), the University of North Carolina's highest honor for faculty in its 17-campus system as well as Honors from the North Carolina Speech, Language and Hearing Association (2017) and the American Speech-Language-Hearing Association (2017).

Carleen "Tenae" Turner—Carleen "Tenae" Turner is from Burlington, North Carolina, and is a graduate of Western Carolina University's class of 2019. Tenae has found a passion for advocating for minority groups and helping those that are underrepresented. While in school, Tenae demonstrated her goal of representation and inclusivity by being a part of the Whee Matter Movement, speaking up for underrepresented students and proposing changes to policies and governing bodies to ensure inclusivity for current and future students. Tenae is a member of Alpha Kappa Alpha Sorority, Inc. and the NAACP. She has had the honor to speak at the 2017 NC NAACP moral march on the topic of education. One day, she hopes to publish works of her own and continue to be an advocate for all. Tenae is grateful for the opportunity to be a part of this process with such distinguished scholars and advocates.

Drew Virtue—Drew Virtue is an associate professor in the Department of English at Western Carolina University. He earned a PhD in rhetoric, scientific, and technical communication from the University of Minnesota. Drew teaches a variety of courses in the professional writing concentration, with an emphasis on technical writing, editing and publishing, and writing in digital environments. His current research examines the intersections of rhetoric, pedagogy, and digital/web literacies, with a special focus on the role of technology in the classroom and workplace. He has presented his scholarship at national conferences as well as published his writing in prominent academic journals.

Emily Virtue—Emily E. Virtue has a PhD in educational leadership from Clemson University and is an Assistant Professor of Educational Research at Western Carolina University. She has served in various student affairs and faculty positions to support undergraduate leadership, engagement, and learning. Her research interests include learning communities, conditionally enrolled students, and pedagogy.

Elwood Watson—Elwood Watson, PhD, is professor of history, gender studies, and African American studies at East Tennessee State University. He is the author of two books, *Outsiders Within: Black Women in the Legal Academy After Brown v. Board* (2009) and *Understanding the Humanities* (2014). He is the author of the forthcoming books *Race in America: Critical Essays* and *Today's Man: Essays on 21st-Century Masculinity*. He has edited numerous collections. He has published numerous articles about race, gender, higher education, popular culture, and American culture in national newspapers and magazines and is a blogger for *Diverse Education*, *Huffington Post*, *The Good Men Project*, *X/Y Online*, *The Black Past*, Medium.com, the *New York Times*, the *North Star*, the *Seattle Times*, the *Boston Globe*, the *Philadelphia Inquirer*, *US News and World Report*, and other publications.

INDEX